To Dad and Ree:
With thanks for all of
your continued support and
encouragement. I couldn't do
what I do without you both!
Keep up the good work,
Love,

★ *The People's Choice* ★

CONGRESSMAN

JIM JONTZ

OF

INDIANA

RAY E. BOOMHOWER

Indiana Historical Society Press | Indianapolis 2012

Printed in the United States of America

This book is a publication of the
Indiana Historical Society Press
Eugene and Marilyn Glick Indiana History Center
450 West Ohio Street
Indianapolis, Indiana 46202-3269 USA
www.indianahistory.org
Telephone orders 1-800-447-1830
Fax orders 1-317-234-0562
Online orders @ shop.indianahistory.org

The paper in this publication meets the minimum requirements of American National Standard for Information Sciences—Permanence of Paper for Printed Library Materials, ANSI Z39. 48–1984

Library of Congress Cataloging-in-Publication Data

Boomhower, Ray E., 1959-
The people's choice : Congressman Jim Jontz of Indiana / Ray E. Boomhower.
    pages cm
Includes bibliographical references and index.
ISBN 978-0-87195-298-1 (cloth : alk. paper)
1. Jontz, Jim. 2. Legislators—United States—Biography. 3. United States—Politics and govern-
ment—1981-1989. 4. United States—Politics and government—1989-1993. 5. Legislators—
Indiana—Biography. 6. Indiana—Politics and government—20th century. I. Title.
E840.8.J616B66 2012
328.73'092—dc23
[B]
                         2011049243

To my first boss, Liza Janco, who took a chance
on a young reporter and introduced me to Jim Jontz.
Thanks for setting me on the right path.

"I do not believe that America was meant to be a jungle
where only the fittest or the richest prosper.

I grew up believing that there's a bargain in our country. When you work hard,
when you pay your taxes, when you're a good parent and citizen and obey the
law, when you play by the rules, you have a right to expect certain things—a
safe job, a decent income, good schools, clean air and water, a chance to enjoy
life, a cushion against problems that overwhelm you, a secure retirement,
a government that cares, a strong country that's free and at peace.

That's the American promise that I believe in,
and that's what I fought for all my life."

*Walter F. Mondale, address to the AFL-CIO convention, Hollywood, Florida,
October 6, 1983, newsclipping with quote found in Jim Jontz's personal papers*

Contents

Preface

In the fall of 1982 I had been employed for a few months in my first job after graduating from Indiana University in Bloomington with degrees in journalism and political science. As a reporter for the *Rensselaer Republican* newspaper in Jasper County, Indiana, I covered everything from school board meetings to volleyball games and county fairs, as well as taking and developing photographs and pasting up the newspaper before it was printed for daily distribution to our subscribers. It was a great learning ground for a budding reporter, but the pay was nothing to brag about. I still remember covering the distribution of some surplus government cheese for low-income families only to discover that I was also eligible for the food. I ate a lot of grilled cheese sandwiches for dinner over the next couple of weeks.

One of the assignments I particularly enjoyed was covering anything related to Indiana politics, a subject I had been interested in from an early age. I remembered the nervousness I felt, however, when I was asked by my editor, Liza Janco, to interview the candidates in the race for the Twenty-fifth District in the Indiana House of Representatives. The first person I interviewed was the Republican candidate, Dave Diener, who replied to my questions in his office at a supply company he owned with his brother in Monticello, Indiana. A member of the Monticello City Council, Diener advocated local control on a number of issues, but spent the majority of his time blasting his opponent, incumbent Democrat Jim Jontz of Brookston. Diener said it appalled him that voters in the district, "for some reason or another," kept electing him to office.

My interview with Jontz occurred at a Monticello pancake house where, between bites of his dinner, the veteran legislator impressed me with his knowledge of and enthusiasm for discussing a wide range of issues from the potential of synthetic fuels to provide jobs for Hoosiers, establishing home care for the elderly, and strengthening laws to help regulate utility companies. During our discussion he did not mention his opponent's name once.

My meetings with Jontz during my days at the *Republican* left me impressed with how hard he worked on behalf of his constituents and his dedication to understanding the complex issues facing government. Before meeting Jontz, I had been inclined to agree with a quote by famed journalist H. L. Mencken that the "only way for a reporter to look at a politician is down." After dealing with Jontz on a variety of stories, my view of politicians changed for the better (it returned to Mencken's opinion in later years as I realized not every politician was like Jontz). My career path changed in subsequent years and I started working in Indiana history. I lost touch with Jontz as he rose to serve three terms in Congress and, after his defeat in 1992, worked for a variety of environmental groups. My last communication with him was an e-mail exchange for a book I was writing on Robert F. Kennedy's 1968 campaign in Indiana for the Democratic presidential nomination. Jontz seemed pleased to hear from me, and I was shocked to learn just a few months later that he had died at the age of only fifty-five.

Jontz's service to the citizens of Indiana inspired me to write about his life and career in the pages of the Indiana Historical Society's popular history magazine *Traces of Indiana and Midwestern History*. My article on him appeared in the fall 2010 issue of the magazine and provoked a positive response from his friends, relatives, and former staff members. Realizing there was more to be said about his remarkable life, I worked with his mother, Polly Jontz Lennon, and sister, Mary Lee Turk, to produce this biography. Without their assistance, this book would not have been possible. They offered insightful comments on Jontz's early days growing up in Indianapolis, and were patient with my requests for additional information as the project progressed.

Those who knew Jontz—his friends, staff members, and colleagues in the Indiana Statehouse and U.S. Capitol—responded with enthusiasm whenever I sought to interview them to learn more about his life. There are too many to list here, but I wish to give particular thanks to Tom Sugar, Elaine Caldwell Emmi, Kathy Altman, Scott Campbell, Brian Mayes, Christopher Klose, and Scott Paul.

Jontz's papers are at the Calumet Regional Archives at Indiana University Northwest in Gary. Stephen G. McShane, the archives' archivist/curator, provided invaluable assistance during my visits and even allowed me to sit in the chair and behind the desk of former Indiana congressman Raymond J. Madden. It felt appropriate to research the life of a congressman at the desk of a congressman. My appreciation also to James B. Lane, professor emeritus of history at IU Northwest and codirector of the archives, for his encouragement, support, and lunchtime companionship. I knew I was on the right track in my research at the archives when I came across a newspaper clipping in Jontz's papers from the December 18, 1982, *Rensselaer Republican*. Jontz had saved a copy of a column I did for the newspaper listing Christmas wishes for Hoosier political figures, including Governor Robert Orr, Lieutenant Governor John Mutz, and Jontz, then a state representative. For the legislator, I wished the following: "A Democrat-controlled Indiana House or Representatives, Senate and a Democrat[ic] governor. Also, any pies left over from Floyd Fithian's [U.S. Senate] campaign. Good eating Jim!"

When asked about his successful writing career, the famous American novelist and screenwriter Elmore Leonard observed that he tried to "leave out the parts that people skip." I have had the privilege of working with editors and others who have aided me immeasurably in the task of presenting a story that will please, educate, and enlighten readers. My wife, Megan McKee, as she has on my other books, has been my inspiration. Without her, none of this would have been possible. At the Indiana Historical Society Press, Kathy Breen toiled away on the manuscript while handling a host of other tasks as well. Her contributions have made the book better. Thanks also to Kris Davidson at the IHS for her skilled design and Becke Bolinger for her tireless efforts to promote the IHS Press's books to a wide audience.

1

"A Large and Courageous Heart"

"Unless someone like you cares a whole awful lot,
nothing is going to get better. It's not."

THEODOR S. GEISEL (DOCTOR SEUSS), *THE LORAX* (1971)

For centuries, the waters of Fall Creek near Attica in west central Indiana
have cut through the steep, walled canyons of the Fall Creek Gorge. The rush-
ing waters swirled gravel with enough force to scoop out circular depressions
known as "potholes"—some as big as six feet in diameter, four- to five-feet
deep, and large enough to trap unsuspecting visitors—in the rock creekbed.
The canyon walls are covered with ferns, mosses, and liverworts, while red-
tailed hawks swoop overheard scanning the tops of white pine trees on the
sandstone bluffs for unwary squirrels and the ground below for cottontail
rabbits. More than two thousand miles away from this midwestern scenic
splendor in the Pacific Northwest states of Oregon, Washington, and California stand old-growth forests of Douglas firs, western hemlock, redwood,
and Sitka spruce. These ancient forests have stood since well before the time
Norse explorer Leif Ericson and his crew became the first Europeans to land in
North America. Sheltered within them live a diverse blend of creatures, including such endangered species as the northern spotted owl. Scientists note
that while the most productive tropical rain forests that have been measured
contain 185 tons of plants per acre, the average Pacific Northwest forest yields
400 tons an acre, while some redwood forests contain 1,800 tons per acre.[1]

These two seemingly different ecosystems do share one thing in common—they can be enjoyed by visitors today thanks to the efforts of a little-
known Indiana politician and environmentalist, James P. Jontz. From an

A view of the potholes at the Fall Creek Gorge in Warren County, Indiana.

early age Jontz, the eldest of two children, displayed a dedication to nature while growing up in the 1960s in the Northern Hills subdivision on Indianapolis's north side—a "semirural setting" that enabled him to develop his deep love of nature. He remained devoted to helping preserve the outdoors as an Eagle Scout, the highest rank one can attain as a Boy Scout; as a student at Indiana University majoring in geology; as a representative and state senator in the Indiana legislature; as a three-term member of the U.S. Congress; and even after he was defeated in the 1992 election. Three years later, he and other environmental activists were handcuffed and led away by police during a protest against timber cutting in Oregon's Siskiyou National Forest. His parents, both of whom were solid citizens of good standing in Indianapolis, were shocked when they learned their son had been arrested. Jontz tried to calm their fears, pointing out that when law enforcement officers hauled him away, "I had my suit on!"[2]

Jontz's long service in politics working for social and economic justice as a member of the Democratic Party came about in no small part because of his interest in protecting the state's natural resources. He entered his first race for public office in 1974 as a candidate for the Indiana House of Representatives in the state's Twentieth District to oppose a multimillion-dollar U.S. Army Corps of Engineers dam project on Big Pine Creek, a tributary of the Wabash River located near Williamsport, Indiana. "I gave a damn about a dam," Jontz said of his first campaign.[3] The dam and the reservoir it would have created threatened to engulf homes, businesses, thousands of acres of cropland and pastureland, and such scenic natural areas as Fall Creek Gorge. A majority of those who lived in the area opposed the project, and the few who supported the dam, according to Jontz, were "the people who were going to get rich off of it and the politically powerful people in the community who were their friends. It just didn't seem right to me that a few powerful people should be able to do something like this." Jontz became a leader in the fight to stop the dam from being built, entered the race for the state legislature, and eked out a narrow victory against his better-known Republican opponent. He spent the next several years working against the dam project at the Indiana Statehouse before finally seeing it abandoned in the 1990s. For years Jontz used this victory of average citizens against a politically powerful foe as an important lesson to young and old alike "who see injustice and want to believe that you can make a difference—you *can* make a difference."[4]

Opal Creek Valley in the Willamette National Forest in western Oregon. The valley includes one of the largest intact stands of old-growth forests in the western Cascades.

When Jontz won election to the U.S. House of Representatives in 1986, representing the Fifth Congressional District, he took his passion for environmental and other social-justice causes with him to Washington, D.C., and became a hero to conservationists for attempting to protect old-growth forests in the Pacific Northwest from logging companies. "I looked around and saw a lot of people were very close to the timber industry," Jontz said. "That's OK: they need some support: but why should they have it all? There are other voices, too. People don't want those other voices to be heard."[5] The zeal in which he pursued protecting nature frustrated and sometimes infuriated congressmen from other states, who saw him as meddling in matters that were outside the district he represented. Jontz's sponsorship of the Ancient Forest Protection Act, which would have forbid cutting stands of ancient

Indiana congressman Jim Jontz appears before the Save the Dunes Council's sunset ceremony at Mount Baldy overlooking Crescent Dune in northwest Indiana on Earth Day, April 22, 1990.

timber in three western states, caused one Oregon congressman to call him "a rank opportunist," while another member of the Oregon delegation became so mad at Jontz during a meeting that he kicked him out of his office. Upset by Jontz's successful effort to end arrangements benefiting timber companies in the Tongass National Forest in Alaska, Congressman Don Young of that state introduced a bill to establish 35 percent of Jontz's Indiana's district, a mixture of farmland and factories, as a national forest. Jontz gave Young credit for his "humorous proposal," and said he kept asking the Alaskan legislator if he could have an autographed copy of the bill. "He's very creative and entertaining," Jontz said of Young.[6]

On a more serious note, to respond to charges that he was interfering in matters that were not his business, Jontz defended his actions. He called the ancient forests in the West "a national treasure, much as the Grand Canyon, Yosemite, and the Everglades are. If we cut the last 10 percent of the ancient forests for short-term greed, they will be gone forever. If we preserve them, future generations, as well as our own, will be able to enjoy their benefits." The trees in national forests, he also pointed out, were not the private

Jontz talks on the telephone at his congressional office at the Longworth House Office Building in Washington, D.C.

property of anyone, but "public lands owned by the citizens of Indiana as much as by citizens anywhere, and they should be managed for the well-being of the public, not just a few." Jontz's passion when it came to helping preserve wild areas puzzled one of his campaign volunteers, Phillip Perdue, who noticed that the congressman often talked about the outdoors, but never did any camping or hiking. "I will someday," Jontz told him, "and I want to know it will be there when I'm ready to enjoy it."[7]

Ironically, the issue that had sparked his political career—the environment—became one of the issues that lead to Jontz's defeat by his Republican challenger Steve Buyer in the 1992 general election. His stand against allowing private companies leases at below market value to cut logs from portions of national forest lands owned by the federal government so inflamed members of western carpenter unions—worried about losing their jobs if firms could no longer harvest the timber—that they traveled to Indiana to campaign against Jontz's re-election. "I played a role in this debate and I paid a price for it," Jontz recalled. "But I don't regret it." He later joked: "No good deed goes unpunished."[8]

Jontz's efforts on behalf of nature continued after his defeat, as he worked with such environmental groups as the Western Ancient Forest Campaign and the Alliance for Sustainable Jobs and the Environment. His labors did not go unnoticed by others who had spent their lives working to protect the Earth. Brock Evans, president of the Endangered Species Coalition, said that of all the people he knew over the years campaigning on behalf of the environment, very few had touched him as deeply as did Jontz, whom he called "one of the most courageous and dedicated persons, always living for his convictions, who I have ever known." John Osborn, an activist for the Sierra Club, remembered Jontz as "one of those marvelous people you meet occasionally in life—committed, upbeat, high energy, 'let's make it work.'" Jontz, said Osborn, was comfortable in a t-shirt in Eugene, Oregon, talking strategy with environmental activists, in a suit on Capitol Hill, or even risking arrest to call attention to illegal logging in national forests.[9]

Throughout most of his political life Jontz had made a habit of winning election as a liberal Democrat (he preferred the term progressive) usually running in conservative districts with a majority of registered voters that identified themselves as members of the Republican Party. Philip Loy, a Taylor University political science professor, reflected that when you were around Jontz he, at first, appeared to be a "sort of a rural country bumpkin. And then you stand back and realize that this is one incredibly complex individual who defies all the normal rules of politics." Jontz even won the grudging respect of his GOP foes, with longtime Indiana Republican state chairman Rex Early humorously noting, "He [Jontz] cuts everybody's lawn. He rides his bicycle backwards and he knows everybody's lost grandson."[10]

Political pundits routinely predicted Jontz's defeat in every election only to see him celebrating another victory with his happy supporters, always wearing a scruffy, hooded plaid jacket from his high school days that he wore for luck. "I always hope for the best and fight for the worst," said Jontz. He noted that voters appreciated that he worked for "the public interest, not special interests." While voters sometimes pigeonholed the positions of Democrats as being for more government and Republicans favoring less government, Jontz described his philosophy as reorienting "government to serve the interests of the average citizen."[11]

During his long career in politics, Jontz won five terms as state representative for the Twentieth District (Benton, Newton, Warren, and White Counties), served two years in the Indiana Senate, and captured three terms

During his time in Congress, Jontz served on a variety of committees, including those dealing with education, labor, veterans' affairs, agriculture, aging, and the environment.

in the U.S. Congress representing the sprawling Fifth District in northwestern Indiana that stretched from Lake County in the north to Grant County in the south. Jontz told a reporter that his political career had always "been based on my willingness and role as a spokesman for the average citizen." His sister, Mary Lee Turk, noted of her brother: "He just worked harder than anybody else. He made a difference." Jontz's mother, Polly, noted that the family often used "to tease him that he went into politics to change the world." Jontz noted that everybody had their own way of doing business, and he always felt most comfortable in "raising issues and taking on interests that I thought ought to be taken on. You pay a price, but that is what I chose to do."[12]

U.S. Senator Dick Durbin of Illinois, a longtime Jontz friend, called him a "bridge builder." While one school of politics said the way to win elections was to divide people into groups and set them against one another, Jontz, Durbin noted, "wanted to build bridges and understanding between groups that too often saw themselves as enemies: organized labor and environmentalists, and family farmers and environmentalists. He was always trying to find some common ground." For example, Durbin noted that Jontz believed one of the ways to preserve family farms was to help farmers be better guardians of the land. "That seemed like a strange idea to some people twenty-five years ago," Durbin said. "Today, it surely makes sense."[13]

Jontz managed to win re-election in his Republican-dominated district thanks to a combination of tireless grassroots, door-to-door campaigning; a relentless focus on serving his constituents through such activities as town hall meetings, a toll-free number for those wishing to question their congressman, and face-to-face encounters at neighborhood coffee shops at all hours of the day (informal meetings called "Jontzings" by *Logansport Pharos-Tribune* reporter Dave Kitchell); and a willingness to listen to dissenting opinions. "You have to disagree sometimes," he noted. "But you have to disagree agreeably." Tom Buis, a legislative assistant specializing in agricultural issues in Jontz's Washington, D.C., office, said Jontz's style involved really listening to people. He always believed that "you don't hear much when you're talking all the time," but by listening he could discover what a person was really concerned about and how to address their issues. "He was one of those people that in his role as a public servant took it very seriously," Buis said of Jontz. "He worked tirelessly at it and encouraged all those who worked for him to do likewise. I think that's a legacy that won't be easily forgotten by those who worked with Jim or for Jim or knew Jim."[14]

Each election season voters in Jontz's congressional district could count on hearing a knock on their front door and seeing the rumpled, tousle-haired Democrat ready to promote his candidacy and talk about whatever issue that might concern them that year. "I campaigned on the personal attention idea," Jontz said. "Issues are important to people, but more important to them is feeling that government is responsive." Tom Sugar, a longtime Jontz aide who later in his career served as chief of staff for former U.S. Senator Evan Bayh of Indiana, said that during a campaign Jontz "believed in knocking on every door that was knockable."[15]

On a typical campaign day, Jontz began knocking on doors on one side of the street at three in the afternoon, while an aide took the other side of the street. The usual conversation began with introducing themselves, telling a homeowner that Jontz was campaigning in the area, and giving them material on his candidacy. If someone was not at home, Jontz left behind literature about his candidacy with a note signed, "Sorry I missed you." Sugar said that the rule of thumb was that the campaign did not "stop knocking on doors until people started showing up [dressed] in robes." The candidate also made it a

Every Fourth of July while in office, Jontz could be found riding his bicycle in parades throughout the Fifth Congressional District. Here, he waves to a crowd in Rochester, Indiana, on July 4, 1990.

habit of scanning newspapers in his district to find such events as fish fries and pancake breakfasts to attend and interact with voters. "He joked to me that he campaigned door to door just to keep his weight down," Perdue recalled.[16]

The congressman remained in Washington only when he had to, spending the rest of his time in Indiana attending to a packed schedule of events; his staff had to create specialized computer software just to keep track of where he had to appear each day. Whenever a community in his district hosted a parade, Jontz, who began his two-wheeled campaigning during his days as a state representative, could be found peddling up and down the street on his sister's rusty, old blue Schwinn bicycle with mismatched tires, waving to the crowd lining the curb, his tie flapping in the breeze—an effort that won him the title of "best congressman on two wheels" from one Indiana reporter. "People used to joke . . . if there were two people together, Jim Jontz would find them," said Kathy Altman, who ran Jontz's district offices in Kokomo and Valparaiso. His tireless campaigning and work on behalf of his district inspired, exhausted, and sometimes exasperated his staff and volunteers. "He was as driven as

A grinning Jontz sits on the steps near the U.S. Capitol during his first term as a congressman in 1987. "He was first and foremost very principled about what he believed," said his sister, Mary Lee Turk. "He would not have compromised any of his stances."

anyone I ever met," said Perdue. "It was as though he needed to work in order to breath." The long hours took a toll on his hardworking staff, who tried, and sometimes failed, to match Jontz's pace. "For everyone on staff, this was definitely a labor of love," recalled Scott Paul, who worked for the congressman in his Washington, D.C., office. "You worked for Jim because you believed in what he was doing and were happy to do the work because he was an unfailingly kind and decent human being and boss, but you knew you were going to put in long hours to do it the Jim Jontz way."[17]

The national media also paid attention, finding Jontz to be a good story, noted Scott Campbell, who served as the congressman's press secretary. "There were other liberal Democrats in the U.S. Congress, there were other conservative districts in the U.S. Congress, but the number of solidly Republican districts represented by liberal Democrats was a number you could count on your hand," said Campbell.[18]

Christopher Klose, who managed Jontz's first run for Congress and served as his chief of staff in Washington, D.C., called his former boss "a true populist," noting he could be just as distrustful of mindless government as he could of reckless corporate behavior. He remembered Jontz saying that issues needed to be examined from "top to bottom, not left to right." One of Klose's favorite memories of Jontz is one culled from the campaign trail. After another long day and night seeking votes, the candidate, after packing up his car for the next day's schedule of events, uttered what came to be known to his staff as the Jim Jontz prayer. "Jim would just shake his head and look up and say, 'Lord, help me win this one, and I promise next time we'll do it right,'" Klose said.[19]

This single-minded devotion to serving the voters—he kept a homemade sign given to him by a supporter on the door to his Washington, D.C., office that read "This Office belongs to the people of Indiana's 5th District"—came with a price in his private life, as Jontz saw his two marriages end in divorce. "He always had a goal," said his first wife, Elaine Caldwell Emmi, who today lives in Salt Lake City, Utah. "He knew exactly what he wanted to do." She recalled one conversation with her husband as their marriage was falling apart in which she told him that every morning she awoke questioning if this is what she wanted to be doing and how should she lead her life. "He looked at me and said, 'I never ask that question. I know exactly what I should be doing,'" Emmi said. "I think he really liked being a public official, a servant of the people—that was really his goal." Being a congressman, noted one of Jontz's aides, became his "all-consuming passion." Jontz never, however, let the power of his office go to his head. Amy Isaacs, for many years the national director for Americans for Democratic Action, the country's oldest progressive advocacy organization, noted she had a friend who worked with the House's Foreign Affairs Committee who told her "these people came into town and had three months when they were people and then they became members of Congress. That didn't happen to Jim. He was always Jim, no matter what." Throughout his life, though, Jontz, kept his private life just that, private, with many of his colleagues and supporters unaware about details of his background. "He tended to compartmentalize his life," recalled Andy Kerr, an environmental activist who worked with Jontz over the years and only learned he had a sister after the congressman's death. "The cause was more important."[20]

Jontz's passion for public service was infectious, even attracting volunteers for his campaigns from as far away as Canada. During his days as a graduate student at the University of Toronto in the mid-1980s, Brian Mayes, no fan of the then American president, Ronald Reagan, decided to satisfy his

Jontz shares a story with Duneland School Corporation students. During his time in the Indiana legislature, Jontz supported a "minimum competency testing" law requiring certain levels in basic skills before a student could graduate from high school.

fascination with U.S. politics by volunteering his services to a worthy Democratic candidate somewhere in the country. After viewing a documentary on Indiana congressman Pete Visclosky, who represented the First Congressional District, Mayes called Visclosky's office, but was told that his efforts might be better appreciated by another Hoosier candidate who was involved in a close battle to serve the Fifth District—Jontz. When Mayes learned that Jontz's Republican opponent, Indiana state senator Jim Butcher, had the support of evangelical minister Pat Robertson and conservative activist Phyllis Schlafly, he signed on as a Jontz volunteer and took a train to Rensselaer, Indiana, to begin his work. "Here was an opportunity to get involved in a close race with the opportunity to sway the undecided," said Mayes, a native of Winnipeg, Manitoba, who was also drawn to Indiana by his "unhealthy affection" for the music of John Cougar Mellencamp. As he learned more about Jontz, Mayes came to admire the politician's attempt to promote an "activist vision that government should 'get back on your side' not merely 'get off your back.'" Mayes was also impressed that Jontz had the courage to oppose such pet projects of

Reagan as aid to the Contra rebels in Nicaragua and the strategic defense initiative ("Star Wars," as it was called then) right "in the heartland of the nation."

Mayes's major involvement with the Jontz campaign included various office tasks and going door to door, handing out leaflets in Kokomo and in such small communities as Russiaville and Camden. His most "powerful experience" came in seeking votes from those waiting in line for distribution of free government surplus food, often cheese, through the U.S. Department of Agriculture. "How do you respond to a haggard farmer telling you, 'If your fellow gets in tell him to put an end to these goddamn breadlines and let these people get back to work'?" Mayes asked. The Canadian also endured a bit of culture shock as he tried to get used to Hoosiers' "near-religious support" for their local high school teams and observed that the car of choice seemed to be the Chevrolet El Camino. "There were ice cream socials and turkey dinners," Mayes noted. "Locking the car door at one of these got me labeled as a 'city boy.'"

Although Mayes and the rest of the volunteers and campaign staff worked hard that fall, nobody exceeded the effort put forth by Jontz, who had earned a reputation as a relentless campaigner during his days as a state representative and senator. One day Mayes decided he wanted to see what a full day with the candidate was like, so he followed Jontz as he worked from early in the morning until late at night—an effort that "almost killed me," Mayes recalled—visiting workers at factories, attending prayer breakfasts, and his usual door-to-door visits across the large district. "He was very good at the door," Mayes said of Jontz. "He didn't dumb it down or try to impress people with his power. He was just himself." The hard work paid off; Jontz defeated Butcher. "Jontz's ability to communicate his priorities on jobs, trade, and farm aid showed that he could speak to the people on their terms," said Mayes, "and take a 'liberal' message and make it one of common sense."

Mayes continued to travel to Indiana every fall to volunteer for Jontz during his campaigns for re-election in 1988, 1990, and 1992, when Jontz went down to defeat. Over the years, Mayes kept in touch with Jontz, and even had the tables turned when the former congressman journeyed to Canada to help Mayes in his unsuccessful campaign for a seat on the Toronto City Council. Today, Mayes is an attorney in Brandon, Manitoba, where he serves on the school board. One of his sharpest memories of his time with Jontz comes from an item in the diary he kept about his time in the 1988 campaign. The entry reads: "Canvas in Medaryville . . . off to Gas 'N Go, check-out lady to

In a rare moment of relaxation, Jontz reads a book at his home in Portland, Oregon. A friend, Lynn-Marie Crider, remembered asking him time and time again to take a few hours off for a hike. "I always lost those struggles," she said.

Jim, 'You're the only reason I go to vote.'" More than any other politician he had known, Mayes added, Jontz possessed the ability to inspire "people to believe in [the] democratic process. That is true leadership."[21]

In 1994 Jontz made his final try for political office, losing a longshot attempt to unseat U.S. Senator Richard Lugar, a fellow Eagle Scout. After his defeat, Jontz left Indiana to work on behalf of a number of progressive causes in an attempt to forge coalitions among labor and environmental groups. He led an unsuccessful campaign to stop the passage of the North American Free Trade Agreement with the Citizens Trade Campaign, helped protect the Endangered Species Act when it was under attack in the 1990s as director of the Endangered Species Coalition, campaigned to save old-growth forests as executive director of the Western Ancient Forest Campaign, and tried to foster progressive causes as president of the Americans for Democratic Action "He always was an activist," said Altman. Jontz worked especially hard in these positions to establish and support strong grassroots organizations and to build bridges between such groups as labor unions and environmentalists. He could be relentless in promoting his cause. Roger Featherstone, who worked with Jontz to save the ESA, said one of the favorite sayings from Jontz was: "When they feel the heat, they start to see the light." Even when he was no longer in office, Jontz used the entrée he had earned as an ex-congressman to further causes he believed in. "He walked the line between folks who do things by the book, and folks who think out of the box," said Bart Chilton, who worked as Jontz's legislative director when he first came to Congress before moving on to a job at the U.S. Department of Agriculture during Bill Clinton's presidency. "He was right on the edge, he knew enough about the system to know how to work it, yet he wasn't complacent and accepting that that's the way you always had to do things. Whatever means he could use that he thought appropriate, he would do it to . . . move forward on his agenda." Chilton recalled that a group from the Pacific Northwest wanted to meet with Secretary of the Agriculture Dan Glickman on a conservation matter and Jontz used his name to successfully arrange a meeting. On the day of the meeting, Jontz, noted Chilton, was nowhere to be found, but Glickman acquiesced to continuing with the meeting as planned. "He walked the line," noted Chilton of his former boss.[22]

According to Lynn-Marie Crider, Jontz's friend from the Service Employees International Union, the former congressman always thought about "how change happens, how one step leads to another, how what looks to others like defeat can be turned into the next step along the path to a goal that we share." Smart, frugal (he bought his copy of the *New York Times* at a Starbucks Coffee Company store near his residence, but he refused to buy coffee there because it was too expensive), with little tolerance for small talk, and a "bit of a hermit," Jontz, said Crider, "thrived on being connected to people in motion." Although he had a deep commitment to the environment, she said he also "understood the struggle of the working class, and he cared deeply about their predicament and was able to marry those concerns in a way that few could."[23]

Jontz moved to Portland, Oregon, in 1999, but Indiana still had a hold on him. He told his mother that his thoughts sometimes turned to one day returning to the Hoosier State to buy a plot of land in the Brown County hills, where he could sit back, relax, and enjoy the magnificent trees. He never had that chance, dying at his home in Portland on April 14, 2007, after a two-year battle with colon cancer that had spread to his liver.

Visiting him during the former congressman's final illness, Sugar recalled walking into a Portland hospital room to see Jontz on a conference call with fellow workers in the environmental cause, offering them his ideas on what to do next. "Jim was always focused on doing the right thing, the good thing, the thing he believed to be right and true," Sugar noted. "People become very cynical about politics today, but Jim Jontz was the real deal." For Campbell, hearing about Jontz's death reminded him of campaign stop the two of them had made to one house in a small town in the Fifth District. "I've never had a congressman come to my door in the twenty-nine years that I've been an adult," Campbell remembered the homeowner telling Jontz. "When you live in some very small town like Royal Center, Indiana, and not just you, but half the

Jontz is lost in the shadows in Washington, D.C. "For him," *wrote Dave Kitchell of the* Logansport Pharos-Tribune *following Jontz's death in 2007,* "fighting windmills wasn't an impossible dream. He wouldn't have wanted it any other way."

CALUMET REGIONAL ARCHIVES, INDIANA UNIVERSITY NORTHWEST

town says my congressman knocked on my door today, that means something," said Campbell.[24]

To the end, Jontz remained optimistic that coalitions could be formed to work together to save forests and other wild areas from destruction. For years he had been inspired in his efforts on the environment's behalf by Doctor Seuss's book *The Lorax*. The book is a powerful comment on the destruction of nature, telling how a greedy character named the Once-ler fails to heed the warnings of the Lorax and ravages Truffula trees to service his factories until the air is polluted and the animals have fled. The sad Lorax floats away through the smog leaving behind a pile of rocks on which are etched the word: "UNLESS."

Suess's book offered some hope, as the now despondent Once-ler hands a young boy to whom he has been telling his story to the last remaining Truffula seed. Throughout his life, Jontz symbolized that same sense of hope. According to his fellow environmentalist Evans, Jontz's most enduring legacy is his constant reminder that "even seemingly hopeless causes can be won. All we need is the right kind of leader, a person of high spirit and sunny optimism, and, above all, a large and courageous heart."[25]

2

An Activist's Awakening

On the eve of Election Day in November 1974, Kathy Altman, volunteer White County coordinator for Democratic candidate Floyd Fithian's successful run to represent the Second Congressional District against incumbent Republican congressman Earl Landgrebe, was driving back with her husband, Jerry, to their house in Monticello, Indiana. The couple had just finished a long day's work setting up a get-out-to-vote effort on Fithian's behalf. Suddenly, the car's headlights flashed into the rainy darkness and lit upon a lonely figure trudging down the road—Jim Jontz, a young, first-time candidate for the Indiana House of Representatives.

Jontz had been staying at the Altman's home while engaging in a dogged door-to-door campaign in the four counties of the Twentieth District. Altman and her husband asked him if he needed any help. "No, it's late," Altman remembered Jontz responding, "but there's a laundromat up there that's still open I think I'll go hit before I quit for the night."[1]

The next day Jontz, a twenty-two-year-old Indiana University graduate with an unpaid job as a caretaker for a local nature preserve, defeated his heavily favored Republican opponent, John M. "Jack" Guy, one of the Republican Party's leading figures in the Indiana House. Jontz had entered the race in the majority Republican district in large part to oppose a multimillion-dollar U.S. Army Corps of Engineers dam project on Big Pine Creek near Williamsport, Indiana. "I must have knocked on half the doors in the district," he said of what he called a "shoe-leather" campaign. "And I found that people like to have someone come to their door and talk to them, even if it is a young kid. I told them that I wasn't a lawyer or politician, but that I was interested in people, in dealing with them personally. And that was about it."[2]

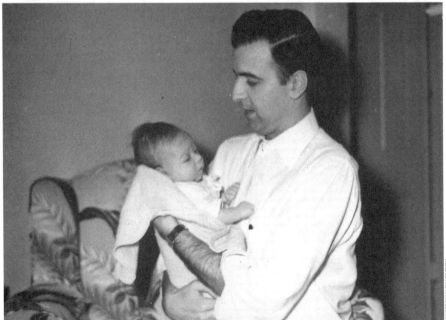

Jim Jontz, born on December 18, 1951, is held by his father, Leland, and his mother, Polly.

The determination that Jontz displayed in his first run for public office was something that had been developed early in his days living in the Hoosier State. Born on December 18, 1951, in Indianapolis, the state capital, Jontz was the first of two children born to Leland D., a local businessman, and Pauline (Polly) Prather Jontz. A daughter, Mary Lee, was born on October 12, 1955. Leland had worked for a time in the marketing department at a meat- processing firm in Indianapolis before opening a furniture store downtown. The business later became Leland's, a fireplace and tool store located on Eighty-sixth Street and Ditch Road. Mary Lee remembered her father, who died in 1995, as an "artistic, kindly, gentle, quiet man."[3]

Although busy raising her son and daughter, Polly found time to volunteer at the Children's Museum of Indianapolis, one of the most respected facilities of its kind in the country. The museum later hired her as its public relations director and she also worked as its development director. "I suspect I was one of the very early women to make the transition from volunteer to paid professional," Polly told a reporter from the *Indianapolis Star*. In 1982 she became president of the Conner Prairie Pioneer Settlement, a living-history museum near Fishers, Indiana, working there until her retirement in 1996. Her work at Conner Prairie won praise from other museum professionals, with one noting that Polly "built a remarkable program that really makes for a wonderful adventure for visitors." Her children, however, could always count on her to be there when they needed her. She remembers rising at the crack of dawn to drive her high-school age son for hockey practice at the Indiana Fairgrounds Coliseum. On another occasion Polly and a friend, Eve Corbin, braved a blizzard to decorate a church hall for a banquet involving Jontz's Boy Scout troop. "The banquet was, of course, canceled [because of the heavy snow], but that church was decorated," Corbin recalled with satisfaction.[4]

In the years following World War II the soldiers who had endured frozen feet during the Battle of the Bulge in Europe and had hacked their way through jungle canopies on Pacific islands in search of the Japanese enemy had returned home to begin new lives and forget, if they could, the horrors of combat. Veterans earned college degrees with the assistance of the GI Bill and, with their diplomas in hand, looked for decent jobs in the booming economy. After marriage, these veterans settled down to raise families in homes located in suburban tracts on the fringes of large cities they purchased with the aid of mortgages guaranteed by the federal government.

A 1958 view of busy West Market Street in downtown Indianapolis (above). The Traction Terminal at Market and Illinois streets across from Block's was a bus station and a major transportation hub for the city. The downtown's shopping supremacy, however, was soon threatened by the growth of suburban malls, including the Glendale Center, a model of which is shown at top.

Indianapolis in the postwar years mirrored changes that were under way in other communities across the country, as families moved to suburban neighborhoods with names such as Devington, Ivy Hills, Greenbriar, Delaware Trails, and Brockton. At the start of the decade, Indianapolis consumers shopped downtown at such large department stores as L. S. Ayres and Company on Washington Street and William H. Block Company on Illinois Street. But as people began moving from the urban center to homes in the suburbs, new developments—shopping malls—sprang up to serve their needs. Glendale Center opened in 1958, ushering in a host of similar shopping centers, including Castleton, Greenwood, Lafayette Square, and Washington Square. Leaders in the local Chamber of Commerce saw this growth as good for business, and were also proud that such leading companies as Ford, Chrysler, and Western Electric opened new factories in the area. The chamber strove, as Indiana historian James H. Madison noted, "to keep taxes low, avoid the snares of federal aid, and maintain Indianapolis as a pleasant city with a small-town feeling."[5]

The Jontz family lived at 1141 East Eightieth Street in a three-bedroom, ranch home located just north of the Indiana School for the Blind between North College Avenue and Westfield Boulevard in Washington Township. The township was undergoing a boom in population, growing from approximately sixteen thousand residents in 1950 to more than forty thousand by 1970. The Jontz home sat on top of a small hill in an area with mature trees and near a creek that became a favorite place for the neighborhood's children to explore. "It was a wonderful place to live," Mary Lee said of the home she lived in until the age of eighteen. There were two large cherry trees in the backyard. Mary Lee and her brother had the chore of climbing the trees when the cherries were ripe, picking the fruit, and placing them in buckets to carry inside. Polly would then use the fruit to make cherry pies until the supply was exhausted.[6]

David Corbin, who grew up in a house just around the corner on Meadowbrook Drive and was a close friend of Jontz's through high school, has fond memories of the neighborhood. Corbin described the area as "sort of a classic, idyllic middle-class suburbia for the 1950s," as it was a safe, close-knit, and egalitarian community with young parents of the baby-boom generation who were establishing themselves in new middle-class careers to support their growing families. "It was a place where there were a great number of kids—you were never at a loss for playmates," said Corbin, who added that the neighborhood provided them with a nurturing environment in which to grow up.[7]

Jontz engaged in activities that marked him as a child of the 1950s, including serving in the Boy Scouts (above), where he achieved the rank of Eagle Scout, and playing baseball at his grandmother's home in Silver Lake, Indiana (opposite).

The young Jontz displayed a liking for organization and a love of nature while growing up in the the Northern Hills subdivision. "Mom encouraged me to chase butterflies, and we bought all the Golden [Nature] guidebooks," he said.[8] At the age of five, Jontz even came up with a sure-fire method for catching butterflies. He advised obtaining some stones and a rake, digging a hole in the ground, and "picking any kind of flowers and take them along with some string. Tie one end of the string onto the flowers at one end of the string and one end of the string onto the rake." After sticking the rake into the hole, Jontz said to pile the stones beside the rake to make sure it stood up straight. "I guarantee if you don't catch a butterfly that you should not read the book and don't try it again," he concluded. Polly helped her son with his moth and butterfly collections, carefully preparing the specimens for mounting and display. Jontz loved exploring the neighborhood's fields and woods, followed

everywhere he went by Herbert, his father's English springer spaniel. The two romped and played until they were called home for dinner by Polly ringing a bell hanging on the back door of the family home.[9]

Nature provided the perfect playground for the neighborhood children. Corbin noted that there were undeveloped woods behind his home and a creek, fed by Windcombe Pond, ran through the area and in front of Jontz's home. "We probably spent the better part of half a dozen years in those woods and in that creek, literally," Corbin remembered. They played games in the woods, climbed trees, examined the insects that lived there, and were fascinated by the crawdads and frogs splashing in the creek. In the winter months, they played pick-up hockey matches on the frozen Windcombe Pond and sledded on a hill across the street from Jontz's house. "That had a pretty substantial effect on both Jim and myself in particular among the kids in our neighborhood given some of his subsequent environmental interests and concerns and the kind of direction my life took," said Corbin, who today is vice president of planning and development for a Colorado ski resort and has been involved in a number of environmental organizations. "I think that physical environment really had a profound effect on him [Jontz]."[10]

Polly remembered her son as "a very intense child, very curious, very serious, [and] very focused." Jontz's kindergarten teacher at Nora Elementary School told his mother that he had been the only student she had taught "who had the dignity to be president of the United States." Jacquelyn Pavey, Jontz's English teacher at Northview Junior High School, said that he was the kind of student "who does not appear often, and when he does he is a true delight." Although he worked well with others while her pupil, Pavey said Jontz was "too much of an individual to 'follow the crowd.'" She also described him as "intelligent, perceptive, and creative as well. His polite and reserved manner cannot hide his quick wit and profound thoughts."[11]

As a young man Jontz also displayed the leadership qualities that served him well during his political career, organizing his friends for impromptu football games (his sister and her friend were recruited to play, but only as offensive linemen) and bicycle races up and down a hilly course through the neighborhood each May during the annual running of the Indianapolis 500 automobile race. Corbin noted that because Jontz was a little bigger and a little stronger than other children in the neighborhood, he usually won those races. "People certainly looked up to him because he was smart as a kid and capable," Corbin said of his friend. "He had a leadership quality that was recognized among us kids from an early age." Jontz did enjoy athletics, participating in Little League baseball and also taking on his sister in some epic ping-pong games on a table in the family's basement recreation room. "He was a fun young man to know because he was interested in everything," said Polly.[12]

On family trips during the summer to historic sites and national parks, Jontz made sure to add to his growing rock collection by stopping at every rock store on the route and hunting for geodes along the roadside with his pickaxe, noted Mary Lee. His other hobbies included music (Jontz played the piano, trombone, and French horn) and a devotion to the ideals of the Boy Scouts of America as a member of Troop Number 117, earning the rank of Eagle Scout while in the seventh grade. "My main aims now are to receive a good education, to become an asset to my community and a good citizen, and to live up to the Scout oath and law," Jontz wrote in his application for

COURTESY MARY LEE TURK

The Jontz family explored a variety of attractions on vacation trips. Here, Jontz is with his father and sister, Mary Lee, during a stop at the Great Smoky Mountains National Park on the North Carolina and Tennessee state line.

Eagle Scout to the BSA Central Indiana Council. He also indicated his interest "in conservation, especially in forestry." When he was older, Jontz continued to support the organization, working summers at Camp Belzer, a Boy Scout reservation near Lawrence, Indiana. "I hope that we engendered in him some kind of early respect for the environment," said Polly, "but I really credit the Boy Scouts." Jontz also maintained his interest in the outdoors by later leading nature hikes through Indianapolis parks for the Children's Museum and serving as a naturalist for the Indiana State Parks system at Shakamak State Park near Jasonville, Indiana, where he also led visitors on hikes through the park's trails, identifying the different flora and fauna participants encountered on the walk. Pat Puckett, who often camped at Shakamak with his parents, remembered going on those Jontz-led hikes on weekend visits and became impressed by his knowledge about the outdoors. "He took his job very seriously," Puckett remembered.[13]

A glimpse into his experiences leading nature hikes can be gleaned from a story Jontz later wrote for *Etchings in Thought*, an anthology of student compositions for students at North Central High School from 1969 to 1970. In his essay, titled "The Law of Nature," Jontz described a hike he led on a clear June day near a lake. Two of the boys along for the day called for his attention when they came across a water moccasin struggling to bring a fish he had caught to shore. "The unsuspecting fish had swum too close to his [the snake's] hiding place in the underwater reeds, and, feeling a twinge of hunger deep inside, the snake had struck with lightening speed," Jontz wrote. He and his young hikers stood enthralled by the spectacle that finished with the snake triumphant. "For ten minutes we stood breathless until the last of the victim's tail disappeared in one great gulp," Jontz noted, "and the fish was no more than a lump in the snake's stomach." As the snake slithered away into the weeds, he said the scene of the struggle looked as though nothing had happened. "Only within us was there a real change," Jontz said. "We had seen the law of nature."[14]

His time with the state parks might have implanted in Jontz the germ of the idea of entering public service. Jontz's boss was a man named Bill Waters. One day Waters picked him up at his parents' home on the north side of town to take him to work at the Indiana State Fair. As the two drove to the fairgrounds, Waters turned to him and asked, "Jim, have you ever given any thought to a career in public service?" Jontz laughed and told him at the time: "No. All I really want to do is be a naturalist." Many years later, when Jontz was in Washington, D.C., as a congressman, Waters retired as director of the Indiana's state parks and took a position with the National Park Service in the nation's capital. Jontz wondered if he would receive a call from Waters to "find out how my career as a naturalist is coming."[15]

Jontz's interest in nature meant that there were often wild animals roaming his family's Indianapolis home. Camp Belzer had a small zoo with rescued wild animals. At the end of one summer, Jontz brought home with him a de-scented skunk that he named Jerome. Although his father built a cage for the skunk, it sometimes escaped and wandered through the house looking for hiding places. During one try for freedom the skunk sought refuge under a bed and bit Leland on the finger when he attempted to retrieve it and return it to its enclosure. Other members of Jontz's wildlife menagerie included a red-tailed hawk that Jontz fed raw meat and a squirming mass of baby rattlesnakes. "You never knew what would be in our house," noted Mary Lee.[16]

In 1967 Jontz, while a student at North Central High School, led local youths on nature hikes in city parks through a program sponsored by the Children's Museum of Indianapolis. At Holliday Park he instructs (from left) Jimmy Root, Beth Root, and Eileen King.

Jontz and Jerome, the de-scented pet skunk he loved, but the rest of the family, at best, tolerated.

Those who grew up with Jontz and went to the same schools he did vividly remember his compelling interest in the natural world. "I remember Jim as a good guy and quite a character," said Frederic M. Martin, who was in eighth grade with Jontz and today is a minister in Bemidji, Minnesota. Martin particularly remembered an assignment a teacher gave them to do a report on a nonfiction book of their choice. For his book, noted Martin, Jontz selected *The Indiana Weed Book*, written by Willis Stanley Blatchley and originally released in 1912 by the Nature Publishing Company of Indianapolis. "It's not a bestseller," Martin said. "It is exactly what it sounds like—a book devoted to describing the weeds that you can find in the state of Indiana. Like I said, Jim was quite a character." Martin was not surprised that Jontz later became heavily involved with the environmental movement. "What would you expect from a guy who read *The Indiana Weed Book* as an eighth grader?" he asked.[17]

Jontz tried his hand at writing while in junior high school in 1967, helping to produce a book titled "The All American Boy Meets the Rather Hairy Beast on the Bridge." The book grew out of an English assignment on the proper parts of speech (nouns, verbs, adverbs, and adjectives) and involved Jontz and his friends Larry Peck and Kent Shields. For the homework assignment, Peck recalled that he had started writing about a "rather hairy beast" and decided to expand the story with the help of his two friends. The friends got together at school and at each others' homes to collaborate on the book. It was a modern fairy tale about a boy who leaves his home seeking fame and fortune, encounters an odd creature (the hairy beast) on his travels, and the adventures the two have along the way back home. After producing a copy of the book on an old typewriter, the boys gave the manuscript to Peck's father, who ran off copies on a mimeograph machine, after which the friends stapled the pages together to make about a hundred books in all. Shields remembered that they took the books to school and were able to sell about forty or fifty copies at twenty-five cents apiece to their classmates, "which was a bestseller in our opinion at the time."

Shields, who produced all of the illustrations while Jontz and Peck provided the copy, said the book was a bit of a "scandal" at the time because they had produced and sold it without any permission from administrators at the junior high. But the adults in charge at the school had the final say on the matter, as they seized upon an item that Jontz had put in the book as an inside joke. On an opening page he had included the statement that all of the bird illustrations inside were drawn from nature by J. J. Audubon (John James Audubon, famous for his colorful paintings of North American birds). There were not, however, any bird illustrations in the book, by Audubon or by anyone else. Jontz had put the statement in to see who would notice, which was "typical of his sense of humor," Shields said. School administrators did not get the joke and insisted that it could no longer be sold at the junior high because of possible copyright infringement. The boys' parents "thought it was all good fun," recalled Shields.[18]

From his parents Jontz learned the lesson of always following his convictions, but expressing disagreement within established structures. Both Polly and Leland were staunch Republicans, and were surprised to hear their son note, after saying something to him about your party, meaning the GOP, "Mom, I'm a Democrat." Despite their political differences, his parents supported Jontz's quest to find a suitable vocation for his devotion to hard work and wide knowledge. Jontz and Polly shared a number of the same personality traits, Corbin noted. "I see a lot of his mother in him," Corbin said of Jontz. They both possessed a "seriousness of purpose, organizational ability, and intellectual rigor."[19]

The high school Jontz and his friends attended, North Central, offered students a quality education that stressed academics. "It was a school full of high achievers," said Peck. The new North Central building had opened in 1963 to great fanfare, with a reporter from the *Indianapolis News* calling it "one of the most modern schools in America." Costing $6.75 million, the school had a state-of-the-art library, numerous science laboratories, a fifteen-hundred-seat auditorium, and a large gymnasium that could seat more than four thousand spectators for basketball games. Shields noted that due to the large number of students (the school had room for approximately three thousand) attending North Central, the experience could be a bit "impersonal," as because of large class sizes it was hard to get to know your teachers and "you tended to lose track of people you had know earlier on" in lower grades.[20]

In addition to its strong academic reputation, North Central became known for fielding capable athletic teams, as it could draw upon its large student body. As William F. Gulde, a longtime history teacher at North Central, noted in his history of the school, students were, perhaps unfairly, seen by other Indianapolis teenagers as belonging to "the sportscar set," with most assuming their families were wealthy. Although the school had no dress code, girls were not allowed to wear short dresses or pants and some boys were suspended because they had let their hair grow down below their ears in the style of their favorite rock band, The Beatles.

Other national issues also intruded on day-to-day activities, including America's involvement in the Vietnam War. Students who were turning eighteen were worried about possibly being drafted in military service; a fate they could avoid by going on to college and receiving a student deferment. In November 1969 a cultural committee of North Central's student council sponsored a seminar on the country's role in the Vietnam War. Approximately 140 people attended the seminar, with speakers on both sides of the issue.[21]

During his three years at North Central, Jontz played trombone in the school's stage band and displayed a keen interest in academics, taking several accelerated classes aimed at improving his chances at succeeding later on at college (during his junior year he achieved a 1,473 overall score—753 verbal and 720 math—on the Scholastic Aptitude Test). "He was very much an academically oriented kid in those days," said Corbin. Another friend, Richard Stock, said that he and Jontz engaged in some "friendly competition" during their senior year in high school. Because the school did not offer an advanced placement class in European history, the two of them did an independent study of the subject. "Jim was amused by the contrast between us because he was already extremely organized and was reading the appropriate textbooks," said Stock, "while I just dabbled around having spent years reading every type of history I could get hold of." Even while he was in high school, Jontz, Stock remembered, had a passion for the natural world that "was more rooted in knowledge than the rest of us. He really had absorbed an environmental ethic that was not yet common."[22]

Although Jontz maintained a serious demeanor when it came to his studies, Peck said that his friend remained "a joy to be around," noting that he "was a very upbeat person . . . and very enthusiastic." Whatever Jontz had his hand in—from being in the band to his involvement in classroom work or in Boy Scouting—he did it in a good mood and possessed an optimism about life that was infectious, Peck added. One of the things that struck Corbin the most about his friend was the person he knew in high school "was indeed a very serious young guy. He was definitely a very good student; he was very capable intellectually if he chose to." However, the Jontz he saw and spoke to in later years when he was involved in politics, had become, not in any derogatory sense, "very much sort of a backslapper and . . . exhibited a kind of casual affability that I would not have attributed to him in high school, but obviously had become part of his persona, and indeed must have been necessary for his professional persona as a public official or politician."[23]

After graduating from North Central in 1970, ranking eleventh academically in a graduating class of 1,100 students, Jontz entered Williams College, a small liberal-arts institution in Massachusetts. He spent only a single semester there, taking classes in art history, Greek literature, Greek philosophy, environmental biology, and geology. He decided to leave the East Coast and return to Indiana. Williams, he said, was just "too academic" for his tastes. "I read 12 hours a day there," Jontz recalled. "I had had enough of that, so when I came to I.U. [Indiana University] I had some spare time."[24]

In January 1971 Jontz enrolled at IU, Bloomington, where he majored in geology. Jontz began his studies at Bloomington during a time when campuses across the United States were in turmoil. Since the late 1960s college students had organized to protest the Vietnam War. The American commitment to assist the South Vietnamese government in its fight against the Communists from North Vietnam had grown from under a thousand military advisers in 1960 to more than half a million soldiers by 1968. The decision by President Richard Nixon to expand the war into Cambodia in late April 1970 had enraged antiwar activists, who responded with demonstrations that sometimes grew violent as police clashed with protestors.

On May 4, 1970, tragedy struck when Ohio National Guard troops opened fire on student protestors at Kent State University. In just thirteen seconds the soldiers fired between sixty-one and sixty-seven shots from their M-1 rifles; the result, four students were killed and nine were wounded. A

Ohio National Guard troops open fire on unarmed students protesting the Vietnam War at Kent State University on May 4, 1970 (above). Mary Ann Vecchio kneels by the body of Jeffrey Miller, one of four students killed that day; nine were wounded (top). One historian called the shootings "a wound in the nation's history."

presidential commission that examined the incident called the shootings "unnecessary, unwarranted, and inexcusable." The tragedy at Kent State incited boycotts of classes at more than a 130 campuses; some protesters became so enraged that they burned down buildings where young army officers were taught in Reserve Officers' Training Corps programs.

At IU, a May 6, 1970, rally drew eight thousand students to Dunn Meadow (a grassy field close to the Indiana Memorial Union in the center of campus popular as a student gathering place). Although students were still upset about the shootings in Ohio, the protest went off without incident.

Author and environmentalist Rachel Carson holds a copy of her best-selling book Silent Spring. *In her book she noted that "only within the moment of time represented by the present century has one species—man—acquired significant power to alter the nature of the world."*

"We don't want to have a Kent State here," said Keith Parker, an antiwar leader on campus. "We don't need any more martyrs to our cause. We have a duty to ourselves and to humanity to speak out against injustice. To be silent is to endorse it."[25]

The student activists involved in the antiwar movement were also attracted to other causes aimed at improving American society. Many were drawn toward the conservation of natural resources. Unlike the efforts of pioneering conservationists in the late nineteenth and early twentieth centuries such as Theodore Roosevelt and John Muir, this was not an attempt to preserve scenic splendor for people to enjoy, but a movement to halt mankind's negative effects on nature, especially the introduction of dangerous pesticides and chemicals into the environment. The growth of this modern environmental movement had been nurtured in part in 1962 with the publication of a book called *Silent Spring* by Rachel Carson, an author and marine biologist who had worked for the U.S. Bureau of Fisheries and later became editor of the Department of Interior's publications. Carson left government service after the success of her 1951 book *The Sea around Us*, a best seller that won the prestigious National Book Award for nonfiction.

The ground was ripe for Carson's new book. Just before Thanksgiving in 1959, consumers were shocked to learn that cranberries for their holiday meals had to be pulled from the market because they had been contaminated with aminotriazole, a weed killer known to cause cancer in humans. In addition, news came from overseas that thalidomide, a drug used by pregnant women to prevent miscarriages, had caused terrible birth defects in newborn babies. First excerpted in the national magazine *The New Yorker*, *Silent Spring* warned that the unrestrained use of pesticides, especially Dichlorodiphenyltrichloroethane (DDT, a synthetic pesticide used to control such insects as mosquitoes and lice), was not only killing birds, but also posed a considerable long-term threat to human health. "I contend, furthermore," Carson wrote, "that we have allowed these chemicals to be used with little or no advance investigation of their effect on soil, water, wildlife, and man himself. Future generations are unlikely to condone our lack of prudent concern for the integrity of the natural world that supports all life."

Powerful chemical companies in the United States spent hundreds of thousands of dollars in an attempt to discredit Carson. Scientists and government officials with ties to the industry unfairly called her a modern-day Cassandra, and former Secretary of Agriculture Ezra Taft Benson went as far as to label her as "probably a Communist." Carson calmly stood firm against the critical barbs thrown her way and defended the quality of her research through interviews with the media. *Silent Spring* became a hit, spending thirty-one weeks on the best-seller list and inspiring a desire in many young people to stop the despoiling of nature. *New Yorker* writer E. B. White called the book the "*Uncle Tom's Cabin* of the environmental movement," comparing Carson's influence to that of Harriet Beecher Stowe's effect on the slavery issue leading up to the American Civil War.[26]

Other ecological disasters that dominated the news headlines encouraged others to rally to the cause of preventing a manmade catastrophe from destroying the Earth's environment. In the 1950s scientists warned of the dangers posed by the aboveground testing of nuclear weapons by both the United States and Soviet Union during the Cold War. Fallout from these tests, especially the radioactive isotope strontium-90, polluted the atmosphere and made its way through the food chain and into people's bodies. Other environmental calamities that shocked Americans included an oil spill in Santa

Barbara, California, that one resident said looked like "a massive, inflamed abscess bursting with reddish-brown pus, and the Cuyahoga River, described by *Time* magazine as the river that "oozes rather than flows," in Cleveland, Ohio, becoming so polluted that it caught fire and burned in 1969. The haunting image of a river actually on fire inspired songwriter Randy Newman to write the song "Burn On," where he sang, "the Cuyahoga River goes smokin' through my dreams."[27]

The world also began to realize how important it was to protect the planet's fragile ecosystem through a photograph of Earth from a perspective none had seen before. American astronauts on the *Apollo 8* mission that became the first time in history men trav-

Astronaut William Anders snapped the famous "Earthrise" photograph on December 24, 1968, during the Apollo 8 *mission—the first manned voyage to orbit the moon. The photo is displayed here in its original orientation, though it is more commonly viewed with the lunar surface at the bottom of the photo.*

eled around the moon also brought back with them stunning photographs of the Earth—including one called "Earthrise," taken from lunar orbit by the three-man crew on December 24, 1968. The image, described by nature photographer Galen Rowell as "the most influential environmental photograph ever taken," shows a lovely, lonely blue-and-white orb floating above the lunar horizon, all alone in the blackness of space.[28]

Responding to the gloomy news about industries belching pollutants into the atmosphere and lakes and rivers strewn with garbage, a group of students at IU had begun attending a weekly Department of Biology seminar taught by Craig E. Nelson, assistant professor of zoology, and Donald R. Whitehead, associate professor of botany, on the environment. "We were beginning to realize that technology was creating many more problems than it was solving," said Whitehead of those days. "We had looked at problems in isola-

U.S. Senator Gaylord Nelson of Wisconsin speaks to an Earth Day crowd in Denver, Colorado, on April 22, 1970. "Our goal is not just an environment of clean air and water and scenic beauty," said Nelson. "The objective is an environment of decency, quality and mutual respect for all other human beings and all living creatures."

tion rather than as part of a connected biosphere." Hoping to do more, the students banded together in September 1969 to start a group called the Committee to Publicize Crisis Biology, whose purpose was "to promote and engage in educational and action projects which work to protect the quality of the environment and to sponsor fund-raising activities to support these projects." Crisis Biology started small at first, offering a prepared series of speeches to give before groups on such subjects as "The Population Explosion," "Air Pollution," "Water Pollution," and "The Effects of Pesticides." Also, the thirty to forty students in the group planned to survey and analyze different areas in the community to gauge their environmental quality. "I should suspect that a core of about 15 to 30 students are doing most of the work," noted Nelson.[29]

Rod Crafts, then a graduate student working toward a master's degree in student personnel administration, served as the committee's adviser and noted that those involved with Crisis Biology were "very genuinely concerned about the future of the planet." Committee members included students majoring in biology, botany, zoology, with a few studying political science or from other related fields, said Crafts. The students who volunteered for Crisis Biology could count on the firm support of faculty members, but Crafts noted that the reaction from their fellow classmates rang the full gamut from some thinking they were "doomsday folks claiming the world is about to come to an end, to others saying, 'This is great, about time,' and everything in between."[30]

The aims of Crisis Biology received a boost due to a one-of-a-kind event that has become a worldwide institution—Earth Day. The nationwide commemoration was the brainchild of U.S. Senator Gaylord Nelson, a Democrat from Wisconsin. During a 1969 speaking tour of the West Coast, where he witnessed at first hand the devastating effects of the Santa Barbara oil spill, Nelson had been inspired from articles he had read about teach-ins against the Vietnam War being conducted at the University of California at Berkeley and at other college campuses. "It popped into my head. That's it!" he recalled. "Why not have an environmental teach-in and get everyone involved?" To help ensure that the project did not smack of partisanship, Nelson was able to convince Congressman Paul McCloskey, a Republican from California, to agree to serve as cochairman. The project had a total budget of less than two hundred thousand dollars and was run mainly by student volunteers, leaving much of the organization up to local communities. "If we had actually been responsible for making the event happen," said Nelson, "it might have taken several years and millions of dollars to pull off."

Earth Day, then known as the National Teach-In on the Crisis of the Environment, had its debut on April 22, 1970—it was a smashing success. Large rallies were held in New York, Washington, D.C., and San Francisco; two thousand colleges and ten thousand elementary and high schools sponsored programs or events; and an estimated twenty million people in all participated. Nelson, who called the event "the biggest town meeting in the nation's history," added that the demonstration had been large enough "to get the attention of the political establishment, and force the issue on to the political agenda. The public was already there, ahead of the politicians. When the people demonstrated their interest, the politicians responded."[31]

The federal government had begun to respond to the new challenges facing the environment even before the first Earth Day. On January 1, 1970, President Nixon signed into law the National Environmental Policy Act, legislation proposed by Senator Henry Jackson of Washington with the assistance of Lynton Caldwell, a public policy expert from IU and Jontz's future father-in-law. The act included a far-reaching provision requiring federal

Students gather near Dunn Meadow at the Indiana University campus in Bloomington, Indiana, for the first Earth Day celebration on April 22, 1970. So many politicians participated in Earth Day activities that Congress had to shut down for a day. One wire service report noted that oratory was "as thick as the smog at rush-hour."

agencies to develop Environmental Impact Statements to cover any possible negative effects to the environment from proposed projects. Other major developments on behalf of nature included the creation of the Environmental Protection Agency, a major federal department charged with enforcing environmental laws; passage of the Clean Air Act that helped decrease air pollution by 80 percent from 1970 to 1990; and key amendments improving the Water Pollution Control Act.

The IU campus played a key role in that first Earth Day, as it was one of only a few sites in the country to host a speech by Nelson. In spite of threatening skies, approximately two thousand students gathered in Dunn Meadow to enjoy live music from such rock-and-roll bands as Pure Funk and the Screaming Gypsies, listen to speeches, and read literature handed out from organizations with "every possible connection to the environment that you might imagine," noted Crafts. As a reporter for the student newspaper, the *Indiana Daily Student*, who covered the event noted, the booths' subject matter

ranged from "Planned Parent-
hood to organic food; from
non-detergent soap to a soft
drink company's use of reusable
bottles."

In his talk to the crowd
in Bloomington, Nelson indicated that it was time to change
mankind's attitudes about the
natural world, noting humans
were the "only animal which
desecrated the environment." He
called for a national policy on air
and water quality to deal with
pollution, as well as setting standards for business and industry
that should be enforced "with
no exceptions." Those attending
the rally greeted Nelson's remarks
with cries

*Jontz reads over some material at the Crisis
Biology offices at IU.*

of "right on" and applause. There was some dissension, however, as a group
of about ten women dressed as witches rushed near the stage, dancing in a
circle and chanting, "Save our bodies, save ourselves" (the women were part
of the group WITCH—Women's International Terrorist Conspiracy from Hell).
According to a report in the *Indiana Daily Student*, the women were demon-
strating for free use of contraceptive devices (Nelson had chaired a Senate
subcommittee investigating the safety of birth control pills) and the ending of
laws restricting abortion. "As I often said," Nelson joked about the minidemon-
stration, "I wonder whether the world is worth saving." An IU student from
Columbus, Indiana, John Goss, who later went on to become director of the
Indiana Department of Natural Resources under Governor Frank O'Bannon,
remembered that first Earth Day as "a real awakening for me and a lot of other
people," inspiring them to work for the environment on campus and in the
state as well.[32]

With his interest in the environment, Jontz was a natural fit to work with
Crisis Biology, an endeavor that soon became his all-consuming passion. While
at IU, Jontz lived in Parks House in a student dormitory called Wright Quad-

rangle, named for former Indiana governor Joseph Wright and located near
the university's main library at the intersection of North Jordan Avenue and
Tenth Street. Jontz roomed with a freshman student named Bob Rodenkirk.
A native of Chicago, Illinois, Rodenkirk originally had been roommates with
a relative of Philippine dictator Ferdinand Marcos, who very quickly flunked
out of the university after spending more time enjoying himself rather than
studying. Jontz proved to be quite different, with Rodenkirk describing him as
a serious and driven student, especially when it came to environmental issues.
"I can't remember a time when he didn't have a to-do list a half a mile long,"
said Rodenkirk, who has worked for many years as a broadcaster in his hometown. "Even then his amazing energy, his ability to multitask on any number
of issues (long before the word was coined), and his refusal to take 'no' for an
answer were in full flower."[33]

Jontz spent much of his time while an IU student with Crisis Biology,
becoming the group's overall coordinator. "Jim was the most visible of that
group," recalled Tim Harmon, who wrote a number of articles on environmental activities at IU while a reporter for the *Indiana Daily Student*. "He believed
very deeply in environmental issues, in the need to preserve the environment."
Harmon, today managing editor of the *South Bend Tribune*, said he sometimes
found it hard to be objective during his days as a student journalist because he
sympathized greatly with what Crisis Biology was trying to accomplish. "With
Jim I found somebody who was a kindred spirit," said Harmon. Jontz became
a trusted source as he was "always available" and could be counted on to offer
him "good quotes" on whatever environmental issue Harmon wrote about. He
praised the work of those in Crisis Biology, saying that they helped to develop
and enlarge "everybody's awareness" about environmental issues that they
could take with them when they graduated and went out into the world to
make their living. Goss recalled that Jontz was "full of ideas" to help create
an awareness at IU about the environment and was determined to organize
activities and not just be a student." Goss became impressed by how hard
Jontz worked and the creative vision he had that if "we talked with enough
people we could do something" to inspire change.[34]

From his office at 205 Morrison Hall, Jontz and others involved in Crisis
Biology worked on a wide range of issues, including trying to decrease the
belching black smoke from the university's coal-fired power plant; trying
to determine why a large sinkhole had opened up in front of Wright Quad;
improving how IU disposed of plastic foodware; studying the ecology of the

Jordan River, a stream that ran through the campus; opposing a dam that threatened the unique Lost River in Orange County; stopping a plan by Public Service Indiana to build a heavy voltage power line through Lilly-Dickey Woods in scenic Brown County; and supporting a decision by the U.S. Forest Service to halt access to trails by such off-road vehicles as motorcycles, trail bikes, and snowmobiles. Crisis Biology members also traveled to Indianapolis to testify at an Indiana Air Pollution Control Board public hearing regarding regulations controlling sulphur-dioxide emissions from industries. The group collected more than three thousand signatures on a petition expressing concerns about the issue to present to the board. "He took no time off and there was never a down moment with Jim," Rodenkirk said of his roommate. "He fell asleep while working the phones on one or more pet projects with his books open in the Crisis Biology office more nights than I can remember."[35]

Obtaining support from a wide number of people at IU became crucial to the group's success. "A large part of an organization's effectiveness is getting people to do things," Jontz explained. As one of its major projects, Crisis Biology instituted a monthlong pilot program at Jordan Hall for something that is considered commonplace today—recycling paper. Planned by J. Michael Jones, a graduate student in zoology, the program included placing specially marked baskets in the building's offices. Those working in Jordan Hall, which housed the Department of Biology, were asked to dispose of their wastepaper in these bins, which were picked up later by custodians. Twice a week student volunteers hauled the paper to Bloomington's Fell Iron Company for recycling (the company paid twenty cents for a hundred pounds of paper). Next, Crisis Biology prepared a feasibility study to present to then IU chancellor Byrum Carter on whether recycling could be expanded to other campus buildings.

In the first week alone, the project recycled approximately two thousand pounds of paper that otherwise would have been buried in a landfill—a total that Jones estimated would have saved almost seventeen trees. Over a four-week period, Crisis Biology volunteers collected approximately five thousand pounds of paper from Jordan Hall. Although the project ran smoothly for the most part, there were a few small snags, "none of which appeared to be unsolvable," Jontz said. Students had to deal with a total lack of interest from some in Jordan Hall to others tossing nonpaper items in the recycling containers. These items included cigarettes, batteries, hypodermic needles and syringes, sandwiches, petri dishes, and dead laboratory rats and mice.

In a survey taken by Jones at the project's conclusion, 94 percent indicated university-wide recycling was possible. "Combining this with the rather precarious and strained position of the voluntary recycling effort," wrote Jones in his report, "it is suggested that the University move as swiftly and efficiently as possible to assume this responsibility." It took many years, however, for university-wide recycling to be instituted at IU, but when it did the success envisioned by those in Crisis Biology came to fruition. In 1993 and 1996 the university's Building Services staff earned the Governor's Award for Excellence in Recycling.[36]

In spite of Crisis Biology's attempts at opening people's minds to the dangers facing the environment, there were some who remained unconvinced. In November 1971 the IU Conservative Club invited Melvin J. Grayson, a former vice president for *Look*, a national news and picture magazine, to speak in Bloomington. In his lecture, Grayson said that the country had entered what he called a "dingaling era" in which untrained "amateur ecologists" had been able to influence not only public opinion but also legislation. These unknowledgeable people, he said, had helped to spawn fears about "horrors of cataclysmic proportions" on such issues as DDT, the population explosion, and automobile safety. Grayson also downplayed the dangers of pollution, saying, for example, that the issue of water pollution had been wildly exaggerated "based on esthetic, not scientific facts.

To those at IU worried about mankind's effect on the environment, Grayson "seemed to us like the devil," noted Harmon, who attended the lecture, as did Jontz. "He [Grayson] appeared to be part of this establishment that was trying to fight against all good things. We who believed in the environmental movement took it extremely seriously, [and] personally," said Harmon. The highlight of the lecture came during a question-and-answer session. Harmon remembered Jontz standing up in the back of the room and saying, "Mr. Grayson, here's all I have to say." Jontz proceeded to reel off a list of animals that had been on the Earth for millions of years, including the turtle, which first appeared approximately two hundred million years ago. He ended his statement by comparing the longevity of animals to the relatively small amount of time modern humans had been around. When finished with his statement, Jontz sat down to thunderous applause from the audience. "I thought that might have been one of the moments when Jim Jontz decided he wanted to be a politician," Harmon recalled. "Jim moved into the political world for a reason. If you're going to get some real change in this country, you're going to have to get into public office."[37]

The long hours he spent as coordinator of Crisis Biology meant that tracking down Jontz during his days at the university could be problematic. He spent little time in his dormitory room at Wright Quad, getting by on just four to five hours of sleep per night—a schedule he kept in later years (one of his favorite quotes was "early to bed, early to rise, work like hell and organize"). Through his work on environmental issues, Jontz also became very involved in state politics, helping

A 1972 photograph of Jontz during his days at IU, dressed in his usual outfit of a button-down shirt and bib overalls.

to write the conservation and recreation platform for the Indiana Democratic Party and serving on an environmental education task force created by State Superintendent of Public Instruction John J. Laughlin. "I used to hitch-hike up to Indianapolis to lobby the Legislature on environmental matters," Jontz recalled. "I was a nobody, but you didn't really have to be anybody. It taught me a lot [about politics]." In addition, he worked to make sure students had a voice in what happened in the Bloomington community by helping organize voter registration drives on campus—an effort that Goss noted helped create the base for the election of Frank McCloskey, a recent law school graduate, as mayor in 1971, defeating two-term incumbent John H. "Jack" Hooker Jr. "We just worked to get out votes," Jontz noted. "We didn't worry too much about who'd they vote for."[38]

Even when he could be found in his dormitory room, Jontz received little rest, fielding questions on environmental issues from such noted Indiana political figures as Governor Otis Bowen and Senators Birch Bayh and Vance Hartke. "The phone calls I would take for Jim were amazing," remembered Rodenkirk. "We answered the phone, 'Jontz and Rodenkirk for a better world.'

Even then, they [political figures] knew who Jim was and the respect was obvious." What scared Rodenkirk was Jontz's habit of reading a textbook lying open on his lap while driving back and forth from Bloomington to Indianapolis to have his voice heard on behalf of environmental issues at the Indiana Statehouse. Jontz always made it back safely, and Rodenkirk was "amazed at how much information he could process. He was a born leader."[39]

Those trips to Indianapolis also involved engagement with the legislature on issues of national importance, including a groundbreaking attempt by environmentalists and lawmakers to have Indiana become the first state in the nation to ban the use of phosphates in laundry detergents. Studies had shown that phosphates contributed to algae growth in lakes and streams, choking off supplies of oxygen and killing fish and other plants. Burnett C. Bauer, a Democratic state representative, had sought to regulate detergents during three sessions of the Indiana legislature, but had failed. When he was defeated in a run for the state senate, Bauer's son, B. Patrick, won his House seat and continued the fight to restrict the use of phosphates in detergents through the Indiana Stream Pollution Control Board—an effort that found success in the 1971 legislative session, as his bill passed the House by a 73 to 11 vote and the Senate by a 38 to 1 margin. For assistance on environmental matters, Patrick Bauer turned to Jontz, who served as his intern and offered his support as soap manufacturers battled to overturn the new law in subsequent legislative sessions. Bauer remembered Jontz as a workaholic and recalled receiving telephone calls from him "at six o'clock in the morning and one o'clock at night." The legislator became impressed by the young environmentalist's intelligence and motivation to work on behalf of conservation matters.[40]

Jontz used his position as a respected state environmental activist to express his frustration with what he saw as IU's biggest problem. In a July 18, 1972, interview with the *Indiana Daily Student*, he said the most important pollution problem on the campus did not come from IU's power plant or the material dumped into the Jordan River, but instead "the attitude the University takes toward the environment of the student." Although he lauded university officials for recently establishing the School of Public and Environmental Affairs, creating a campus health and environment committee, and offering courses on the environment, those traditional responses were not enough. "People's attitudes don't develop by means of a formal academic process," said Jontz, but by example. He pointed out that students see the university building parking garages and therefore "come to feel it's perfectly okay to drive all

Jontz leads the discussion as part of the environmental subcommittee for the Indiana Democratic Party's platform committee in the early 1970s.

over campus instead of walk. They see it not doing anything to clean up the air around the power plant, and not doing anything to clean up the Jordan River, and therefore are taught it's all right to tolerate the degradation of the environment." Instead of looking at what might be cheaper initially, he said, a broader view needed to be taken. "In the long run, it is cheaper to use paper cups and containers, rather than plastic or Styrofoam ones," Jontz said. "But the University fails to realize this—it thinks the few cents it saves in initial costs are more important."[41]

To help prod the IU campus into taking environmental problems more seriously, Jontz used the bully pulpit of the campus newspaper, writing a weekly column focusing on environmental issues for the *Indiana Daily Student* in the spring of 1972. In his column Jontz campaigned to add additional acreage to the Indiana Dunes National Lakeshore authorized by Congress in 1966, lambasted the Indiana legislature for passing a watered-down version of an Environmental Management Act that left power in the hands of the Indiana State Board of Health (criticized by Jontz for its "inefficient track record and demonstrated lack of concern for the public"), questioned the sincerity of the U.S. Army Corps of Engineers' attempt to improve its image as an "environmental despoiler," opposed construction by the Corps of Engineers of a number of reservoirs in the state, called upon the U.S. Secretary of the Interior Rogers Morton to allow public hearings on the proposed oil pipeline in Alaska, and advocated taking a small step on behalf of the environment by having Indiana communities approve ordinances promoting the use of returnable bottles.[42]

In addition to these larger national issues, Jontz focused on matters closer to home, including trying to protect a sinkhole—a natural depression in the ground—located near his dormitory from being filled in by IU's physical plant. His thoughts on the issue brought into sharp focus the way he thought about environmental issues at that time in his life. Jontz noted that even a sinkhole has a "special value . . . because it is in part, at least a little bit, wild." Environmentalists realized that the "engineering mentality" insisting the sinkhole should be drained and planted with grass reflected the attitudes spawning the ecological problems the country faced. He wrote: "Man has told Nature she must measure up to our standards, and we have used our technology with neither understanding nor appreciation to the natural systems with which we are dealing to get nature 'in shape.' We dam her rivers, cut down her trees, kill her animals, pave her meadows, tear up her hills, and if we don't stop damming, cutting, killing, paving, and tearing up, she will die and we will along with her." Jontz added that saving the sinkhole was also important because the opinions of the thousand residents who lived at Wright Quad were important. "The 1,000 residents are 1,000 voters, 1,000 taxpayers, 1,000 citizens who will be voters and taxpayers and citizens in what may be the most crucial time in all of man's—and nature's—existence," he wrote. "The 1,000 must learn that a 'sinkhole,' or swamp or a river or the Grand Canyon, is not a bad place once you get to know it, and deserves to be saved."[43]

In 1972 the work of Crisis Biology merged with another campus organization—the Indiana Public Interest Research Group—as its environmental division. A student-run activist group that Jontz had been a part of since its inception, InPIRG, and other organizations like it at college campuses across the nation, had been the outgrowth of a public interest law firm started by consumer advocate Ralph Nader. Students in Minnesota, Oregon, and Massachusetts had been the first to organize such groups, and other like-minded activists followed suit on other campuses, including IU. "We wanted to take charge of our own destiny," noted Goss, who served as head of InPIRG for a

COURTESY ELAINE EMMI

*Wedding photograph of Jontz and Elaine Caldwell, who are flanked by the bride's parents
and grandparents. Lynton Caldwell is on the far right, and his wife, Helen, is on the far left.*

time. "Jim was involved on the ground floor, helping people to think how to
organize it." As Kathy McCord, a member of the InPIRG projects committee,
said at the time, the merger between the two organizations was proposed
because "every time we [InPIRG] wanted to begin planning an environmental
activity, we would run to Crisis Biology because they not only had good people
but were always aware of what was going on. . . . We both saw a lot to gain
from the move."[44]

Jontz's work with Crisis Biology, InPIRG, and his subsequent role as president of the Eco-Coalition, a loose federation of fourteen environmental groups
in the state, brought him into contact with another student activist, Elaine
Caldwell. She was the daughter of Lynton Caldwell, the nationally known
professor of political science at IU famous for being one of the principal archi-
tects behind securing environmental impact statements for federal projects,

while her mother, Helen, was a sculptress who always had season tickets to the opera and enjoyed seeing plays. The Caldwell family had moved to Blooming-ton when Elaine was six years old and quickly fell in love with the area's woods and fields, spending a lot of time outdoors. "In our family," said Elaine, "God was outside."

Although Elaine had observed Jontz in geology and folklore classes they shared, the two did not become close until she helped arrange a trip with other IU students to Washington, D.C., to lobby on wilderness issues before a U.S. Senate subcommittee for an environmental law class she was taking. Through her father she was able to find accommodations for the group in the basement of a church on Capitol Hill for just seventy-five cents a night. "He really wanted to make a difference," Elaine said of Jontz, whom she married in June 1973. (The couple spent their honeymoon on a train traveling to Washington, D.C., to lobby before Congress on environmental issues. For part of their journey they even had to sit apart because they could not find a seat together.) "His mom told me he was never a kid, this was an adult in a little body. I think he always was purpose driven." Although Elaine hated public speaking, Jontz rel-ished such occasions. "And he got better at it every day," she said. "He remem-bered everyone's name and took delight in walking into a room full of people as no one was a stranger—there just were people he hadn't yet befriended." Although it might sound too grandiose to say that Jontz wanted to save the planet, Elaine noted "that was his ultimate goal, to be a spokesman for those that couldn't speak—the trees, the animals, the air, the water."[45]

For Jontz, saving the environment made sense not only on an intellectual basis, but also on a financial level. In a letter to the *Indianapolis Star* from his position as president of the Eco-Coalition, Jontz noted that nobody knew just how much man's lifestyle had to change in order to insure the planet's survival, but there were things people could do now that would have a positive and immediate effect. Quoting a study made by the National Wildlife Federa-tion, he pointed out that the nationwide bill for damages from air and water pollution—including costs for damages to materials and vegetation, increased needs for health care, and lost recreational opportunities—stood at $28.9 billion annually in the United States, or $481 per family. "Reasonable cleanup costs, reducing water pollution by 90 percent and air pollution by two thirds," said Jontz, "would be $10.2 billion annually or $170 per family. This cleanup would reduce pollution damage by $22.2 billion annually, or $370 per family. Thus by 1980, net savings of $12 billion annually, or $200 per family, would result." It simply would be "irrational" to not proceed with some efforts to improve the environment, including looking at ways to improve communities' mass-transit systems. "We do not pretend to have all the answers," he said, "nor does anyone else. Neither do we believe that it is necessary to have all the answers before taking a first, obvious step."[46]

Graduating from IU in 1973 with Phi Beta Kappa honors, Jontz continued his interest in conservation matters, working for a few months in Chicago as program director for the Lake Michigan Federation, which had been formed in 1970 as a result of a of a 1969 conference of conservationists from Wisconsin, Illinois, Indiana and Michigan. The organization's mission was "to restore fish and wildlife habitat, conserve land and water, and eliminate pollution in the watershed of America's largest lake." Jontz returned to Indiana to become executive director and editor of the monthly newsletter, *Hoosier Conservation*, for the Indiana Conservation Council, an affiliate of the National Wildlife Federation. "I had responsibility for both pursuing the conservation objectives of the organization, and seeing after administrative responsibilities, including fund raising and membership," he remembered. Jontz later became the group's conservation director, concentrating his duties on representing the organization on conservation matters and working "for the wise use of our natural resources and protection of our environment" and editing *Hoosier Conservation*. In the newsletter Jontz had a regular column called "Hook, Line and Sinker" in which he shared his thoughts on issues with the ICC's members, including the need to protect the state's rivers and streams, the expansion for wilderness areas for Hoosiers, the importance of environmental impact statements, and opposition to open the Hoosier National Forest for use by off-road vehicles. "The same solitude, beauty, and vastness which are attractive to the backpacker and the sportsman would be enjoyed by the day visitor to the wilderness, too," Jontz wrote. "Certainly these types of experiences are needed by all of us, whether we have the time and inclination to spend several days in remote areas backpacking or not—and a wilderness would offer such an opportunity."

In a July 1973 column Jontz addressed the view held by some that environmentalists and conservationists were "too negative and 'against everything.'" Although he disagreed with the view, he said it was something to be conscious of and when considering campaigns to halt destruction of the country's natural resources there needed to be steps taken to ensure "implementation of wise practices which will help ensure that man's activities are in harmony with our environment." He pointed to a recent announcement by

Hartke outlining his opposition to a proposed dam and reservoir on Big Pine Creek in Warren County, Indiana. Hartke had written a letter to John C. Stennis, chairman of the Public Works subcommittee of the Senate Appropriations Committee, explaining his decision. Jontz agreed with Hartke's stand that asking to withhold funds for the project was not a "negative action. Rather, I see it as an opportunity to explore those alternatives whereby a stream of extraordinary natural value and inherent recreational potential might be preserved for use by generations to come." Jontz and Hartke supported having the creek designated as a state natural, scenic, or recreational river under legislation passed by the Indiana General Assembly, or possibly have it included in the National Scenic Rivers system.[47]

Jontz soon had much more to say on the issue. The potential ecological threat of the reservoir drew Jontz and his new wife to move their belongings to Warren County in November 1973 to help preserve the wild area near Big Pine Creek. The dam and the controversy it created among local citizens put Jontz on the first step to his long career in Indiana and national politics.

3

The Dam

For those struggling to survive during the height of the Great Depression in the 1930s, dams, great earthen or concrete structures that controlled rampaging rivers or created cheap hydroelectric power, were viewed with pride as marks of progress and prosperity. In the 1940s and 1950s, the U.S. government sought to control flooding on the Wabash River basin in both Indiana and Illinois. The U.S. Army Corps of Engineers drew up plans to build thirteen dams on tributaries of the Wabash and more than a hundred other projects to meet the needs of the 33,000-square-mile watershed until the year 2020. One of the proposed dams and resulting reservoir and lake was to be constructed on Big Pine Creek, which flowed from southwestern White County south through Benton and Warren Counties before entering the Wabash River near Attica.

Along its route Big Pine Creek ran through scenic sandstone cliffs and Fall Creek Gorge, noteworthy for the large potholes carved into the floor of the steep-sided canyon. In October 1965 the U.S. Congress, in its Flood Control Act, had authorized the Corps of Engineers to build an earth and rockfill dam on Big Pine Creek at an estimated cost of $28 million. Once the engineers had finished building the dam, the resulting reservoir and lake it created would cover more than a thousand acres northeast of Williamsport, Indiana. This new recreational area would join the other reservoirs already built by the Corps in the state over the years: Cagles Mill (1953), Cecil M. Harden (1960), Monroe (1965), Salamonie (1966), Mississinewa (1967), and Huntington (1968). William J. Watt, administrative assistant during Indiana governor Otis R. Bowen's two terms in office, noted that state legislatures were glad to endorse such projects "because of their recreational benefits and the perceived economic growth brought to surrounding areas in the form of enterprises to serve tourists and the increased value of residential land."[1]

The dam, which received support from Republican congressman John T. Myers, who represented the Seventh Congressional District, as well as the powerful Wabash Valley Association that represented business and political interests in the region, drew protests from state environmental groups, who viewed such projects as a blight on the land. "If all the dams, channelization, and stream 'improvements' are built," noted Thomas E. Dustin, Indiana executive secretary of the Izaak Walton League, "by 1985 Indiana will have said good-bye forever to its best remaining scenic streams." In their place, Dustin added, would be "silent muddy waters, stagnating behind huge rolled earth or concrete structures." Environmentalists and the Corps of Engineers had often battled over such projects. Many of those who worked on behalf of the environment believed, as Indiana University professor Lynton Caldwell noted, that government agencies such as the Corps had emerged "more often than not as a partner, promoter, or protector of activities that diminished the quality of the environment."[2]

The approximately nine thousand residents of Warren County saw the planned Big Pine dam as a dagger aimed at the heart of their way of life. A poll conducted by a county newspaper, the *Williamsport Review-Republican*, indicated a ten-to-one margin against the project, with most viewing it as "another dam senseless squandering of the taxpayers' money." Local groups opposing the dam, including the Committee on Big Pine Creek and the Friends of the Big Pine Creek, charged that if it were to be constructed it would engulf sixty homes, ten commercial properties, 2,347 acres of cropland, 2,200 acres of pastureland, and 1,995 acres of woodlands. The project also threatened such uncommon plants as the walking fern and snow trillium, and threatened to destroy habitat for the bigeye chub and bluebreast darter, as well as badgers— all species considered rare or endangered in Indiana and the Midwest. "The Corps of Engineers wants to build the Big Pine dam because it would make more work for them," said Bill Parmenter, president of the Committee on Big Pine Creek. "A lot of government agencies think that way. They won't lose any land, their neighbors won't have to move away, they don't pay taxes in Warren County, and they could care less about the beauty of Pine Creek."[3]

Hoping to protect a portion of the area from destruction, the Nature Conservancy in the late spring of 1973, with the help of a $20,000 loan from a Purdue University janitor, bought a forty-three-acre site in Warren County— property that included the Fall Creek Gorge. "This is a place that needs to be preserved because there is not another place like it in this whole area of

Fall Creek Gorge in Warren County, Indiana.

Northwestern Indiana," said Helmut Kohnke, vice chairman of the Indiana chapter of the Nature Conservancy. "This is why we are so fussy about this, because it is unique. Not unique, period, but unique for this area."[4]

To help protect and promote what the area had to offer, the Nature Conservancy turned to Jim Jontz, who had spoken out against the Corps of Engineers' reservoir projects while still a student at Indiana University during his time as president of the Indiana Eco-Coalition. While still working for the Indiana Conservation Council as its conservation director, Jontz was picked by the Nature Conservancy to serve as an unpaid caretaker and program director for the Fall Creek Gorge beginning in the fall of 1973. In a November 21, 1973, letter addressed to his friends, Jontz wrote he had moved to the Fall Creek Gorge property to serve as its "resident caretaker," and reminded them to become ICC members, as that was where "my salary comes from." He lived in a small, handmade house in Liberty Township next to the preserve. Joining him there were his new wife, Elaine, two dogs (Brother and Sister), and two cats (Vance and Birch, named for Indiana's two U.S. senators at that time, Vance Hartke and Birch Bayh, both Democrats). In his letter, Jontz invited his friends to "come by some time, visit the Gorge, and enjoy Big Pine Creek.

Opportunities exist here for some of the finest camping, hiking, canoeing, fishing, and nature study in the Midwest. Give me a call ahead and/or stop in at the Gorge (I'll send you a map) and I'll do what I can to make your visit enjoyable."[5]

Elaine remembered that she and her husband each had a desk in one tiny room and there were two compact bedrooms, a kitchen, and a bathroom. Jontz later decorated the walls with posters stating "We Care About Endangered Wildlife," "Save Our Wetlands," and "Ecology: A Wild Idea." A stuffed owl peered down from a shelf high on a wall on bookcases with volumes on Indiana's natural resources, covered bridges in the Midwest, and classic works by writers such as Homer and Sophocles. In the winter months, Elaine had to walk down to Fall Creek to haul water back to the house so they could flush the toilet. Her father, Lynton Caldwell, sometimes visited, working to get rid of poison ivy and helping to pull trash out of the creek. Although Caldwell and his son-in-law sometimes did not see eye to eye when it came to policy on environmental issues, Elaine said the two of them enjoyed a cordial relationship during their marriage. "Jim was disdainful of academics," she recalled. "I think in his effort to be 'of the people,' he probably went overboard." Elaine also noted that Jontz was not "a party person" and it was even a problem for her to get him to either of their parents' houses for holidays. "We would drive the two and a half hours each way to Bloomington without spending the night," she said. Jontz did improve his attendance at family holiday gatherings in later years, especially Thanksgiving and Christmas, where he recited the poems "When the Frost is on the Pumkin" by James Whitcomb Riley and "Ain't God Good to Indiana" by William Herschell.[6]

Jontz organized crews to help maintain the trails, ran summer events to introduce visitors to the beauties of Fall Creek Gorge, and hosted board meetings for the Nature Conservancy. "There was always something going on," said Elaine. Jontz helped make ends meet by taking a job filling gumball machines at stores in the nearby rural communities he reached by driving his AMC Gremlin (an automobile *Time* magazine listed as one of the fifty worst cars of all time). Although raised in a big city, Indianapolis, he soon came to appreciate what Warren County had to offer. "It's close-knit," he said of the area. "Many are opposed to change. They like the quiet lifestyle and there's a backwoodsy atmosphere in parts of the county."[7]

Often dressed in his trademark blue-jean bib overalls, Jontz quickly became one of the leaders in the fight against the Big Pine dam, which his wife

Jim Jontz during his days as the caretaker at Fall Creek Gorge.

called "a total boondoggle." Parmenter, who knew Jontz from earlier state environmental gatherings, said that he had the ability to "make people do things— more than they thought they would be able to do." While there were plenty of people involved in trying to stop the dam, Jontz served as the "sparkplug" for the effort. "We were so young then," Parmenter remembered, "with so much confidence in our rightness. Well, we *were* right, and the Corps of Engineers, the Congress, and the Indiana legislature, to say nothing of the Wabash Valley Association, were wrong." Laura Ann Arnold, a student at Purdue University at that time and one of the leaders of Purdue Environmental Action, a student chapter of the Izaak Walton League, remembered Parmenter and his wife, Penny, bringing Jontz to one of the group's meetings. Arnold quickly became impressed by the young environmentalist's enthusiasm and commitment to the cause. "Jim was one of those people whose leadership style was to roll up his sleeves and to be involved right along with the troops," said Arnold. "He wasn't just somebody who barked out orders and expected everybody else to do the dirty work. He was there working beside you—usually working twice as hard as anybody else."[8]

Jontz's beloved American Motor Corporation Gremlin. Introduced to the buying public on April 1, 1970, the Gremlin was marketed as America's first subcompact car.

Using his IU degree in geology, Jontz, with the assistance of another ICC staff member, David Dreyer, prepared a thick report outlining the arguments against building the dam on Big Pine Creek. Dreyer, who went to high school in Richmond, Indiana, had been with the Peace Corps before returning to Indiana. Because he had worked with state government on a tax package that had been passed by the legislature during the administration of Governor Otis Bowen, Dreyer concentrated on the economic side of the dam proposal, while Jontz worked on the conclusion. "Cowriting with Jim was difficult," Dreyer recalled. "I tended to be a little more poetic, and he just wanted the facts somehow to be poetic in themselves. He rewrote a lot of what I wrote."[9]

Issued in March 1974, the report blasted the plans of the Corps of Engineers and predicted that the dam on Big Pine would have "disastrous environmental consequences" for the area. These included replacing "excellent sport fishing, whitewater canoeing, and other rare outdoor recreational opportunities with poor quality fishing and extremely limited boating in an aesthetically undesirable reservoir which does not meet the real recreational needs of the region." Jontz and Dreyer said the project was a waste of taxpayer's money and, in the end, would destroy people's lives and their rural lifestyle forever. Instead, they advocated including the Big Pine Creek in a state or national scenic river system, asked Warren County government officials to institute proper zoning and land-use policies, and sought for environmental groups such as the Nature Conservancy to purchase additional land in the area for protection. The report also included part of an editorial by Henry Cripe of the *Williamsport Review-Republican* that noted: "We should keep trying to improve our community and meet the challenges of changing times. But, we shouldn't make drastic changes in the name of progress unless we're really sure we're going to like it afterward. No one is going to restore Warren County to its present state once the reservoir is built, even if it all proves to be a big mistake."[10]

The powerful political figures in the area, including Congressman Myers and Indiana State Representative Jack Guy, who represented the Twentieth District (Benton, Newton, Warren, and White Counties), lined up to support the dam. Jontz attempted to find someone to run for the state legislature against incumbent Guy, a Monticello attorney, in the rural district. Jontz believed that having someone who opposed the project in the legislature was essential because the Indiana General Assembly could halt the project in its tracks by refusing to appropriate funding for the state's share of the federally built dam's costs. "Without state approval, the Corps of Engineers simply couldn't build he dam," he noted. "It would be dead—just as dead as if it were deauthorized at the federal level. I think we need a State Representative who will stand up against the schemes of the federal bureaucrats and work to cut wasteful federal spending, not promote it."[11]

Unable to find someone to run as a candidate for the Democratic Party nomination, Jontz approached party leaders in the area and told them he wanted to run for the state representative post (he had thought about running for state senator, but was not yet old enough to do so). In spite of his young age (twenty-two), Jontz said that party leaders "were tickled to death that someone wanted to do it." Jontz ran unopposed in the Democratic primary and prepared to tackle Guy, the majority leader of the Republican-controlled Indiana House, in the general election that fall. Few, if any, political pundits believed the rookie candidate could pull off the upset against such a powerful figure as Guy. Announcing his candidacy, Jontz said his campaign would be based on "the disappointment which my neighbors sense about what is going on in Indianapolis. People aren't upset about their taxes if they know their money is being spent wisely. They aren't upset about granting powers to their

The relentless pace Jontz maintained during his run for state representative took a toll on his shoe leather.

government if they feel those powers are being used responsibly. Yet, people are upset, and there is good reason."[12]

With help from his wife and a few friends, Jontz began a shoe-leather, door-to-door campaign, visiting every house in such small communities in the district as Boswell, Brook, Brookston, Chalmers, Fowler, Goodland, Kentland, Monon, Morocco, Otterbein, Oxford, Reynolds, West Lebanon, Wolcott, and many others. An advertisement for the Jontz campaign that ran in local newspapers under the title "I'll Be At Your Door Soon" included a photograph of a grinning Jontz, his tie loosened and displaying the sole of one of his shoes battered and full of holes from his door-to-door effort to introduce himself to voters. "I realize people are busy and my purpose is not to inconvenience anyone," he said. "If someone has a question for me or wants to tell me something, I will be pleased to stay as long as necessary. Otherwise, I will simply leave a piece of literature with my phone number and address, so I can be contacted in the future." Jontz also spread the word about his candidacy by attending every community fish fry he could find and going to three straight weeks of county fairs, shaking hands with countless potential voters. "I campaigned on the

Jontz and his wife, Elaine, speak out against the Big Pine Creek reservoir at the annual Pine Creek Settlers Day.

personal attention idea," Jontz said. "Issues are important to people, but more important to them is feeling that government is responsive."[13]

By his side throughout the campaign was Jontz's wife, Elaine, who acted as his unofficial campaign manager. She remembered sending out letters and press releases, placing leaflets on car windows, organizing meetings, and rounding up farmers and their wives to go to Washington, D.C., to testify against the Big Pine dam. "We always tried to keep the level of awareness up," she noted. They did everything they could to fight the dam, including raising money for the cause by raffling off canoes at county fairs and even having one of the farm wives give belly dancing lessons. "I really believed in what he was doing," she said, remembering life with her husband as "a constant campaign." The expense of fighting the dam and running for the legislature meant that the young couple was often broke. Elaine remembered trips to the grocery store where she wandered up and down the aisles wondering what she could prepare for meals with the five dollars she had for buying groceries. Luckily, Jontz's favorite food was Senate bean soup with white beans and ham, which she could make very cheaply.[14]

Scenes from Jontz on the campaign trail, including an activity that became a regular part of his every attempt at public office—riding his bicycle in local parades (top).

In the literature he handed out to voters, Jontz emphasized that he was not a lawyer or an experienced politician (both of which Guy were). "I don't have anything against lawyers," he noted, "but I do think we need more different kinds of people in the General Assembly." If elected to the legislature, Jontz said he "would bring a fresh perspective, some youthful energy, and a few new ideas to Indianapolis." To connect with the mostly conservative voters that inhabited the district, he called for reducing "excess government expenditures," recommended cutting down on unwise public work projects, and said he knew the problems of "trying to pay upper-class prices and upper-class taxes with a middle-class income and middle-class values."[15]

The young candidate also endeared himself to rural voters through his self-deprecating, sometimes corny humor. To put audiences at ease and to break the ice, noted Elaine, Jontz first apologized for being late (he often ran behind because of his busy schedule), saying he was driving to the meeting in a hurry when he rounded a bend in the road and ran into a huge pig. "I stopped my car to check and sure enough it was dead," he continued. "I felt really bad and went up to the farmhouse to apologize to the farmer. I asked him if I could replace his pig. He looked me up and down and slowly replied, 'Well, you're a bit skinny, but I guess you'll do!'" (Elaine also remembered that her husband practiced his campaign jokes by telling them to their dogs, and remembered his favorite dog joke: "How do you stop a dog from smelling? Why, you cut off his nose!")[16]

Guy, who had started his career in the legislature in 1971, touted his experience as his biggest asset and downplayed Jontz's calls for a debate. In interviews and advertisements, the Guy campaign said that while it was "commendable" that Jontz had traveled throughout the district to meet voters, there was "more to being a representative of the people than "knocking on doors, saying hello, and then vanishing into the political night leaving vague promises of change." But Kathy Altman, a longtime Democratic Party worker in White County along with her husband, Jerry, remembered Guy as being overconfident, believing he could cruise to an easy victory over his rookie opponent. Altman witnessed firsthand how hard Jontz worked to connect with voters. After campaigning for the day in Monticello, an exhausted Jontz would stagger to the Altmans' home "and eat like he was ravenous—just a huge appetite after he had been out door to door all day and had not stopped to do anything but talk to people."[17]

The issue that dominated Jontz's campaign was his opposition to the Big Pine dam. At a July 1974 meeting in the Williamsport school's gymnasium, staff from the Corps of Engineers's Louisville district were greeted by nearly two thousand residents, out of which only four spoke in favor of the project. Jontz quickly energized the audience by asking for those attending to stand up if they were for or against the dam. "He basically ran the show, much to the chagrin of the Corps," Elaine remembered. The crowd reacted with suspicion to anything the Corps of Engineers presented. When one Corps official pointed to the recreational activity at a lake project in Ohio, estimating forty thousand to fifty thousand people visited over a weekend, an audience member reminded him that the reservoir planned for Big Pine would sometimes have its water level seventy-five feet below its banks. "What are you going to do," asked the local resident, "build steps, or let people slide down to the water?" (Those in the audience might have been even more upset if they had known that officials in the Indiana Department of Natural Resources had already estimated the reservoir's lake would be too small for its visitors to use motorboats.)

Other aspects of the project also came under fire. At the meeting, Dreyer rose to state that the Corps of Engineers' claims of a flood control benefit "is actually a subsidy to a select group of downstream landowners which helps them increase their profits at the expense of others." It would be cheaper for taxpayers, Dreyer continued, to make direct cash payments to farmers affected by flood damage than to spend the millions of dollars for building the Big Pine dam.[18]

Even before the meeting with the Corps of Engineers, dam opponents had taken direct action against those who supported the project. For a number of years the Warren County Republicans had held a golf outing to raise funds for Congressman Myers. The fifth annual event, held at the Big Pine Golf Course, had some unexpected visitors as between two hundred and three hundred Warren County residents showed up to protest Myers's support for the dam. Late in the afternoon a caravan of approximately a hundred vehicles descended on the course full of farmers and their wives and children bearing signs proclaiming "Save Our Land, Stop the Dam," "Farmers Produce More than Motorboats," and "Dam the Corps." A plane flew overhead towing a banner reading: "Please John [Myers] No Dam."

The peaceful protesters handed out a letter asking Myers and Governor Bowen, who attended the golf event, to halt their support of the dam and a group gathered to discuss the issue with Myers. "We weren't there to disrupt Golf Day or debate the merits of the dam, but simply let our Congressman know we are upset about it," said Jontz, who appeared at the rally dressed in his usual bib overalls. As one county resident added, "We'd just like to have someone listen to us for a change." The demonstration failed to change Myers's position. He told a reporter that the mail he received consistently ran two to one in favor of the Big Pine dam and he intended to continue his support of the project. His only intention on supporting the project, the congressman later said, was a "sincere desire to do what we can to stop the senseless flooding of the farmland and to provide an adequate water supply for future generations."[19]

The controversy about the Big Pine dam in 1974 had drawn the attention of officials in the Bowen administration in Indianapolis. Natural resources advisers to the governor were worried that controversies about reservoirs would only worsen as time passed. According to Watt, "it was necessary to devise workable philosophies to assess the value of individual projects." He noted that he met with Joseph Cloud, DNR director, and John Hillenbrand II, longtime DNR commission chairman, to research the matter and they had agreed that the project on Big Pine Creek "should be scuttled." Although they urged Bowen to drop state support for the dam, he turned down their recommendation. "The timing was not yet right," Watt said of the governor's decision. "He was reluctant to trigger what surely would be a nasty confrontation with Myers over a project in the congressman's home district."[20]

National events that summer may also have given a boost to Jontz's first-time efforts for public office, as well as the campaigns of other Democrats across the country. On August 8, 1974, President Richard Nixon announced his resignation. Two years earlier, on June 18, 1972, a team of burglars organized and funded by Nixon's presidential re-election campaign had been caught and arrested inside the offices of the Democratic National Committee in the Watergate office complex in Washington, D.C. What a White House spokesman called "a third rate burglary" mushroomed into a huge political scandal and cover-up that saw a number of senior presidential officials go to jail for their crimes and led to Nixon's leaving office in favor of Vice President Gerald Ford, who declared upon assuming the presidency, "our long national nightmare is over." (On September 8, 1974, Ford announced a "full, free and absolute" pardon for Nixon for any offenses he "has committed or may have committed.")

The momentous events in Washington trickled down to Jontz during his door-to-door campaign for state representative in Indiana's Twentieth District. So many voters asked him what he thought about the Watergate scandal and Nixon's resignation that he issued a press release on the matter. Instead of debating past misdeeds by both political parties, Jontz said voters should resolve to make sure such abuses did not happen in the future. Although he pledged never to lie to voters as a candidate or as an elected official, Jontz said what was more important than any candidate's pledge "are the responsibilities of all of us as citizens. There is, indeed, only one way I know of and one way I can recommend as a means of stopping abuses of power. This is for all of us to do a more conscientious job as citizens."[21]

The fallout from Watergate and voters ire about the GOP-controlled legislature's doubling of the state sales tax the year before resulted in a huge win for Democrats in Indiana in the 1974 election. Five incumbent Republican congressmen—Earl Landgrebe, William Bray, David Dennis, Roger Zion, and William Hudnut—lost their re-election contests (Myers survived the debacle), and Indianapolis mayor Richard Lugar fell to incumbent Bayh in the race for the U.S. Senate. Democrats captured such statewide offices as secretary of state, state treasurer, and state auditor, and also took control of the hundred-member Indiana House of Representatives, the first time they had enjoyed such an advantage since 1965. One of the closest races that year involved Guy and Jontz. In spite of all their hard work, in the end Elaine did not think her husband would win. Late in the evening of Election Day, November 6, it appeared as though Jontz had failed in his attempt to unseat the Republican incumbent. Elaine remembered returning to their small home late in the evening and she could tell that Jontz was thinking what his next move might be if he lost.[22]

Jontz finally went to bed believing he had gone down to defeat after hearing a report from the final precinct in Warren County indicating he was behind by only two votes. "It was a total shock when we heard the news the next morning," Elaine said. There had been an error and Jontz had won by the same slim margin. "One more vote than I needed to win!" he exclaimed. Photographs of Jontz examining election returns that appeared in area newspapers showed him wearing a scruffy brown-and-gold hooded, plaid jacket from high school that he would go on to wear for good luck every subsequent election night. His razor-thin victory earned Jontz the nickname "Landslide Jim" from his wife. Jontz credited his victory to his opposition to the Big Pine dam. "Guy refused to oppose the dam and that hurt him," he said. Jontz noted that although Democrats were a minority in the district "and often don't think it's worth their time to go out and vote, this time they were encouraged. And the independents were more inclined to look favorably on the Democrats." He added that Democrat challenger Floyd Fithian's defeat of incumbent GOP congressman Landgrebe in the Second Congressional District also helped, as Benton, White, and Newton Counties were part of that district.[23]

COURTESY MARY LEE TURK

Jontz's upset win of better-known opponent, Republican Jack Guy, inspired this 1974 cartoon.

A weary Guy, who, in 1977, returned to the legislature as a state senator, expressed deep disappointment about his loss to Jontz. "I quite frankly thought that what I had done for the people in the 20th House District deserved better support than I received," he told a reporter. Especially upsetting to Guy was seeing the four-thousand-vote margin he enjoyed in the election two years earlier in White County (his home county) fall to less than eight hundred votes in 1974. The unexpected result stunned election officials, with one deputy clerk in Warren County marveling, "I never before realized just how important that one vote can be."[24]

Jontz's win over Guy in the general election survived a recount (the final tally certified by the Indiana House Select Recount Committee had Jontz winning by thirty votes, 10,463 to 10,433) and he traveled to Indianapolis to take his seat in the legislature. He joined a number of other young Democratic newcomers to the House who had been swept into office, including Stan Jones of West Lafayette. Jones noted that at first the two of them were sometimes mistaken for pages—student volunteers—by the older lawmakers. "We became pretty close friends almost immediately after getting elected because we were very young, from the same part of the state, and had similar ideas," said Jones, who became known for his expertise about educational issues. From his first days in the general assembly, Jontz earned a reputation as a "very responsible legislator," said Jones. "He didn't miss votes, he came to every committee meeting, he read bills—not every legislator reads bills." (As for Jontz, he said of Jones that he was "as close to him [in the legislature] as anyone.") The increase in younger members revitalized the legislature during this period. Edward Ziegner, political correspondent for the *Indianapolis News*, noted that "the general quality in [the] House and Senate is high, probably as high as it has ever been . . . and there is a legitimate seriousness of purpose which was infrequent a decade ago and almost unheard of 20 years ago."[25]

Jontz worked as hard during his days as a legislator as he had during the campaign. He was often the last person working in the House at night and the first to report for duty early the next morning. A reporter covering the Statehouse noted that Jontz earned a reputation as "one of Indiana's most industrious legislators and among the best informed." Fellow Democrat Lee Clingan said that in his many years in the general assembly he could not "recall anyone who has worked harder than Jim Jontz." Other lawmakers turned to him for his expertise on the environment and on health issues. Although he still served as an unpaid caretaker for the Fall Creek Gorge preserve, Jontz had to quit his job with the ICC to avoid a conflict of interest, meaning he could devote his full time to his work as a legislator. "There was no downtime," said Elaine. "I think that was one of the problems that came between us [the couple divorced in 1975]. He was really all about work—it was hard for him not to be working." The husband and wife scoured every newspaper in the four-country district, clipping out articles about people in the news, pasting them onto official Indiana House stationery, and having Jontz write a personal note congratulating them on whatever honor they had achieved. "Sometimes we would be up very late at night and get really silly," she said, "concocting imaginary headlines—'County Commissioner Arrested for Stealing Hubcaps' or 'Honor Student Arrested for Prostitution Ring.' You can imagine the gales of laughter that resulted." Jontz continued the practice throughout his state legislative career, sending handwritten cards congratulating constituents on special events in their lives.[26]

Early during his time as a state legislator Jontz learned that his newfound status did not always impress everyone. One of Jontz's friends was leaving town on vacation and asked him to run his gasoline station in West Lebanon, Indiana. During his time at the station, Jontz did fine pumping gas for customers, but, of course, refused any requests to do mechanical repairs on

Jontz relaxes in the Indiana Statehouse, where he had the best attendance record of any legislator. In 1984 Michael K. Phillips, Democrat leader of the Indiana House, noted that Jontz's record of eight sessions of 100 percent attendance for roll-call votes "is unique. No other legislator comes close to matching this demonstration of commitment."

Jontz at work in the Indiana Statehouse.

the cars that stopped by, citing his inexperience in such matters. One morning a "local character" stopped and struck up a conversation with Jontz, during which he found out he was speaking to a state representative. Unimpressed, the man said he thought the station's owner "would have found a senator or a judge at least" to take over his duties during his vacation.[27]

Dependent as he was upon his salary (approximately $7,000 a year at that time) as a legislator to earn a living, Jontz maintained a frugal lifestyle while representing his district in Indianapolis (he did later supplement his income as a lecturer at Purdue and Butler Universities and as public relations director for the Sycamore Girl Scout Council in Lafayette). He found a small apartment on Meridian Street within walking distance of the Indiana Statehouse that he rented for $100 per month (he later often stayed at his parents' house and returned home on the weekends). The conditions at the apartment were so bad that Elaine refused to stay there, returning to Warren County to their handmade house at the Fall Creek Gorge preserve. "It was grim," she said of the apartment. State legislators were often plied with expensive dinners and alcoholic beverages from lobbyists for special-interest groups, as well as being offered tickets to local sporting events, but Jontz, who did not drink alcohol, turned down such perks. "He never took gifts of any sort from lobbyists or business groups—no free tickets to games," Elaine recalled. "But he would attend an event and accept free food if he was allowed to give a speech!" The opening of each legislative session also meant that the 150 lawmakers in the general assembly could have their pick of receptions to attend sponsored by a variety of organizations. "There are more receptions than what anybody could go to," said Jontz. "My rule is if I have a constituent driving clear from Northwestern Indiana, then I attend. Otherwise I do my homework." During his first term in office he tried to be diligent about returning any free passes he received, but in later years he just tossed them in the wastebasket. For most of his daily meals, Jontz prowled the city looking for cheap restaurants at which to eat, including the Capital Tavern located across the street from the State-house. He complained to a reporter, however, that his favorite inexpensive restaurants had the habit of going out of business.[28]

Keeping his campaign promise to stop the Big Pine dam became one of the first legislative tasks Jontz undertook during his first two-year term of office. With his cosponsor, Republican William L. Long of Lafayette, Jontz introduced House Bill 1478. The measure would have repealed an act passed by the 1967 Indiana General Assembly that directed the DNR to cooperate with the Corps of Engineers to construct the dam. On February 20, 1975, the House voted by an 83–8 margin to pass the bill. For the measure to become law, however, it still needed to pass the Republican-controlled Indiana Senate and be signed by GOP governor Bowen. Unfortunately for dam opponents, Jontz's bill never made it out of a Senate environmental subcommittee and died for that session.

Dam opponents received a boost just under a year later when the Army Corps of Engineers' Louisville district recommended that the Big Pine project be abandoned. The decision came thanks to a process initiated by Jontz's father-in-law, Caldwell, who had been responsible in the late 1960s for helping write legislation requiring environmental impact statements for all federal projects. The Corps found that the Big Pine dam would significantly harm the wildlife and natural features in the area where it was to be built and its economic benefits did not justify its costs. "The Corps' credibility is at stake all over," said Colonel James N. Ellis, district engineer. "We are going to continue to take a hard look at all of our projects."[29]

During his time in the Indiana General Assembly, Jontz worked to toughen the state's laws on toxic waste, sought cheaper prescription drugs, improved prenatal care for Hoosier babies, and expanded coverage of Indiana's criminal laws against abuse, neglect, and exploitation of the elderly. Jontz saw himself as an advocate "for the interests of consumers, farmers, working people and the elderly."

In spite of the Corps' recommendation, the fight over the Big Pine dam continued to drag on for years, as its supporters continued to seek funding for the project in Washington, D.C. The end finally came on January 12, 1990, when the Corps formally deauthorized the project, as well as a dam on Wildcat Creek near Lafayette, as Congress had allocated no funds to construct either one. "This deauthorization is the result of the efforts of many committed conservationists and area residents over the years," said Jontz, by then a U.S. congressman. "People who make their homes in these areas will finally have the peace of mind of knowing that these projects are no longer on the books."[30]

Although environmental causes were always important to Jontz, he also worked on a variety of other issues as a state representative—a position that he treated as his full-time job, as opposed to many other legislators who viewed their lawmaker duties as a part-time position to their regular jobs back in their districts. "If I were to operate in the legislature only as an environmentalist," he said, "I would be doing a disservice to my constituents." When the general assembly was not in session, he could be found in his district, attending meetings of service clubs such as the Rotary or Kiwanis and any other local event he could find. "The job of a legislator," said Jontz, "is to listen and identify problems." Jones noted that "everyone in that district knew who Jim Jontz was." Jontz often talked with voters and turned their concerns about issues into legislation. After speaking with a grade school teacher in Wolcott, he introduced a bill requiring reading and writing tests for high school graduates, an idea that became law. In addition, he fought to keep utility companies from charging their ratepayers for unfinished power plants, worked to keep nursing homes safe for their elderly residents, instituted preventive health screening for children, created solar energy tax credits and tax credits for the elderly, helped start a state cancer registry, tried to aid the chronically mentally ill, and became the driving force behind Indiana's child abuse, spouse abuse, and elder abuse laws. "My district is very Republican and very conservative," said Jontz, "but my constituents want someone to go to Indianapolis and speak for the little guy." He attempted to answer each letter he received from his constituents with problems and tried to solve them when he could. "Some legislators are conscientious about responding to letters, but not conscientious in responding to the problem," Jontz noted. He also gauged public opinion in his district through surveys printed in weekly newspapers. "I get about 20 to 30 a day from that survey," he told a reporter for the *Lafayette Journal and Courier*. "If they've just answered the questions, the surveys go in one pile. If they need an individual response, they go in another pile." Jontz noted that the approximately $15,000 he received in salary, expenses, allowances, and reimbursements was "more than adequate . . . I could live with less than that."[31]

Michael E. Thrall first met Jontz when he served as an intern with the House Democratic Caucus in 1978. Hired as a full-time legislative assistant for the general assembly in 1979, Thrall, a graduate of Ball State University with a degree in political science, worked as an aide to a number of representatives, including Jontz. Thrall helped the lawmakers write letters to constituents, aided voters with any problems they had with state agencies, corresponded with Indiana and other government officials, and researched issues for possible legislation. During his time assisting Jontz, Thrall developed the "utmost respect" for the state representative. "In all the time I worked for him, he was always an exemplary legislator," Thrall recalled. "If all governmental officials and politicians were as hard working and sincere as Jim Jontz and truly cared about their constituents as he did, government and politics at all levels would be much more effective." That respect and admiration was shared by the people Jontz represented, who seldom made any critical comments about their legislator, added Thrall. "In fact," he said, "the opposite was the norm. Many of the constituents expressed to me how helpful he had been to them and the tremendous respect and admiration they had for him."[32]

As an attorney for the nonpartisan Indiana Legislative Services Agency, Terry Mumford, a graduate of the IU School of Law, worked with both

Democratic and Republican lawmakers in the Indiana House and Senate to draft hundreds of pieces of legislation for each session during the twelve years she worked there. Even today, she retains vivid memories of Jontz during his days as a state representative. "The mental pictures I have of him are striding through the Statehouse with a purpose—he was going somewhere, he was always on the move," said Mumford, a partner with the Indianapolis office of the Ice Miller legal firm. She also remembered him as someone who was happy in his work and a legislator who continually thought deeply about issues. "He wasn't necessarily accepting the conventional wisdom on either side of an issue," Mumford noted. "He really wanted to understand it and really wanted to figure it out." This trait manifested itself whenever Jontz worked with Mumford on drafting legislation, and she considered him as an example of a good lawmaker to work with. One, he had a really good idea of what his goal was with each bill, was willing to let the bill drafter think about the technical issues of how legislation went together, reviewed the draft, and shared his concerns. "If he asked you to do something," Mumford recalled, "it was because he thought that the policy needed to be carried out and he wanted to know if there were any problems with it and how it would work. He was just a really, really good legislator."[33]

Jontz's dedication to his duties—he never missed a day and during a ten-year period missed just one roll-call vote out of a total of six thousand recorded votes at the Indiana General Assembly—became legendary. Longtime state representative Marilyn Schultz of Bloomington noted there was "no harder worker in the legislature than Jim Jontz. He was the first one there in the morning and the last to leave." That hard work resulted in victories at the polls each November. Jontz won re-election to the Indiana House in 1976, 1978, 1980, and 1982 (that year in the new Twenty-fifth District that included Benton, Newton, White, and portions of Carroll and Pulaski Counties). "He just went out of his way to be responsive to people," noted Arnold. She added that even people who did not agree with Jontz on issues, they still respected him "for the amount of dedication and attention that he gave to everyone." Although Jontz often won those races against his Republican challengers by as much as 64 percent of the vote, he never took his re-election for granted. He continued his shoe-leather campaign tactics, attempting to visit every home in his district in spite of the dangers he sometimes faced. As the *Williamsport Review-Republican* joked during one campaign swing through

*Jontz and his second wife, Donlyn Meyers (center), at the annual dinner for the Sycamore
Girl Scout Council. Jontz worked for a time doing public relations for the council.*

Warren County, Jontz had been bitten by two dogs, "and neither of the dogs
were seriously injured."[34]

The unremitting pace Jontz maintained during his time as a state representative contributed once again to a failed relationship. In 1977 he had
married again, this time to an art teacher in the Benton Central Community
Schools near Fowler, Indiana, named Donlyn Meyers. The young teacher might
have been warned what she faced by her first meeting with Jontz, which came
during one of his famous door-to-door campaign swings. The two lived at the
small house on the grounds of the Fall Creek Nature Preserve and, like Emmi,
Meyers found herself alone there for long stretches of time. When the legislature was in session, Jontz stayed in Indianapolis, returning home on the weekends to host town meetings and attend dinners at area fire halls. "He was a
workaholic," noted Meyers, who aided her husband in his political campaigns.
She silk-screened yard signs and knocked on so many doors in the district that
she could tell someone what dogs would bite in a town. "You get so you don't
want to do that all the time, you want more in your life," said Meyers, who

obtained an amicable divorce from Jontz in 1981. "Jim was made for it—loved it, thrived on it, truly enjoyed meeting people, truly enjoyed finding things he could do to help people. He was everything he appeared to be."[35]

In the 1982 campaign Jontz faced tough criticism from his GOP opponent David Diener for moving from Williamsport to Brookston in White County because his district had been altered by the Republican-controlled legislature. To remain in office in his old district, he would have had to run against fellow Democrat Jones. "I had to move into my [new] district because it was the Republican legislature that put my home in another legislator's district," Jontz pointed out. "That was by no means necessary and was done to get me out of the legislature." If his opponents sought to defeat him, he said they would have to do so "fair and square. I'm not going to roll over and play dead because of a sneaky underhanded maneuver like that."[36]

Jontz surprised political pundits who had predicted a close contest by cruising to an easy win in his new district. He won fifty-eight of the district's sixty-four precincts and even defeated Diener in his home city of Monticello. "I made a niche for myself some time ago," Jontz said of his standing with voters. "I looked at the issues and saw that there were ones where the established interests were vying for positions and others where no groups were speaking out. I decided a long time ago to raise issues that weren't otherwise going to be discussed." He noted that such powerful institutions in the state as utilities, oil companies, and banks all had lobbyists in Indianapolis pressuring legislators at the Indiana Statehouse for their causes, and he had "tried to see there is someone speaking on behalf of those who have no army of lobbyists."

Although labeled as a "liberal" by his opponents, a description used to paint him in a negative light with voters in the conservative district he represented, Jontz said he preferred the term "progressive," as it more closely reflected his views on a wide range of issues. He noted that when it came to problems such as the regulation of utilities (gas, water, and electric power) in the state, the time-worn liberal versus conservative distinction made very little difference to consumers, who believed their opinions mattered little in decisions regarding utility rates and regulations. "I'm always accused of pulling the wool over the eyes of my constituents when I run for re-election," Jontz said. "But I think there's a populist flavor to my approach that's appealing in rural Indiana where the people often feel that the major institutions have overlooked their problems."[37]

Jontz's passion for the causes he supported often put him at odds with his fellow legislators, who did not appreciate anyone speaking out against the bills they sponsored. "I think people [legislators] were pretty frustrated with him, but he was very effective," Jones said of his fellow Democrat. "He was just determined to get things accomplished and it really didn't matter to him that they might be upset by that." In her dealings with Jontz's colleagues at the Statehouse, Mumford had the impression that some of them "just wished he weren't so enthusiastic, he didn't care so much, that he would give them a break." Schultz, who Jontz knew from his days at Indiana University and whom he had advised on environmental issues during her first campaign, was Jontz's seatmate in the legislature for a number of years. As brilliant and as hard working as he was, said Schultz, Jontz never seemed able to enter into the camaraderie of the legislative process. "What they [other legislators] saw of Jim was the fighter and his speaking style was pretty didactic," she recalled. "We would always look at his notes he was taking up to the podium and try to snatch them away so he would have to do it [speak] extemporaneously and be shorter and more communicative. His main problem was that kind of grinding, didactic approach when he spoke because he tended to just turn people off." Another longtime Democratic legislator, B. Patrick Bauer, said it took Jontz a long time at the Statehouse before he learned "you can't put in fifty amendments a day and speak and speak and speak. It was a learning process."[38]

Those in the legislature, state representatives and state senators, serve two quite different constituencies, noted Louis Mahern, an Indianapolis Democrat who had a seat in the Indiana Senate from 1976 to 1992. One are the people who vote on whether or not they will remain in office, he said, and the second are the other members of the legislature, who they have to get along with in order to obtain passage of their bills. Mahern said that he and Jontz were at the opposite ends of the spectrum. "He played very much an outside game," said Mahern. "I don't think he cared very much at all what other legislators thought of him. He was very much directed to the outside [the voters]." Because he ran in a relative safe Democratic district, Mahern said it was easier for him to gain some measure of influence with other members of the general assembly. Jontz himself said that the worst part of his job as a legislator were the decisions he made "about how much to rock the boat. I've done my own share of boat-rocking; it hasn't always made my life easier with other legislators."[39]

Because of his outspokenness on a number of issues, Jontz found it difficult for his bills to receive a fair hearing. "The best way to get in trouble around here," he said of the legislature, "is to talk against [other legislator's] bills." Jontz later recalled sensing an "undercurrent of disapproval" from his fellow House members when he rose to try and explain his position on various issues. In fact, many Republicans seized the opportunity when Jontz spoke to go out for a coffee break or troop to the bank of telephone booths outside the House chambers to return calls they had received during the day. Jontz, however, measured his effectiveness as a legislator not on the amount of bills he passed, but on the number of issues he convinced his fellow lawmakers to consider. "Every campaign," Jontz said, "that's one of the things my opponent raises, 'You don't get bills passed.' But that's just the price you pay when you march to a different drummer." Realizing the barriers he faced, Jontz decided to concentrate on offering amendments to improve legislation on issues of concern to him. "I'm not going to get something passed just because of my name or power," he said. "I have to convince them [other legislators] of the merits of an idea." For example, during the 1980 legislative session, Jontz introduced an amendment requiring the Indiana Department of Revenue to deposit checks received from taxpayers within thirty days of their receipt. "They're losing interest because of a considerable backlog in deposits," Jontz noted, who complained one check he wrote them took seventy-three days to be deposited. Although his amendment went down to defeat on a partisan-line vote, Jontz remained optimistic. "But I'm persistent, I'm persistent . . . at least I got a chance to talk about the problem," he told a reporter. Schultz noted that Jontz was always trying to find ways to move the issues he cared about forward. "He was more concerned about the issues than he was about the ownership of having done something," she said. "He didn't need the credit, he just wanted it done. He was a true believer. He wanted to make the world a better place and it didn't matter what people thought about him. He was just going to keep trying to do it in whatever way he could. Such an incredible guy."[40]

A February 13, 1984, article in the *Indianapolis Star* perfectly captured the often difficult path Jontz had chosen for himself in the general assembly. The article, part of the newspaper's regular "Inside the Legislature" column, pointed out that Jontz had become a familiar sight walking up to the micro-phone to offer amendments on pending legislation, usually seeing them voted down by more conservative Republican members. "I read the bills and I know

One of the most frequent questions Jontz received during his time in the state legislature was how he got along with the other, for the most part, older lawmakers. "The legislature is divided into cliques, but it doesn't break down into age groups," he noted. "I've had no trouble working with fellow legislators of all ages."

what's in them," he said. Jones remembered seeing Jontz walk into the House chambers at the start of a session with eight to ten amendments in hand on different bills that he would parcel out to different legislators to introduce, realizing he could never get so many approved on his own. He said he was willing "to fight the losing battle" in order to get the issues he cared about before fellow legislators. "You just have to be patient," said Jontz. "Just because you lose today doesn't mean you'll lose tomorrow."[41]

Jontz's patience earned dividends on two key issues. During the 1982 legislative session, he quietly worked behind the scenes on a major reform of the state's nursing homes that toughened standards for such institutions. At the 1983 legislative session, Jontz was able to gain ground on a controversial matter that he had been concerned about for years—keeping electric utilities from passing rate increases along to their customers to help cover the costs of building new power plants (an issue known in those days as construction work in progress). He convinced another Democratic lawmaker to introduce an amendment banning utilities from doing so, and the measure helped spawn a major utility reform law that required utilities to obtain permission from the Indiana Public Service Commission before constructing new power plants. The new law also prohibited utilities from seeking rate increases within fifteen months after they had last filed for a general increase. "The bills may not pass with my name on them," said Jontz, "but they get through." Arnold, who has worked on renewable energy issues during her time in Indiana, noted that on environmental issues during the days when the Republicans controlled the Statehouse she and her allies would sit down with Jontz to draft legislation, without his name on it, and then try to find a Republican to serve as the legislation's main sponsor, with Jontz signing on as the measure's cosponsor—a method that worked well, including gaining a solar tax credit for individuals and businesses in 1980. Jones noted that although Jontz never gained a position of power in the legislature, "he was clever enough to get things done. He's more devoted to public service than anyone I know." Running for office every two years took its toll on Jontz, who always attempted to imitate his first campaign by knocking on as many doors as humanly possible."I thought I was a hard campaigner because I would knock on several thousand doors during a campaign," said Jones, "but he would literally knock on every single one of them, probably several times. He was very committed to connecting to his constituency." Jontz estimated he devoted five to six months every two years to campaigning.[42]

In 1984 Jontz decided the time had come for a new job, announcing he would seek the seat in the Indiana Senate being vacated by its incumbent, Guy (the legislator he had beaten in his first run for public office). Being a state senator attracted Jontz because they served for four years instead of two years. He also believed he might fit in better in the Senate, as it was "a more deliberative body" and offered him "a little better forum to work from." Jontz described Senate District Seven, which included all of Jasper, Benton, Pulaski and White Counties, and portions of Newton, Carroll, Starke, Tippecanoe, and Warren Counties, as similar to the House district he represented, as it was a part of the state that included small towns, farms, small businesses, retirees, and average working people.[43]

Indiana's Republican Party saw the District Seven race as an opportunity to finally rid themselves of Jontz and keep a firm hold on its majority in the state senate. Seeking to retain the seat formerly held by Guy, the state

GOP pledged twelve thousand dollars to help fund the campaign of Jontz's opponent, Rensselaer businessman Mike Smith, a first-time candidate. Smith touted his candidacy with television advertisements at the beginning and end of the popular national program *60 Minutes*. Gordon Durnil, the state GOP chairman, attacked Jontz's record as a state representative, especially the small number of bills he had managed to write and pass through the legislature. Such criticism was nothing new to Jontz, who pointed out that the Republicans who controlled the legislature had "virtually adopted a rule that bills had to have a Republican name first" before they would be considered. "You could put in a bill," he noted, "but if you want it to go anywhere, it had to have a Republican's name on it first. I've seen situations where people [legislators] have put in motions to flip the names just to get bills considered." The GOP, he added, created the situation and then turned around and used the issue to help them in campaigns against Democrats.[44]

Altman, who worked with Jontz on all of his campaigns, remembered the state senate race as one of the hardest ones during his career. The candidate had his headquarters in a former doctor's office in Monticello divided up into tiny rooms. The tense nature of the race even got to the normally unflappable Jontz, who would return to the office late at night to review letters to potential supporters. He ended up criticizing some of the letters and throwing them out because they looked so sloppy, Altman said. Jontz responded by doubling his efforts. Michael Riley, Jasper County Democratic Party chairman, remembered Jontz as the hardest working candidate he had ever run across. "He did not have a walking list of registered voters or Democrats or independents or Republicans," Riley said. "He just went door to door. If a farmer was in the field, he would get out of his car and wave him down." In a small county such as Jasper, word got around and people were impressed by how hard Jontz worked to win their votes.[45]

Although outspent in the Seventh District race by nearly a two-to-one margin, and surviving a landslide re-election for President Ronald Reagan against Democratic challenger Walter Mondale, Jontz defeated Smith. Jontz won 55 percent of the vote and captured seven of the nine counties in the district to win by more than four thousand tallies. "We wanted to minimize our losses in the new counties and maintain the plurality in the areas I have represented," Jontz said, adding that it had not been a good year for Democrats in the country. "Reagan has always been popular in Indiana and it was just a question of how big the margin would be. That makes it difficult for us at the bottom of the ticket." For Smith, the results were "hard to understand," but he took comfort in the fact that he ran a "respectable race. We came closer to beating him than anyone else has."[46]

There were some in the Indiana House who were sorry to see Jontz leave the chamber for the state senate. Two of his closest colleagues, Jones and Schultz, sent him a humorous memorandum addressed from "abandoned House members" saying they would be sending him legislation on a daily basis. "We hope you can prepare the amendments in a timely fashion as to give us enough time to read them before we introduce them," the memo stated. "Also, we request that you accompany each amendment with a 'poop' sheet so that we can incorporate those facts into our floor presentation." Katie Wolf, a Democrat who took over for Jontz as state representative for the Twenty-fifth District, remembered that he was "a hard act to follow," especially given the long hours in put in during his days in the House. "One thread weaves through all the stories—Jim worked harder than any state representative," said Wolf. "Some even told me they suspected he slept somewhere in the Statehouse because he was always there." She also remembered his advice to her to listen to what others might have to say on issues in the legislature, but never to "compromise our initial request from our people." For Jontz, said Wolf, the legislative process involved always doing the right thing "because it would make life better for others."[47]

Early into his first term in the Indiana Senate, Jontz had a rare opportunity to broaden his political reach beyond the state. On July 12, 1985, Elwood "Bud" Hillis, who had served as U.S. congressman for the Fifth Congressional District for eight two-year terms, announced he would not seek re-election in 1986. Hillis, the grandson of Kokomo inventor and automobile pioneer Elwood Haynes, had decided it was time to "shift gears," finding life in Congress "demanding and confining." Called by one political observer as a "quintessentially Middle American district," the massive Fifth stretched from Lake County in the north to Grant County in the south and included suburban areas near Gary and factory communities such as Kokomo and Marion. Although Jontz calculated that the Republican candidate would enjoy an advantage of about six percentage points in the polls at the start of the race, it could "be overcome with a good campaign." In August he announced his candidacy for the Democratic Party's nomination. "It will not be easy for a

Democrat to win election to Congress in the 5th District," he told the press. "But in my 11 years in the General Assembly, I have not often taken the easy path." It would be a path on which he wore out a lot of good, old-fashioned shoe leather in the next several months.[48]

4

Mr. Jontz Goes to Washington

The Howard County Fair in Greentown, Indiana, offers the usual variety of attractions—carnival rides, cotton candy, and animals of all shapes and sizes—for those seeking fun and excitement during a hot Hoosier summer. The fairgrounds also proved to be the perfect place to forge a political partnership. In the summer of 1985 Tom Sugar, a Howard County native attending Indiana University at Kokomo, received a telephone call from Allen Maxwell, his political science professor at the school. Maxwell asked Sugar if he might be interested in meeting a fellow Democrat running for Congress who needed someone to help organize the county for the fall election.

Sugar agreed to the meeting and went to the fairgrounds during the middle of the day when the crowd was slight and saw the candidate, Jim Jontz, shaking hands with as many people as he could find. "I'd seen a photo of Jim in the paper before, and, bless his heart, he wasn't the most telegenic guy in the world," said Sugar. The two men found a picnic table where they could sit down and talk. Sugar, who had never before participated in a political campaign, knew about Jontz's Republican opponent, Jim Butcher, a local attorney and state senator, because his parents had sponsored a fund-raiser for him at their home. Although Sugar remembered Jontz looking as though he had slept in his suit, he was impressed by the twinkle in his sharp, blue eyes and it became clear to him "how passionate he was about what he was doing." Sugar walked away from the meeting not completely sure what he had signed up for and realized they had a long road to climb to beat Butcher, who was beloved in the area, but "thinking there was something there."

For the young Sugar, just in his twenties, the meeting with Jontz was his introduction into what came to be a grueling effort to convince those in the Fifth Congressional District that Jontz was the best man to represent them in Washington, D.C. Assisted by local members of the United Auto Workers union and environmentalists from Indianapolis, Sugar set out a schedule for Jontz to meet voters in the county at factory gates early in the morning and at their homes in the afternoon. On a typical day, Jontz started knocking on doors on one side of the street beginning at 3 p.m., with Sugar or another campaign aide taking the other side. The usual routine included introducing themselves, telling a homeowner that Jontz was visiting the neighborhood, and giving them material on his candidacy. If someone did not answer, Jontz would leave behind his literature with a note signed, "Sorry I missed you, Jim."

After the Jontz campaign staff had completed their first canvas of the county, every house that could be visited, Sugar quoted the candidate as saying, "'OK, let's do it again.' So we did it again." Two days before the November 4 election, the second canvas had been completed, but Jontz decided to do it one last time. His exhausted campaign staff threw up their hands in exasperation and sent the candidate out on his own for another round of knocking on doors. "He believed in working until the last dog died," said Sugar. Typically working twenty-hour days, the pace Jontz set left one of the volunteers who attempted to keep up with him one day "a bleary-eyed wreck." An old-fashioned, door-to-door, grassroots campaign, Jontz believed, was the best way to find out what the people were thinking about issues and an excellent way to gauge what a community was like.[1]

Jontz needed every bit of his legendary work ethic to reach the hearts and minds of those residing in the Fifth District, a sprawling area that included fourteen counties in north central and northwest Indiana (portions of Lake, Porter, and Kosciusko Counties, and all of Newton, Jasper, Pulaski, White, Carroll, Howard, Cass, Miami, Wabash, Grant, and Fulton Counties). Voters in the district had grown comfortable being represented by Republican Elwood "Bud" Hillis. Perhaps as a nod to the large number of UAW members in Kokomo and Marion, Hillis, one political observer noted, had a voting record in Congress "just a bit more favorable to organized labor than most Indiana Republicans." Before deciding to retire from his post, Hillis had won a massive victory in the 1984 general election. He defeated his Democratic opponent, Maxwell, with 68 percent of the vote.[2]

Maxwell, who had also lost to Hillis in the previous election, remembered that Jontz was the first person to call him to offer his support and help after the deadline closed to file to run as the Democratic nominee for the Fifth District race in 1982. Maxwell used a Maxwell House coffee can, passing it around and asking supporters to "put something in the can to put a Maxwell in the House." Unfortunately, General Mills, the makers of Maxwell House coffee, got wind of what he was doing and sent a letter alleging the use of their product violated trademark laws. The controversy, Maxwell ruefully noted, brought him the most publicity in both of his runs for public office. In the 1982 race Maxwell, who had trained in international relations and had taught courses on the United Nations and foreign policy at IU Kokomo, sought to make the danger of nuclear weapons an issue, but soon discovered that jobs and agricultural matters dominated discussion in the district. In addition there were a number of one-issue voters, especially when it came to abortion. Maxwell would knock on a door and greet a voter and start talking about his campaign only to be interrupted by the question, "Well, what's your view on abortion?" The minute he told them he had a pro-choice stance they responded by thanking him for coming and closing their door. "It was a very conservative district," said Maxwell.[3]

One of Jontz's colleagues in Indiana's environmental movement, Laura Ann Arnold, believed she was the first person to know of Jontz's decision about the Fifth District race. The two of them were driving to Pittsburgh, Pennsylvania, to attend a telephone utility consumer conference when they heard over the car's radio that Hillis had decided not to run for another term in office. "In that seven-hour drive from Indianapolis to Pittsburgh," she recalled, "Jim decided that he was going to run for Congress." Jontz may have been helped with his decision by not having to face an incumbent, and from a conversation he had at the conference with Jay Rockefeller, former Democratic governor of West Virginia and a U.S. senator. "An open seat in Congress doesn't come along very often," Jontz noted to a reporter. "I came to the conclusion that if I ever wanted to serve in Congress, it's now or never."[4]

Some of those who were involved in politics outside of the state viewed Jontz's quest to fill the Fifth District seat as a lost cause. Louis Mahern, a fellow Democrat who served with Jontz in the state senate, recalled that he traveled to Washington, D.C., early during the 1986 congressional campaign and ran into a lobbyist for some major American oil companies. The two men engaged in some casual conversation and the subject turned to the upcoming election in Indiana's Fifth District. Mahern told the lobbyist, a firm supporter of Republican causes, that he should not discount Jontz's chances at beating the odds and winning the race, as he was well known as a tireless worker. The lobbyist responded by telling Mahern: "He cannot scrape enough windshields

Jim Jontz poses with U.S. Senator Ted Kennedy from Massachusetts in 1982 at a meeting in Washington, D.C. Kennedy wrote a note to Jontz that read: "It was good to get together with so many legislative leaders and discuss problems of mutual interest and concern, and I was just delighted you were able to join us, Jim."

to win out there." Meaning, as Mahern explained, that if he needed to, Jontz was so dedicated that he would awake early every morning and scrape the snow off a voter's windshield in order to gain his or her support.[5]

Jontz was not the first Democrat to announce for the Fifth District seat. Jill Long Thompson (Jill Long at that time), a member of the Valparaiso City Council, had already made the decision to challenge Hillis before the GOP congressman had decided to retire. The two Democrats had already established a friendship (she called Jontz a "truly good person"), so when Jontz decided he would also seek the nomination for Congress, he called and spoke with Thompson about his intentions. Thompson recalled running into Jontz during a Democratic event on the *Madam Carroll*, a cruise ship on Lake Freeman outside of Monticello, Indiana. She asked Jontz to dance, and when he replied that he did not know how to, Thompson, perhaps thinking of their upcoming primary contest, joked: "I'd be very happy to lead, Jim." In conversations with Congressman Andy Jacobs, a Democrat from Indianapolis, however,

Thompson said Jacobs told her that Jontz would be difficult to defeat in a primary, as he was better known in the Fifth District because his state senate district included counties that were part of the congressional district. Jacobs noted that the Democrats did not have a candidate to face off against incumbent GOP U.S. senator Dan Quayle, who had defeated Birch Bayh for that office six years before. Although that also would be a difficult race, Jacobs said by running a strong campaign Thompson could build up some name recognition for herself in state political circles. Thompson decided to challenge Quayle, and although she lost that race, called her choice "a good decision."[6]

A battle of another sort occurred on the Republican side. Challenging Butcher for the GOP nomination was Julian Ridlen, who at the time was in his second term as Indiana State Treasurer. A Logansport lawyer and former city judge, Ridlen received solid backing from the Republican Party establishment, including endorsements from eleven of the fourteen county chairmen in the district. Butcher and his candidacy represented a relatively new force in American politics in the 1980s, as he had the support of conservative fundamentalist Christians. The Fifth District had a strong evangelical presence, as Marion was home to the headquarters for such groups as the World Gospel Mission and the Wesleyan Church. "The difference in campaigning will not be votes, but prayer," Butcher told a campaign rally in Kokomo. "Money is necessary, volunteers are necessary, but the prayers will make the difference." He called for a constitutional amendment protecting unborn children from abortion and advocated passage of a law permitting prayer in public institutions such as schools. Philip Loy, then chairman of the Taylor University political science department, pointed out that Butcher had been quite successful in winning the support of evangelical Christians in the Fifth District. "He established himself with this sub-group of the population by saying, 'I'm one of you, and what we need is more people like us, because we understand the truth,'" Loy said.[7]

The growth of conservative Christian organizations such as the Moral Majority (lambasted by its critics as neither moral nor a majority), created in June 1979 by Reverend Jerry Falwell, a well-known television evangelist from Lynchburg, Virginia, galvanized fundamentalists across the country to participate in political causes and helped to add millions of new voters to the Republican Party. This increased participation in politics by conservative Christians targeted such liberal Democratic stalwarts as George McGovern, Birch Bayh, Frank Church, and Gaylord Nelson, and backed the presidential effort of former California governor Ronald Reagan, who easily defeated incumbent President Jimmy Carter in the 1980 election. These new converts to political action, however, sometimes spelled trouble for Republican candidates who were deemed not conservative enough for their tastes. These motivated voters proved particularly effective in primaries, where they were able to outwork and overwhelm party regulars—as Ridlen soon discovered.

On Primary Election Day, May 6, Butcher won the race for the GOP nomination for Congress in the Fifth District. "All along we were hoping for a heavy voter turnout from the mainstream of the Republican Party, and that didn't happen," said Larry Hopkins, a Ridlen campaign spokesman. "That was a major contributing factor." Other Republican leaders blamed Ridlen's defeat on a national antiabortion group's endorsement of Butcher, its financial contributions to his campaign, and the thousands of telephone calls the group made on his behalf in the district. "Our assessment is that is what did it," said Ridlen. According to Butcher, a radio advertisement from his opponent's campaign attacking him hurt Ridlen's standing with GOP voters. "I think what we got through was . . . I was the only Republican candidate with legislative experience," Butcher said of his campaign.[8]

Jontz faced his own difficulties in securing his party's nomination for Congress. Because the Fifth District contained areas in which he was not well known, Jontz had to deal with a lack of name recognition with a variety of influential figures. Jack Williams, then political director for UAW Local 685 in Kokomo, said he had never even heard of Jontz before the candidate asked to meet with him to try and win union support for his race for Congress. In subsequent years Jontz liked to claim that Williams made him sit in the union hall's lobby for an hour before coming out to meet with him, a story the union leader laughingly disputes as an exaggeration. Williams does remember that Jontz's appearance did not inspire much confidence, as his suit was wrinkled and his hair was unruly. As they two men talked, Williams became more and more impressed with the candidate, especially his vision for working on behalf of the average citizen. "He was a people person," Williams said of Jontz. "If you ever went on the campaign trail with him, you found that out."[9]

Democratic Party leaders in the district had also met with Jontz, who had the security of knowing that even if he lost, he still maintained his seat in the state senate. They called on him to change the usual way he raised money to fund his campaign. In all of his previous runs for public office, Jontz had refused to take donations from political action committees, known as PACs—

Jontz poses with fellow Democrats Floyd Fithian, who served as congressman for Indiana's Second Congressional District, and Katie Wolf, who took over Jontz's old Indiana Senate seat. "He was truly a man of the people," Wolf said of Jontz, "and his heart was in the right place."

private groups organized to influence elections or legislation through their donations. "Jim was a pragmatist," remembered Michael Riley, at that time chairman of the Democratic Party in Jasper County and one of the leaders involved in convincing Jontz to run in the Fifth District race. "He figured out for him to be competitive he would have to do that [take PAC money]." Although Jontz agreed to do so, he never really warmed to the idea of depending upon PACs for funding a campaign. "Jim was more interested in a $10 contribution from a senior citizen than he was a $1,000 check from a political action committee," said Mike Busch, who worked for Jontz during his entire congressional career. "It meant more to him that someone on a fixed income was giving $10 of their money to him. That's what made him tick."[10]

Because the majority of his PAC money came from labor unions and environmental organizations, Jontz in later years described the money he received from such entities as from "little people who were laborers," noted Kathy Altman, a Democratic Party activist from White County and a longtime Jontz supporter, volunteer, and staff member. "I wish we weren't as dependent on

PAC money," Jontz later said. "I wish I could go out there and raise it $10 at a time from concerned citizens, but it's tough." To be successful against his usually well-financed Republican opponents in the Fifth District, Jontz indicated he needed a campaign war chest of at least $500,000, only half of which, at best, could be raised from individual contributions. "I get support from people I agree with. The advantage you have with PAC money is you know where it comes from," he said. "Voters can look at it and make their own assessments. Those who think getting rid of PACs will eliminate special-interest money are being naïve." The second condition was a little easier to take, as Democratic officials asked Jontz to buy a second suit (a campaign aide recalled that a lawyer in Marshall County actually bought the new clothes for the candidate).[11]

The story of how Busch came to work for Jontz during the 1986 campaign is typical for others who joined forces with him during that first congressional race. Busch had a longtime fascination with politics. As a senior in high school he ran as a delegate to the Indiana Democratic Party's state convention. Busch had left college with one semester to go intending to stretch out his last year in school. He returned to his parents' home in Logansport for the spring and summer expecting to spend his time sitting on the couch and watching Chicago Cubs baseball games on television—a plan his parents did not approve of.

Busch's leisure was interrupted by Jontz, who came by the family's home to gain the support of Busch's father, the president of the local postal workers' union. Busch met Jontz and the two of them discussed the possibility of Busch helping out with the campaign. Jontz later asked him to visit his office after the Memorial Day weekend. Busch went to the office expecting to do some volunteer work, perhaps stuff a few envelopes with promotional flyers, but within the first fifteen minutes he received an offer to work for the campaign at a weekly salary of $125. Busch believed he could work a few days a week and make his parents happy. Instead, he and other staff found themselves "putting in seventy-five to ninety hours [of work time] every week," and found that the schedule "got crazier as we believed we were going to win this thing. It was the greatest summer."[12]

Christopher Klose's story of joining the 1986 Jontz campaign echoes that of Busch. Klose grew up in Richmond, Indiana, where his father taught economics at Earlham College. Both of his parents had been active in Democratic Party politics, especially on behalf of Congressman Phil Sharp. Klose worked for Sharp's office in Washington, D.C., before returning to Indiana to serve as chairman of the Democratic Party in Wayne County and to work as communication director for the Indiana House of Representatives Democratic Caucus. Having lost a primary race for a state senate race in Wayne County, Klose had talked with Jontz about a job with his congressional campaign as its press secretary. He went up for a job interview and actually stayed for two days before returning home for just enough time to pack a bag and return to Jontz's headquarters in Monticello for the rest of the contest. Within a month, Klose had taken over as Jontz's campaign manager. Altman recalled that Klose became so busy he did not even have the time to get his broken eyeglasses fixed until after the election was over. She jokingly called his change of jobs a "battlefield promotion."[13]

Early polls had Butcher leading Jontz by double digits, and Democrats in the Fifth District had grown accustomed to losing the congressional seat to the GOP. As a field organizer for the Jontz campaign, Phillip Perdue of Delphi, Indiana, had the responsibility of going into a county, meeting with local Democratic leaders, and convincing them to get behind Jontz. "You practically had to grab people and shake them," said Perdue, who told them they had a real chance of electing one of their own to Congress if they worked hard enough. In addition, Perdue helped organize house parties as fund-raisers around the state in such cities outside the Fifth District as Anderson and Lafayette. Jontz attended these meetings, which were hosted by a local couple at their home, and discussed his core progressive values. These talks varied a little bit, said Perdue, who joked that the closer they got to Terre Haute the more the candidate talked about one of that city's favorite sons, labor leader Eugene V. Debs, a Jontz favorite. "Jim wanted government to work for people," Perdue recalled, "he was very much the populist." Although Perdue said that Jontz was by no means an expert when it came to economics, he added that the candidate's straightforward message—"I think the economy works best when everyday people have some money in their pockets"—appealed to voters of both parties, as well as independents.

Perdue spent a lot of time with Jontz driving him around in his pickup truck to events (the Democrat's staff estimated that Jontz averaged six thousand miles a month by car the last three months of the campaign). One of Perdue's favorite memories of those days revealed much to him about the candidate's "youth and his remarkable mind." The two men were driving past Disko, Indiana, in Wabash County, and Jontz, perhaps using the knowledge he had gained while earning a degree in geology at IU, turned to Perdue and began talking about the Disko High Bogs, a rage geologic formation created by the last glaciers. When he had finished talking about the bogs, the hit song "Bad, Bad Leroy Brown" by singer-songwriter Jim Croce came over the car's radio. "I don't remember who started first," said Perdue, "but soon we were singing along at top volume—two guys in dark suits in a pickup truck headed to a meeting in Akron letting it wail for all the cows and corn to hear." Reminiscing about that day in the car, Perdue was struck that Jontz, still only in his thirties and already a "well-seasoned politician," knew all the words to Croce's catchy tune. "He made the most of the time he had and made a real difference for the people of Indiana," Perdue said of Jontz.[14]

Establishing Jontz's name in the minds of voters became a constant problem for his volunteers. Brian Mayes, a Canadian who spent ten days in mid-October with the campaign, recalled that with simultaneous elections for everything from the U.S. Senate to sheriff, county coroner, and county surveyor, voters "tended to be wrapped up in a ball of confusion." One morning Mayes was at a plant gate in Kokomo the day after the city's mayor had called Republican city council member Jim Johnson "a blubbering idiot." Mayes heard one woman worker, upon entering the factory, remarking to Jontz that the mayor had torn "a strip off your hide yesterday"—a remark that prompted quick attempts to convince her that it was a different candidate the mayor had been talking about. "It also had to be drilled into people that Jontz was running for 'Washington' and not re-election to the State government," Mayes added. In spite of these problems, Mayes said that during the campaign Jontz's ability "to communicate his priorities on jobs, trade, and farm aid showed that he could speak to the people on their terms, and take a 'liberal' message and make it one of common sense."[15]

Busch also marveled at Jontz's ability to discuss the issues of the campaign with anyone, even those who disagreed with him. "He framed every issue in terms of how it related to the people in the district—the average citizen," Busch noted. What Jontz meant by the term "average citizen," he added, was someone who goes to work every day, raises a family, has bills to pay (including a mortgage on a home), works hard, and hopes to somehow put their children through college so they could have a better life than their parents. Busch said that description probably included 70 percent of the people residing in the Fifth District. In Jontz's estimation, he benefited from the district having a high percentage of union households (approximately 30 percent) and the support he received from farm families. Those groups, along with senior citizens, gave him a solid base to work from for every election.

Although the GOP attempted to convince voters that his stands on issues put him out of step with the district, Jontz said his populist philosophy of "getting government back on the side of the average person" proved to be effective with "an independent-minded constituency like this one."[16]

Because of the open seat with Hillis's withdrawal, the Fifth District race drew the attention of national political groups, especially the Democratic Congressional Campaign Committee, which works to elect Democrats to Congress. The Jontz campaign received strategic advice from a DCCC Midwest field representative named Rahm Emanuel, later White House chief of staff for President Barack Obama and mayor of Chicago, and David Axelrod, a political consultant and later a senior adviser to Obama. Klose remembered Emanuel coming down from Chicago to "monitor the campaign, sometimes it was to kick my ass."[17]

Emanuel's annoyance, however, might have been directed more at the candidate than at his staff. As political consultant Chris Sautter noted in an article for *Roll Call*, the newspaper of Capitol Hill, "Jontz drove Emanuel to fits by his insistence on doing things the Jim Jontz way rather than the DCCC way. To Jontz, precinct targeting was helpful to ordinary candidates. But since he intended to knock on every door, targeting was superfluous." California congressman Tony Coehlo, DCCC chairman, also displayed a keen interest in Jontz's race, making it one of the committee's top priorities in capturing open House seats. In spite of the advice offered by these powerful national figures, the campaign's most effective tool was the candidate himself. "The best thing would be to send the candidate out and talk," Perdue said of Jontz. "He was really good at connecting with people. Even Republicans would have to say, 'Well, he is a good guy.'"[18]

Jontz also turned to Hollywood for help. In late September and early October actress Bonnie Franklin campaigned on Jontz's behalf. Franklin had starred for nine seasons (1975 to 1984) on the hit CBS television network situation comedy *One Day at a Time*. She played the character Ann Romano, a divorced mother of two teenage daughters who leaves her broken home in Logansport, Indiana, for a new start as an advertising executive in Indianapolis. A Democrat, Franklin came to Logansport, a community she had never before visited, on September 30 to speak on Jontz's behalf and be honored with "Bonnie Franklin Day" by the city's mayor, John Davis. "I'm in Indiana because I know he [Jontz] will be a better representative and I know voters will be proud they elected the right Jim," said Franklin in a press conference at the Holiday Inn. In addition, she stressed that the GOP was not the only political group valuing patriotism and moral behavior. "It makes me crazy when the flag, Christianity, church and love belong 'just' to the Republican Party," Franklin noted. "They belong to all of us, not one group, no matter how big it is." After the press conference, she met with local and civic groups, toured Logansport's downtown business district, and ended the day at a fund-raising hog roast for Jontz.[19]

As the election neared Altman took over as the scheduler for Jontz's congressional campaign. She juggled her life as a mother with her commitment to getting her candidate elected. After getting her four children off to school in the morning, she worked on the campaign until they had to be picked up from school. After seeing to extracurricular activities such as dance lessons, making dinner, and putting her kids to bed, Altman turned her attention back to politics. Late at night Jontz would end an exhausting day of campaigning in the district by returning to his headquarters in Monticello, "and that's when the real business of the day would start," she recalled. "I could talk to him and figure out what he wanted to do schedule wise and what he didn't want to do." One Sunday night while they burned the midnight oil, the Monticello office had an unusual visitor—Butcher, who noticed the lights were on and knocked on the door. "He came in and we gave him cookies and punch," Jontz recalled.

One of the issues Jontz and Altman discussed in those late-night strategy sessions (as his race for Congress neared the end the candidate found time for only three or four hours of sleep) involved a standard part of any election—the design of the yard sign publicizing his campaign. Yard signs promoting candidates perennially pop up like mushrooms on neighborhood lawns every fall election season. For his yard sign, Jontz tried to emphasize his dogged door-to-door, shoe-leather campaign method by selecting the outline of the sole of a boot with the words "Jontz for Congress" in white letters emblazoned across it on a blue background. "I well remember when that artwork was created—how extremely fussy Jim was about the exact shape of the boot that he wanted," Altman said. "Every night he'd come into the campaign office at 10 or 11—when there were no more possible events he could attend—and make suggestions for revisions. Staff would relay the ideas to the artist, who would do another draft before the next night." Once the artwork met his meticulous standards, Jontz used it for his subsequent congressional campaigns. "People loved them," said Altman. "And the logo was extremely

The campaign sign used by Jontz in each of his races for Congress.

effective—to this day it is the only yard sign I've ever seen with a graphic and unmistakable message."[20]

Another part of Jontz's congressional campaign that became a fixture in the years to come concerned an item borrowed from his sister, Mary Lee Turk—a rusty, blue Schwinn bicycle with a wire basket dangling from the front (in later years a sign hung from each side of the back wheel with the words: "Congressman Jim Jontz"). Taking a cue from his campaigns for the state legislature, Jontz rode the bike, and others like it, in community parades. For such outings he only used bikes with coaster brakes so he could have a free hand to wave to the crowds that lined the sidewalk or to slap the outstretched hands of younger parade watchers. On July 4, 1986, he set a personal best by riding his bicycle in seven parades (a record he matched two years later). "That bike is magic," said Altman. "It really is. It gives you his image: He's on a bike rather than sitting on the back of a convertible waving like Queen Elizabeth." In addition, Jontz cemented his common-man approach by an item he gave away to help spread the word about his race—old-fashioned potholders.[21]

The two congressional candidates' divergent views on issues came into sharp focus during a series of five debates held in such communities as Kokomo, Marion, and Manchester. Butcher attempted to present himself as a fiscal and moral conservative prepared to uphold traditional family values, saying that for far too long politicians and officials in Washington, D.C., had been chipping away at the three main pillars of American society—traditional, American, and family values; the work ethic; and personal, business, and religious liberties. Jontz described himself as someone who would work on Capitol Hill to protect the interests of the district's average citizens. "What's made our country great has not been the Wall Street bankers or the Philadelphia lawyers," said Jontz. "It's been average working people in Marion, Indiana, and throughout our state and our nation who work hard and try to provide better for their family and try to get ahead. We need a congressman in Washington who will speak up for them."[22]

During the debates, the candidates jockeyed back and forth on such national and international issues as abortion, education, a balanced-budget constitutional amendment, continued American aid to Contra rebels fighting the Sandinista National Liberation Front government of Nicaragua, utility rates, taxes, and economic sanctions on the apartheid government of South Africa. While Butcher and Jontz agreed on the need for a balanced-budget amendment to the U.S. Constitution, they disagreed sharply on abortion, with Butcher opposed the procedure unless a physician determined a mother's life was in danger, and Jontz defending a woman's decision to have an abortion after consulting with her doctor, family members, and her clergyman. "It's not the government's role to make that decision," he said. The two men also differed on the conflict in Nicaragua, with Butcher supporting President Reagan's decision to send arms and supplies to the Contras, warning that the Sandinistas had "established a totalitarian government close to our own borders" and if nothing was done other Central American countries would also fall like dominoes. Jontz termed Butcher's reasoning "ludicrous," as it was a "ludicrous thought that a tiny, poverty stricken country like Nicaragua is going to be knocking on our door to bring us to our knees. Our biggest enemies in Central America are hunger and poverty."[23]

In a tactic that other Republican opponents of Jontz had used, Butcher, during the campaign, had contrasted himself with his opponent by emphasizing the Democrat was a bachelor and had spent most of his adult life in public office. "Jim Butcher and Jim Jontz don't think alike and don't vote alike, or

The photograph of Jontz with his mother, father, and grandmother he circulated during his first campaign for Congress when faced with the criticism that he had no family.

Polly and Leland Jontz proudly wear their son's campaign button during a campaign event in October 1986.

very rarely," Butcher noted. Butcher particularly attempted to contrast his personal history with Jontz's, noting that during his life he "had 16 jobs, working my way through college, that I worked 4½ years in the steel mills of Detroit and Gary." Butcher argued that Jontz was somebody who "talks about jobs, but he's never had a full-time job, to my knowledge." And although Jontz talked about family values during the campaign, Republicans were quick to point out that he was a bachelor and had no family. That last charge drew a sharp rebuke from Jontz's grandmother, Louise Jontz. She circulated a letter under her name noting Butcher's charge that her grandson did not have a family. "You can imagine what a surprise that was to Jim's parents and me!" she wrote. Louise pointed out that her family had lived and worked in north central Indiana for four generations and that Jontz was named after his grand-father, her husband, who had worked at the Commercial State Bank in Silver Lake for more than thirty years. "I've been a Republican all my life," said Louise, "but I'll be supporting Jim this year." With her letter she included a Jontz potholder to remind each recipient to vote for her grandson on Election Day.[24]

The Monday afternoon before the Tuesday, November 4, election, the Jontz campaign seemed to be headed for a crushing defeat at the ballot box. A poll conducted by Brian Vargus, a respected Indiana University–Purdue University political science professor and pollster, had Butcher winning 52.5 percent of the vote to only 20.8 percent for Jontz. The long odds failed to deter Jontz from trying to sway as many voters as possible to his side. On Election Day he started his final campaign push by working for four hours in a voting precinct in Howard County before heading back to White County to cast his ballot and check in at his Monticello headquarters. He arrived in Grant County at two o'clock in the afternoon to greet voters at the county's largest precinct (1,705 registered voters) in Upland. Asked by a local resident who saw him standing outside the Upland Community Building why he picked to visit that community, Jontz tried to win him over by responding: "It's the quality of the voters." When a reporter from the *Marion Chronicle-Tribune* sought his prediction on the election, Jontz grinned and joked: "I don't make prognostications. I predict the candidate with the most votes will win." After spending about an hour and a half in Upland, Jontz drove to Marion, remaining at a voting place near the Memorial Coliseum until it closed. He did tell the *Chronicle-Tribune* reporter that he needed to win or run close to Butcher in the district's larger counties—Howard, Grant, and the portions of Lake and Porter—in order to have any chance of capturing the race.[25]

All of Jontz's hard work paid off. He confounded the pollsters by defeating Butcher in the Fifth District with 51.4 percent of the vote to 48.1 for his opponent (Jontz won by approximately five thousand ballots). Maxwell had a simple answer for the victory: "Jim Jontz simply outcampaigned him." Each candidate won seven counties in the fourteen-county district, but Jontz won the largest county (Howard) and lost Grant County by a slim margin (only 146 votes). The loss disheartened GOP officials, particularly Jontz's strong showing in usually heavily Republican areas such as White County. "They [Butcher supporters] all worked so extremely hard for him," noted Mary Beth Drumm, White County Republic Central Committee chairman. "We did the best we could but they [the voters] split their tickets, they *really* split their tickets! I just don't know how to explain it." Drumm did admit that Jontz had always been strong in White County—a fact reflected by his winning there by approximately two thousand votes. One political observer noted that Butcher's defeat of the party-backed candidate Ridlen in the primary meant that Butcher was never able to "bring party Republicans back on his side. He never really tried. The Republican Party never really opposed him, but it never really embraced him either." Rex Harris, Cass County Democratic chairman, said not having Ridlen on the ticket hurt the Republicans, as he "was a very strong candidate, well-liked and popular. I'm sure his loss took away some of the enthusiasm from the Republicans."

On election night Butcher told reporters that he believed he had been ahead until the campaign's last few weeks, when the momentum started to swing his opponent's way. The surge to the Democrat may have come as a result of radio advertisements Jontz's campaign ran criticizing Butcher's voting attendance record in the Indiana Senate, especially missing some time from his legislative duties in order to attend a fund-raiser with television evangelist Pat Robertson. "About 10 days to two weeks ago," said Butcher, "we saw a drastic change in our polls. No one could explain it. There was no national event or local event that could have impacted the polls the way it did." He noted that a poll taken by his campaign on the Sunday night before the election still showed him with a comfortable lead (61 percent to 31 percent). "We won't know for days or weeks what caused the changes, but I do know that there was approximately a slide of nine or 10 points when he [Jontz] began attacking my voting attendance record," Butcher said. "It gradually deteriorated after that." Butcher expressed surprise at not winning his home county, Howard, and only being able to squeak out a narrow victory in Grant County. "Those two surprises, that probably led to our defeat," he said. "I still believe I would have needed to win in Howard County to be successful."[26]

Sugar compared election night in 1986 as one of his favorite memories, alongside such momentous life events as a wedding day or the birth of a first child. He said the campaign knew that capturing Howard County, because of its population, was the key to winning the race. When the first returns came in showing Jontz leading in the county, Sugar remembered he and Jontz ran the three blocks from the Howard County Democratic headquarters to the courthouse, just the two of them, nobody else in the streets in downtown Kokomo, running and looking at each other like two giddy children and thinking, "My God, this is going to happen." Although never very good with numbers, Sugar said he will always remember that they ended up winning by 1,762 votes over Butcher in Howard County.[27]

Sugar's admiration for Jontz and the character he showed during the campaign deepened in the hours after Jontz's congressional win. As the celebration was winding down at Jontz's headquarters in Monticello, the candidate came up to Sugar and suggested that the two of them return to Kokomo early the next morning to greet workers at the Chrysler transmission plant they had visited at the start of the campaign. Williams remembered attending a victory party election night at the home of the Democratic chairman for Howard County and late in the evening, about 1 a.m., receiving a telephone call from Jontz. "How he found me there, I don't know," said Williams. After congratulating the newly elected congressman, Williams said Jontz thanked him and then asked what he was doing that morning as he wanted the union leader to join him for the visit to the Chrysler factory.[28]

Sugar and Jontz were able to snatch a few hours of sleep before awakening at 5:30 a.m. for the drive from Brookston to Kokomo. Sugar remembered that a sign on Jontz's bathroom mirror still read: "Why aren't you in Kokomo or Marion or Valparaiso?" Arriving at the Chrysler facility, Jontz stood at the plant's gate to greet the groggy automotive workers as they started their early shift, jolting them awake with his words: "Hey, thanks a lot guys, I won't let you down. I really appreciate your support yesterday, I will not forget." Most of the workers acted as if this was the first time a candidate had ever thanked them personally for their vote just hours after winning an election. Williams, his voice choking with emotion as he recalled the visit years later, said Jontz spent about an hour shaking hands with anywhere from 100 to 150 workers, "but you would have thought he shook hands with every guy in the plant. It was really something." For Sugar, Jontz's visit served as "an example of everything our campaign stood for. We meant it. We're really going to fight for working folks." After his thanks to union workers, Jontz realized that for the first time in many months he had nothing on his schedule. He decided to eat a bite of breakfast and stop at the Kokomo City Hall for more thank-you calls before returning to Monticello.[29]

With his victory, Jontz found himself in an unusual position. During his time in the state legislature he had been used to being in the minority, as usually Republicans were in the majority in the Indiana House of Representatives and Indiana Senate, as well as occupying the governor's office. In the 1986 election Democrats had held on to the majority in the U.S. Congress and even added to it, gaining five seats. "When I left the Indiana Senate, there were 20 Democrats. We could get together in a small room," Jontz told a reporter. "Here [in Congress] there are 258 Democrats and you've got to talk to dozens of people if you want to build a coalition on legislation." Still, there were perks, including obtaining credit for the work he did. "At home," he said, "if there was a bill you introduced and they [Republicans] liked it, they stole it." Jontz kept busy, learning the ropes of his new job by attending a weeklong seminar at Harvard University's School of Government and finding a place to live in Washington, D.C.—a small efficiency apartment located just a few blocks from where congressmen had their offices. "It's basically a place to sleep," said Jontz. Maxwell remembered visiting Washington and having the congressman offer his apartment as a place to stay during his visit. When he got there, Maxwell noticed there was not much furniture and no curtains on the windows. He checked the refrigerator and found that the only thing inside was a bottle of water. "He lived a very Spartan existence," Maxwell said. In the coming years representing the Fifth District, Jontz spent as little time as possible in his dinky apartment—he had too much to do and rarely enough time in the day to get all he wanted to do accomplished.[30]

5

A Public Trust

On January 6, 1987, Jim Jontz took the official oath of office as a member of the U.S. House of Representatives. The bachelor was accompanied by his four-year-old niece, Katie Turk, the daughter of his sister, Mary Lee Turk of Chicago, at the swearing-in ceremony officiated over by Speaker of the House James Wright of Texas (Jontz's nieces Katie, Beth, and Emily accompanied him at such ceremonies in subsequent years). Katie expressed her excitement at being able to be there to see her uncle get "sworn at." For his part, Speaker Wright reminded the new legislators what a "great privilege" it was to serve in Congress. "The word 'representative,'" he said, "is our descrption as well as our title. We are ordinary men and women, grappling with extraordinary problems. This is the people's House, the nation's town hall." Kathy Altman, appointed as the director of the congressman's Indiana offices in the Fifth District, remembered sitting high in the rafters with Jontz's parents and sister to witness her candidate finally taking office "and I swear I took that oath with him." Although many of the forty-nine freshman congressman left the House floor after the ceremony to attend receptions, Jontz remained behind. "I stuck around," he said. "I wanted to get a sense of the place." In feeling his way around Capitol Hill the first few months in office, Jontz drew upon the lessons he learned as a state legislator, noting the course of legislation was often influenced by the personalities of the individuals involved. "A key for freshman congressmen is to focus on an area where a need is apparent but there's not legislative activity—where there's enough room in the forest so a voice can be heard," said Jontz.[1]

His voice was heard immediately on an issue that more often than not has inflamed the passions of taxpayers everywhere—a congressional pay raise. For Jontz, used to getting by on his pay as a state legislator, the $77,400

Jim Jontz's nieces, Katie, Beth, and Emily, often accompanied him on the floor of the House of Representatives when he was sworn into office with other congressmen.

yearly salary he was set to receive as a congressman seemed more than adequate to meet his needs. With Congress set to receive a 15.6 percent salary increase, Jontz decided to use the extra money to establish a scholarship fund for students in his district, believing it would be a "better investment" than returning the funds ($13,200 after taxes for 1987 and 1988 combined) to the U.S. treasury. "Establishing a scholarship fund with the money which I will receive from the pay hike we never should have received is a way of turning lemons into lemonade," he said. A bipartisan, districtwide committee representing all fourteen counties of the Fifth District oversaw the scholarship fund. From 1987 to 1991, twenty-eight students in the district were awarded scholarships totaling $15,500.[2]

The rookie congressman maintained the same intense pace in office as he had on the campaign trail. During his first year in office, he was one of only eight of the 435 members of Congress to have a perfect voting record, being present for 511 roll-call votes. "The voters in my district have placed a great deal of trust in me and being there for every vote is an important way of honoring that trust," he said. "I've done exactly what I told people I would

Jontz at work in Washington, D.C., May 10, 1987. "It's soaking in very slowly," he noted during his first days in office. "People have high expectations for me, and I'll work hard not to disappoint them."

do." Fellow Hoosier congressman Peter J. Visclosky, who represented the First District, had been impressed with what he saw during Jontz's initial service in Washington. "I would characterize him as being extremely diligent, a student of the institution," said Visclosky. "You can certainly see his state legislature experience shining through." He also called Jontz "aggressive in the good sense," in that he worked hard and sought out additional responsibilities on Capitol Hill. Jontz also received favorable marks for his work from Congressman Thomas Petri, a Republican from Wisconsin, especially for his commitment to aiding those who lived and worked in his district.[3]

Jontz ran his four-room congressional office to emphasize constituent service, placing more staff members back in Indiana at his offices at 104 West Walnut Street in Kokomo and at 302 East Lincolnway in Valparaiso than in Washington, D.C. "We're very district intensive," noted Christopher Klose. Staff worked to help people who had problems collecting their Social Security or veteran's benefits, or farmers looking for help after a natural disaster, handling a total of 1,800 constituent requests for help in 1987. In comparing

Part of a congressman's responsibilities is meeting with people from his or her district on visits to Washington, D.C. Here, Jontz meets with students from Twin Lakes High School (top), a group of Future Farmers of America (center), and members of the Fulton County Farm Bureau (above).

notes with other congressional offices, Klose found that Jontz's staff had a far greater constituent caseload than any other delegation, with the closest office handling only a third of the casework the Indiana congressman's office did. "Every time he [Jontz] would go out and say, 'Tell me your problems,' there were plenty of problems people wanted to tell you about," said Klose.[4]

Barbara Koonce began work as a caseworker in Jontz's Valparaiso office in January 1987. During the three years she spent with the congressman, Koonce, a Crown Point native, described her job as a mixture of diplomacy, persistence, and the ability to listen. "We inform the individual citizen about what's available to them and where to go for help," she told a reporter from the *Valparaiso Vidette-Messenger*. "People have no idea where to find information, so they call. I do a lot of listening." Those who called her office seeking assistance usually fell into two categories, she noted: "A, they've tried everything, and B, they don't know where to go." She kept in touch with various local, state, and federal agencies, but constituents had to make the initial inquiry to such departments before she could step in and try to help. "I try to deal honestly with people and not give them false hopes," Koonce said. "I explain the procedure we go through and what the outcome might be."

Most of the mistakes made by government agencies were usually the result of human or computer error, said Koonce, and sometimes could be easily solved. However, those who called seeking assistance often had the mistaken assumption that a congressional office possessed unlimited power when it came to obtaining information or changing an agency's policies. "Obviously, you don't get a response everytime you ask," Jontz himself noted, "but sometimes you do. That's why you keep asking." Koonce had the ticklish job of explaining that her office was subject to the limitations and regulations established by Congress. One of the worst parts of her job involved trying to get this point across to the public in a diplomatic manner. "I tell the constituents, 'Sorry, we can't break the rules. We can't help you on an aspect because of regulations.' Then I listen to them yell," she said. Still, she enjoyed her job, noting it was "self-fulfilling being able to help people." Koonce also served as a link between Jontz and the public. "The attitude of a case worker should be: I don't know if I can change this, but I won't know if I don't try," she said. "If I don't ask, we aren't going to know."[5]

Letters from constituents seeking solutions to problems or voicing their opinions on issues facing Congress deluged Jontz's Washington office. Bart Chilton, a graduate of Purdue University who had worked in the office of

Jontz takes a soft-drink break while meeting with his congressional staff members. To Jontz's right is Bart Chilton.

Illinois congressman Terry Bruce before becoming Jontz's legislative director in Washington, remembered that Jontz faced a difficult task even before
he had assembled a complete staff. The minute a new congressman is elected
constituents start writing letters asking for assistance. These letters pile up
by the thousands and represent a daunting amount of work during the days
when offices in Washington had only a few computers, instead depending
upon a couple of IBM Selectric typewriters. "Here you are, a new member of
Congress," said Chilton, "you've been so in touch with people [during a cam-
paign], so responsive, and now before you've been sworn in, you're behind the
eight ball right away. Our first job was to catch up, put systems in place, and
map out an action plan for his agenda."

Jontz proved to be a demanding boss because he wanted to make sure
that the people who sought help from his office "felt like they mattered," said
Chilton. Staff had to overcome a big logistical hurdle in trying to get language
approved on each position Jontz took on various issues before Congress
so that if someone wrote in with opinions on the defense bill, the strategic
defense initiative ("Star Wars"), or aid to the Contra rebels in Nicaragua, a
letter could be prepared for Jontz to send out that included his stand on those

Jontz reads his mail at his Longworth House Office Building office. "Certainly one of the things I've learned is that no part of the job is more rewarding than being able to get things done for the people you represent, for your state, and for your country," Jontz said.

issues, as well as a personal message if he knew the person who wrote the letter. Given that Jontz had won his first state legislative contest by only two votes, Chilton said, "he viewed every individual as important, so he wanted to get the letters correct. He wouldn't want a response to appear bureaucratic. He wanted to make sure that the people knew we were writing to them," and not just receiving a form letter. Jontz usually stayed so late into the night at his office because he wanted to personally sign all the letters that went out and even edited a number if they failed to meet his exacting standards. "The people whom he represented should be pleased they had a member of Congress who was so diligent on their behalf," Chilton said. "That doesn't mean it was easy for staff all the time—it wasn't." The staff worked hard to document how and why Jontz voted on each issue that came before the House, as they never knew what question might be lobbed their way late on a Sunday night. "My job was to make sure we were prepared to respond to anything," Chilton recalled.[6]

As they sorted through the correspondence that deluged their office, Jontz and his staff were confronted with a wide range of concerns. Issues involved everything from a woman in Valparaiso concerned that the price of her cable service was on the rise to a man in Lake of the Four Seasons outraged at the *Exxon Valdez* environmental disaster involving an oil tanker spilling thousands of barrels of crude oil after running aground on Alaska's Prince William Sound. The congressmen also wrote letters congratulating a nurse for her thirty-five years of service at the Marion Veterans Center, seeking help from a Department of the Interior official for designating the middle fork of the Vermilion River in Illinois as a National Scenic River, and thanking a man in Griffith for suggesting that closed military bases be converted for use as minimum security prisons. He also had to be a diplomat when responding to "issues" out of left field, including a letter from a Russiaville man claiming he would never vote for him again because Jontz had endorsed beer drinking. The congressman wrote back and expressed his confusion about such an endorsement (odd for someone who did not drink alcohol). "I have never told anyone that I endorse the drinking of beer," Jontz wrote. "If you have any literature which claims that I have, it would be very helpful if you could send it to me."[7]

Some of Jontz's best efforts in responding to his constituents' concerns came on the controversial matters that House members had to contend with in the mid- and late 1980s, including abortion, gun control, and a proposed amendment to the U.S. Constitution allowing Congress to prohibit the desecration of the U.S. flag, including burning a flag as an act of political protest. Answering a 1991 letter from members of American Legion Post 34 in Indianapolis expressing support for such an amendment, Jontz said that although he did not approve of "flag burning or flag burners," he had joined a number of his other colleagues in the House in voting against such an amendment because "the arguments against a constitutional amendment outweighed the arguments for." He went on to write:

> Regardless of how much we disagree with someone else's thoughts and expression, the flag stands for the right of every American citizen to speak his or her own mind, the right of political expression, which is central to our democracy.
>
> It's a freedom that is much easier to support in the abstract than in the specific, especially when the method of expression is flag burning or some other act that we find so offensive. But if you start passing constitutional amendments undoing the Bill of Rights, where do you stop? Would use of flags on articles of clothing or disposable items be

considered abuse of the flag? Do you protect other sacred symbols of our nation, copies of the Constitution, or likenesses of the President with additional amendments?

Our nation has withstood a civil war, the Great Depression, two world wars this century, and countless other crises without once amending the Bill of Rights in 200 years. Do the actions of a few publicity seekers, encouraged by media attention getting them a couple of minutes on the evening news, justify a change in that precedent? I think not. I believe, were we to pass a constitutional amendment now, we would later regret having taken such a step. The overwhelming majority of Americans love our flag and that isn't going to be changed by a few flag burners.[8]

Another hot-button issue during Jontz's time in office involved funding for the National Endowment for the Arts, a government agency founded in 1965 that over the years has given grants totaling $4 billion to "to support artistic excellence, creativity, and innovation for the benefit of individuals and communities." The NEA came under fire in 1989 when the Reverend Donald Wildmon of the conservative American Family Association denounced the organization during a press conference for funding "anti-Christian bigotry," citing the work of artist Andres Serrano, especially a photograph showing a crucifix submerged in his urine. The work of other artists, including photographer Robert Mapplethorpe, also drew censure from such conservative lawmakers as Republican senators Jesse Helms of North Carolina and Alfonse D'Amato of New York.

Over the next few years, as Helms and other conservative critics continued to question grants given out by the NEA, some called for the organization to be abolished. Responding to a 1991 letter from a Kokomo constituent who supported such a course of action, Jontz agreed that taxpayers should not be expected to support paying for "obscene and offensive artwork," but also expressed frustration about cuts to student loans for college while such "wasteful" multibillion-dollar programs as the International Space Station, the Superconducting Supercollider, and foreign aid were kept alive. Although he supported measures in Congress placing some limitations and greater accountability on the part of the NEA, Jontz said he "would find other legislation that would abolish the NEA completely, difficult to support because I believe, in spite of recent controversy, the NEA does accomplish

Jontz watches action on the House floor on a small black-and-white television set in his congressional office. The congressman remained cautious about promising too much to his constituents. "I simply have to pick priorities; I can't do everything," he noted.

a lot of good work in promoting the art in our state, and throughout the nation."

He pointed out that in 1990 the NEA had awarded more than $1.7 million to Hoosier artists and art organizations, none of which had been controversial—the Trails of Courage Living History Festival in Fulton County, the master design plan for the Wildcat Creek Reservoir Park in Kokomo, and artist-in-residence programs at more than sixty-six Indiana schools, including a number in the Fifth District. "These NEA funded programs have enriched our community," wrote Jontz, "and I think that the benefits of the NEA's support for public art and arts organizations is such that we should try to maintain the agency if funding of questionable projects can be stopped."[9]

The explanations Jontz offered for his stands on issues were just as detailed when his constituents agreed with his actions. In May 1991 Jontz was one of only eighty-three Democrats who voted against House Resolution 7, better known as the Brady Handgun Violence Prevention Act. The legislation was named to honor Jim Brady, President Ronald Reagan's press secretary, who had been seriously wounded and partially paralyzed for life during the attempted assassination of Reagan by John Hinckley on March 30, 1991, in Washington, D.C. Brady and his wife, Sarah, had campaigned for several years to institute a background check and seven-day waiting period to help stop felons, youths, and mentally unsound people from purchasing handguns by providing false information on their applications. (Although the Brady Bill passed the House by a 239 to 186 vote in 1991, the measure did not become the law of the land until November 30, 1993, when President Bill Clinton signed the act.) Writing a Marion, Indiana, couple, who opposed the Brady Bill, Jontz said he had voted against the act because he had "doubts that the bill would be effective in reducing crime," as the legislation did not require police departments to actually do a background check during the waiting period and offered no help to those departments who did do so. "I am also concerned that the Brady Bill will not stop criminals from obtaining firearms," Jontz wrote. "According to a Task Force of the U.S. Attorney General, most criminals obtain their weapons through illegal means."

As an alternative to the Brady Bill, Jontz supported an amendment offered by Congressman Harley Staggers Jr., a Democrat from West Virginia. The defeated Staggers amendment duplicated a system instituted in Virginia requiring an immediate check by telephone by gun dealers to screen out those trying to illegally purchase handguns. According to Jontz, such a system "would operate like credit card or check cashing verification systems. Gun store dealers would call a toll-free number to check a potential customer to make sure that he or she does not have a criminal record." Other positives from instituting such a method included police not being "burdened with additional record keeping" and "honest citizens would not be forced to forsake their constitutional rights," he noted.[10]

Jontz used a variety of methods to maintain contact with those in the Fifth District, including dedicating a wall at the entrance to his office for a display of artwork from students. "Every office is proud of the products that are homegrown, and nothing grown at home is more important than children," said Jontz. He also instituted a weekly "Dial Your Congressman" program whereby constituents could use a toll-free telephone number to call and state their views on an issue or ask a question every Tuesday evening when Congress was in session. By using his 1-800-544-1474 number, constituents' telephone calls were actually routed to Jontz's Kokomo office. The staff there relayed the names and numbers of the callers to Jontz in Washington, and the calls were returned by the congressman from his office in the Longworth House Office Building. During the first evening for the program,

CALUMET REGIONAL ARCHIVES, INDIANA UNIVERSITY NORTHWEST

With newspaper in hand, Jontz walks to his work in Congress from his efficiency apartment located three blocks from the Capitol. "People don't expect freshman [congressmen] to work legislative miracles," Jontz said during his first term in office.

Jontz received forty-three calls from all areas of the Fifth District. Although scheduled to run from 6:00 p.m. to 8:00 p.m., the congressman was not off the phone until 9:15 p.m. "People usually don't call in and ask, 'What's your position on this?'" Jontz said. "People just want to talk. . . . It's a political reality that people are much more concerned about individual matters that effect them than they are with big policy matters. It doesn't hurt me to listen."

At one of the weekly sessions a reporter from the *Gary Post-Tribune* listened in as Jontz responded to his constituents' questions and concerns. During his time there, the reporter heard from Jontz about a women in Peru discussing her divorce, a man in Crown Point worried he might lose his Social Security benefits if he took at part-time job, and a man in Valparaiso upset because his landlord had sharply increased the cleaning deposit required for tenants with pets. "If I were designing a schedule to isolate myself, I'd never do this," said Jontz. "But my first priority is to provide good service." The calls sometimes even influenced how Jontz voted on an issue, as when he voted in favor of a sixty-five-miles-per-hour speed limit for interstate highways. "Now I'm getting cards from people who are against it," he noted. "They should have called."[11]

When Congress was in session, Jontz, who served on the agriculture, education and labor, and veterans' affairs committees, maintained a packed schedule, often not leaving his office until well after midnight. On a typical start to his work week Jontz arrived in his office to find his desk piled high with letters that needed his signature, legislation to study, and possible amendments to introduce. During the day Jontz raced back and forth from his office to the U.S. Capitol to cast his vote on various bills or amendments, met with representatives from a variety of interest groups, greeted and had his picture taken with visitors from his district, scheduled events back in Indiana with his staff, and ended the day by tackling the pile of paperwork that still awaited his attention. Tom Buis, an agricultural expert on Jontz's staff, remembered walking into the office late at night after meeting on legislative matters to find that everyone else had already left for the day, but the congressman had remained behind to finish his work. "He read every letter that he put his name on and every letter that constituents sent in to make sure that their concerns were being addressed," noted Buis. "If his constituents were paying him by the hour, he was working for less than minimum wage, because he worked around the clock. They got their money's worth."[12]

Jontz remained in Washington only when he had to, usually from Tuesday through Thursday when Congress voted on bills. He spent the rest of his time back in the district attending to a packed schedule of events; his staff had to create specialized computer software just to keep track of where he had to appear each day. For most of his time in politics, Jontz said he had heard voters complain that they sent representatives to Washington, D.C., and would never hear from them again. Deciding he never wanted to hear that said about him from one of his constituents, Jontz worked like a demon to show voters he had not forgotten where he came from. The hardest position on Jontz's staff was scheduler because of his intense desire to be efficient with his time. Altman remembered Jontz becoming "totally frustrated" on a holiday such as Mother's Day because there was nothing for him to do. "People used to joke . . . if there were two people together, Jim Jontz would find them," said Altman. Chilton said the staff in Washington made sure both the district offices and the congressman had been briefed on what to expect when he returned to Indiana for events, including giving Jontz reminders—"he had a real good memory"—from time to time on what issues he had discussed with particular individuals.[13]

Karen Davis, who served in the Jimmy Carter administration as deputy assistant secretary for health policy in the Department of Health and Human Services, met Jontz during his early days as a congressman at a Library of Congress briefing for new members of Congress held in Williamsburg, Virginia. "I was speaking on health policy issues facing the Congress and he not only asked excellent questions during the session but came up afterwards to pursue several points," said Davis, who added that Jontz had the "most

Jontz always tried to spend as much time as possible back in the Fifth Congressional District, including visiting the Eaton Company in North Manchester (right), attending a town meeting in Monticello (top), and meeting with representatives of the Bruce Lake Association to check on silt and weed problems at the Fulton County lake (above).

inquiring mind" of anyone she had ever known. The meeting sparked a twenty-year friendship that saw Jontz call on Davis to help with a town meeting in Kokomo on health care along with Congresswoman Barbara Kenelly, a Democrat from Connecticut. "It was an opportunity to see how hard Jim also worked back in the district—hitting multiple events at breakfast, lunch, and dinner. As he dashed off, he asked two Miss Senior Kokomos (both age eighty or over) to give me a tour of Kokomo including the stuffed Hereford two-thousand-pound bull Big Ben in the town park and the Delco-Remy battery plant." The experience, she added, came in handy when she testified before Congress and explained why Medicare physician fees "with a geographic adjustment based on area professional wages (including those engineers at Delco) were higher in Kokomo than anywhere else in the nation!"[14]

Another person impressed by Jontz's commitment to serving his district was a fellow member of Congress, Marcy Kaptur, a Democrat who represented Ohio's Ninth Congressional District. As a young girl Kaptur handed out voter guides with her uncle, a veteran of D-Day in World War II. First elected to office in 1982, Kaptur recalled that Jontz appeared to be an outgoing, gregarious person when first meeting other members of Congress. She quickly learned how devoted he was to the Fifth District and the cause of working people. "I don't think I knew anyone who worked harder," Kaptur said. She remembered visiting Jontz in Indiana and having him show her the beauties of the Indiana Dunes and seeking her cooperation on doing more for the Great Lakes ecosystem. "He was completely meant to be a member of Congress," she noted. "He was utterly dedicated to it." Jontz shared what he learned on his frequent visits back to his district with other members of Congress, something that is lacking at Capitol Hill today, she added, as representatives and congressional leaders are more and more concerned with how much money they can raise for the next election cycle. The drive for campaign funds has taken away time from constituent relations, from committee work, and from discussions with colleagues on policy issues, Kaptur said.[15]

For Sugar, who marveled that the congressman had town meetings where there were no towns, one of the most memorable experiences he had while working for Jontz as a field representative for Howard, Grant, and Wabash Counties occurred during an early morning trip from Kokomo to Burket in Kosciusko County to meet with farmers in a local restaurant. "Those farmers could not believe it," Sugar said. "I'm sure they talked about that for the next

A typical day for Jontz when he was back in the Fifth District involved a lot of time traveling from one community to another via automobile.

two years—that Jim Jontz walked in at five o'clock in the morning and had coffee with them and talked about agriculture policy."[16]

Scott Paul, who worked in the congressman's Washington office, still remembers a poll done of the Fifth District where voters were asked how they had heard about Jontz. Those who conducted the poll were shocked and could not believe the high percentage of people who responded they knew Jontz through firsthand, personal contact, and not secondhand by hearing his name through radio, television, or newspapers. "It's the way he did politics," said Paul. Even Republicans in the Fifth District marveled at the Democratic congressman's ability to remember their names and hometowns. Although one GOP supporter criticized Jontz for never working at anything other than politics, he had to admit, "Of course, that's why he's so good at it."[17]

The challenging schedule maintained by Jontz could be hard on his staff, with some believing he worked them too hard. "Jim worked incredibly hard hours," said Klose, "and he expected everyone else, not quite to match him, but certainly to be inspired to work as many hours as he did. That does take its toll." Busch still remembers a memorable twenty-two-hour day with the congressman that began with him leaving Logansport at 4:00 a.m. to pick up

Jontz in Fishers, where he was attending a breakfast meeting with the Ancient Forest Rescue Expedition, a group that hauled around a huge portion of an ancient Douglas fir to highlight the issue of protecting public old-growth forests. Busch met Jontz in Fishers at 6:00 a.m. and then drove him to a full schedule of events in Marion, Wabash, Peru, Logansport, and Kokomo. The congressman finished the day with a dinner in Chicago with the president of Cyprus (a favor for one of Jontz's supporters). The dinner lasted until about 10:30 p.m., and Busch dropped off Jontz in Monticello before returning home, exhausted, to Logansport. David Bozell, another Jontz field representative, noted that the congressman and his staff accom-

Jontz speaks at a meeting of the Grant County Farm Bureau. As a Democrat in a Republican-leaning district, Jontz realized he needed to win over every possible voter. "This race is on everyone's list in Washington, D.C., and Gordon Durnil's [state GOP chairman] list in Indianapolis," Jontz noted in 1988.

plished their marathon travel days during a time before the widespread use of cell phones, but Jontz managed anyway. "Jim absolutely knew where every pay phone was located in the entire district," recalled Bozell. "We frequently stopped for him to make calls along the way during the course of the day."[18]

Each Saturday Jontz scheduled anywhere from four to five town meetings in his district (by 1991 his staff estimated he had held more than three hundred such events). At these meetings, which usually lasted for an hour, the congressman opened by talking about the major issues before Congress at the time before moving on to focusing on one or two key pending issues he believed were important to the people in his district. He ended the meeting by opening it up to questions and comments from those in attendance. "Jim was a horrible public speaker," Busch remembered. "He could not give a speech and when he had to give a speech it was horrible. [But] he was an excellent talker."

Students at Purdue University in West Lafayette, Indiana, take time out to question Jontz about the issues of the day. Jontz remained interested in education issues throughout his career. "Our ability to compete in the world economy is closely linked to how well we prepare the young men and women of today for the jobs of tomorrow," he said.

Jontz could talk to anyone, said Busch, and rarely had to end a conversation by saying, "We just have to agree to disagree." Jontz believed that the key to being a successful politician involved being prepared for any type of discussion with voters. "If you can't answer their questions—at least be knowledgeable in the discussions of their concerns—you won't last very long," he noted.[19]

A reporter who followed Jontz during a visit back to the Fifth District in 1990 agreed with Busch's assessment of the congressman's skill when it came to dealing with his constituents. Writing in *Nuvo*, a weekly alternative newspaper in Indianapolis, writer Bill Craig noted how deftly Jontz's staff, in this case Bozell, shepherded his boss from one stop to another during a busy day on the road "without ever uttering a word; everything is communicated by facial expression or gesture. . . . Only in extreme cases does he interrupt a conversation." Instead, Bozell carefully positioned himself "in the congressman's line of sight and glances at his watch. Jontz knows what that means." On the day Craig traveled with Jontz, the congressman started in Indianapolis at the

Jontz is joined by fellow congressman Charles Hayes, a longtime Chicago labor leader (left), at the Miami County dairy farm of Larry Boys (right).

Pork Growers' breakfast at the Indiana State Fair, attended a forum in Marion protesting an attempt by out-of-state trash haulers to open a landfill there as well as a meeting of United Senior Action, met with auto parts workers at a plant in Gas City, and ended the day with door-to-door campaigning back in Marion. During these various stops, Craig was able to capture the everyman quality that made Jontz successful with voters, noting: "Jontz does not come across as a polished orator, but something in his delivery invites empathy. He is slightly slouched and wrinkled, with both hands in his pockets. He pauses too long between words, sometimes making you worry that he might be stuck. But like most politicians, he is never really at a loss for words; he just takes a little longer to measure his."[20]

Jontz's staff could, at times, become frustrated with their boss. Sugar remembered that after a while he was at wit's end trying to find someplace new for Jontz to visit in the counties he covered. For example, it seemed as though they had seen "every man, woman, and child," in Wabash, Indiana, and there was nowhere else for the congressman to visit. An exasperated Jontz said that could not be true, grabbed a copy of the local Yellow Pages telephone directory, threw it down on a desk, opened it, jabbed his finger on the page and asked Sugar if they had been to the spot he was pointing at. The two men looked down and discovered that Jontz's finger had landed on the name of a Wabash dog grooming parlor. "That's where I took him," Sugar said. The parlor had only "one person and a lot of dogs," so Jontz was only there for about five minutes. When they got back in the car, Sugar asked Jontz if he wanted to do more visits of that sort. The congressman agreed it might not have been the best use of his time, but added, with a twinkle in his eye, that the parlor owner would tell everyone she knew about the visit. "You know what," Sugar admitted, "he was right."[21]

One of the most satisfying aspects of being on staff for the congressman, however, noted Busch, involved having Jontz bring members of Congress from other districts to see firsthand what problems were facing residents of the Fifth District. Visitors included a Chicago congressman, Charles Hayes, who had never seen a cow before in his life, to share concerns on dairy legislation. Some of the other influential politicians who toured the district were Dan Glickman of Kansas to talk about agricultural issues and Les Aspin, chairman of the Armed Services Committee, to ponder additional funding for Grissom Air Force Base in Peru. "I heard a lot of politicians say Jim Jontz was the ultimate or consummate politician," Busch said. "I always took offense at that because he was the ultimate and consummate public servant." Those who were cynical about Jontz's efforts, including those who ran against him, believed he did what he did because he was looking for people's votes. But Busch said Jontz operated the way he did because "that's the way he believed a congressman should run his office. It was a job"—and a job that could not be done while on the golf course, on the beach, or on a trip to Hawaii in the middle of winter for a congressional junket.

Although a loyal supporter of Democratic issues from fighting to keep American jobs from moving overseas to finding health care for those who could not afford such coverage, Jontz did stray from the party line from time to time. "He framed every issue in terms of how it related to the people in his district—the average citizen," Busch remembered. Jontz's support of the Second Amendment right to keep and bear arms—he wrote that "the right of Americans to own firearms is guaranteed under the Constitution, and should never be abridged"—was so strong that he received an endorsement from the powerful National Rifle Association in 1988. Jontz also became one of a handful of Democrats to support a balanced-budget amendment to the

U.S. Constitution mandating that the federal government spent no more on expenditures than it collected in income, serving as a cosponsor of the measure since his first term in Congress. Jontz believed the federal government should live within its means, except in times of acute distress, such as wars or depressions. Paul noted that other progressive members of Congress "thought he was crazy" for supporting such a plan, but Jontz wanted to first straighten out the budget mess and then have a debate on the priorities—what programs to keep and what ones to cut. For example, is Social Security a higher priority than paying $10 billion for a Superconducting Supercollider, or should funding be appropriated for health care or education as opposed to more money for the International Space Station? Jontz, said Paul, believed the budget would be balanced when enough members of Congress had "the courage to vote 'No' on programs that are not important."[22]

From his first years in office, Jontz proved remarkably effective at getting bills affecting his district through Congress. "Above all else," he said, "I want to get the government back on the side of average American men and women: men and women who work hard, pay their taxes, and often don't get back from the government what they have paid for." As he had during his days in the Indiana General Assembly, Jontz used his personal contacts with people from his district to help shape his legislative agenda. The very first bill passed by Congress came about as the result of conversations he had with representatives from the Indiana Association of Cities and Towns and officials from several communities in his district. The federal Farmers Home Administration had planned to sell loans used by rural communities for development projects (for example, water treatment plants, sewage treatment facilities, and firehouses) to Wall Street at a discount. "It just didn't seem right that banks could buy these loans at a discount, while not allowing the communities to do so first," Jontz said. As a result of legislation he authored, thirteen cities and towns in his district saved nearly $6 million from the Farmers Home Loan Buy-Back Act. Indiana communities that found savings through the program included Union City ($1.3 million), Denver ($259,126), Kewanna ($340,959), Orland ($131,803), Wolcott ($123,745), and Sheridan ($704,545).[23]

Buis recalled one remarkable night on Capitol Hill when Jontz became a hero to staff members for a committee engaged in a marathon six-day effort to work out a compromise on differences between the House and Senate versions of a farm credit bill. In the bargain, Jontz might have ensured the survival of his rural community loan buyback effort. Involved in one late-night session,

Jontz listens to remarks by U.S. Department of Agriculture secretary Richard Lyng during a Congressional Drought Task Force meeting in 1988. Also pictured are, from left: Senator Kent Conrad, Representative Tim Johnson, Senator Bob Dole, Senator Christopher Bond, and Doctor Norton Strommen, chief USDA meteorologist.

Buis realized he had forgotten his key to the office and left the meeting to retrieve it, knowing that Jontz would probably still be in his office. When Buis got back to the office he saw Jontz sitting at his desk with his reading light on and told him he would give the congressman an update on the group's progress when they were finished. When Jontz asked him how things were progressing, Buis replied that those in the meeting were getting a little grouchy with one another because they had not had anything to eat for a while. "It probably wasn't a half an hour after I got back up there that the door opened and here comes Jim with two big bowls of popcorn," Buis recalled. "He became the hero for the thirty staff [members] in there. They were just floored that, A, they got a snack, but B, it was delivered and popped by a member of Congress. But Jim never thought of himself as someone with a title above anyone else. That was part of his appeal to people, too." The popcorn might have paid off in another way; the farm credit law eventually signed by President Reagan

Jontz helps Colonel Russell W. Fitch Jr., commander of the 305th Air Fueling Wing, cut the ribbon on a new transportation management office at Grissom Air Force Base near Peru, Indiana. The $1.6-million facility replaced a World War II-era building that previously housed the office.

included Jontz's provision allowing rural communities to repurchase the FHA loans.[24]

Other Jontz success stories included a law aiding students who were in default on their guaranteed student loans by offering a one time, six-month grace period to pay back their loans (saving taxpayers an estimated $30 million in 1990), legislation making low-interest loans more accessible to farmers suffering from the effects of a severe drought that hit the county in 1988, and a measure allowing veterans a second chance to qualify for education benefits under the GI Bill when they left military service. He also made sure to see to the needs of projects back in his district, securing appropriations for updating facilities at Grissom Air Force Base in Peru and the Veterans Administration hospital in Marion, as well as $3.4 million in funding for the development of a Hoosier Heartland Industrial Corridor helping to improve road conditions from Interstate 65 in Indiana to Interstate 75 in Ohio.

A meeting with another group of Jontz's constituents brought national attention to an issue that had been damaging the lives of more than four hundred thousand Vietnam-era combat veterans—posttraumatic stress disorder, a readjustment condition caused by exposure to combat or other dangerous events. PTSD was known by other names in previous conflicts, including "shellshock" in World War I and "combat fatigue" in World War II. According to the National Vietnam Veterans Readjustment Study conducted by the Research Triangle Institute in North Carolina for the VA from 1984 to 1988, more than 479,000 of the 3.1 million Vietnam veterans (15 percent of males and 8 percent of females) suffered from the disorder, which was not recognized by the government or mental health officials until 1980. The high rate of PTSD among Vietnam veterans were attributed to the ambivalence soldiers and civilians back in the United States felt about the country's involvement in the war, as well as the poor homecomings and counseling the veterans received that could have served as therapy for their war-related stress. Families wondered what could be wrong as they saw returning soldiers suffer from such maladies as flashbacks, nightmares, social withdrawal, hypervigilance, substance abuse, and survivor guilt. "The men and women in Vietnam faced a different situation," said Jontz. "There were no welcoming parties when they came home." Despite the high rate of PTSD among Vietnam veterans, only 10 percent had received help from the Veterans Administration in the last year of the Research Triangle's study.

In 1989 Jontz met with Vietnam veterans concerned about the possibility that a PTSD treatment program at the Marion VA Medical Center might be closed (it stayed open). Inspired into action, in August he introduced House Resolution 3037, the Veterans PTSD Treatment and Psychological Readjustment Act. Under his bill, which had 129 cosponsors and drew support from such groups as the American Legion, Veterans of Foreign Wars, and the Vietnam Veterans of America, Jontz sought to present a "balanced, cost-effective approach to help resolve the PTSD problem that . . . had been often neglected over this past decade." The legislation expanded inpatient treatment for the disorder by adding thirty centrally funded inpatient PTSD units to the sixteen then in place nationwide. "The problem is not one of quality of care so much as it is quantity," said Jontz. In addition, the measure added forty Vet Centers to the 195 that existed at the time to provide readjustment counseling for all Vietnam veterans, expanded a scholarship program for mental health professionals who specialized in PTSD, and established a pilot program for PTSD care in halfway houses. As long as the Vietnam combat veterans were "bearing the burdens of untreated wounds such as PTSD, the government hasn't met its moral and legal obligations to them," Jontz stressed.[25]

Jontz worked with Lane Evans of Illinois, chairman of the House Veterans' Affairs Subcommittee on Oversight and Investigations, and Congresswoman Jill Long of Indiana, to seek support and information on the PTSD issue. The subcommittee held hearings in September 1989 at Huntington North High School in Huntington, Indiana, and at a forum at an annual Vietnam Veterans Reunion in Kokomo. At the Huntington hearing, Darlene Mays, a Rochester housewife, said she and her husband, Daniel, a Vietnam veteran, did not know he suffered from the disorder until nearly two decades after he had returned from his service overseas. "The Vietnam War has continued for the past 20 years in the bedrooms, kitchens and living rooms of America," said Mays. "I can't begin to tell the world of the stress that is around my Vietnam veteran." More than eighty veterans and their family members attended the Kokomo event, with many complaining about the government's parsimonious funding for PTSD treatment and public ignorance about the problem. Vickie Foy of Marion related a story about her husband with PTSD who donned his military uniform, grabbed a gun, and went off for a "night patrol" in the woods. "They have no place to go without this program," said Foy.[26]

Although Jontz's legislation failed to make its way through the House, he did see his work rewarded when, in March 1991, the House Veterans' Affairs Committee approved more than $7 million in additional funding to treat PTSD, as well as having the full House pass a supplemental appropriation that included $4 million to create eight new PTSD inpatient units at VA medical centers across the country and $1.4 million to provide readjustment counseling for returning veterans of the Persian Gulf War. "We're already years overdue for providing adequate treatment to veterans with PTSD," Jontz said. "But finally Congress is recognizing that the VA must meet its obligations to the hundreds of thousands of American veterans suffering from PTSD." Jontz staff member Paul said one of his most vivid memories of working for Jontz came when the Veterans' Committee approved the funding. Paul remembered that an audience of Vietnam veterans in the committee room that day all stood up and gave Jontz a round of applause as he left the room. "I think they felt like their voices were heard for the first time in many years," said Paul.[27]

The work Jontz did while a congressman drew the attention of both Indiana and national media. The son of a New Jersey political reporter and

a graduate of Harvard University, Scott Campbell of Cambridge, Massachusetts, served as Jontz's press secretary after the first press secretary left after
only one fast-paced week. Perhaps it was not surprising then that Campbell's
first impression of his new boss was summed up in two words—"very ener-
getic." According to Campbell, Jontz enjoyed cordial relations with the media
in his district because he was respectful of the function the industry served,
as well as the professionalism of individual reporters. "He recognized the value
of the press. In a far-flung district with no political television coverage, and
so many different media markets, he knew the way to reach people was
through journalism, and he was very patient with the print and radio
media," Campbell noted.

A combination of factors contributed to Jontz drawing the attention
of the national media. Campbell noted that the Fifth District consisted of a
healthy mix of agriculture and industry, as well as maintaining a strong union
presence, giving a lot of material for reporters to work with. Jontz also fascinated them because he managed to maintain a progressive voting record while
representing a supposedly conservative Hoosier district (Jontz ranked among
the leaders in Democrats voting against policies favored by the Reagan administration). "There were other liberal Democrats in the U.S. Congress, there were
other conservative districts in the U.S. Congress, but the number of solidly
Republican districts represented by liberal Democrats was a number you could
count on your hand," said Campbell. "He made a good story." As Jontz himself
noted, he had earned a reputation in politics as someone who won races he
was not supposed to win. Campbell added that Jontz offered a stark contrast
to the typical politicians whose "shirts are always pressed, their ties are always
expensive, their hair is always moussed and in place, and again, there's many
of those, [but] very few of the kind of retail politician that Jim was. Someone
who could relate to anybody, regardless of how sophisticated or unsophisti-
cated the person he was dealing with was."[28]

Voters must have liked what they saw, as they rewarded Jontz by returning him to office in 1988 and 1990 against two determined Republican
opponents—Patricia Williams, a former member of GOP congressman Elwood
"Bud" Hillis's staff, and John Johnson, a millionaire businessman from
Valparaiso. "It's taken me longer to get those guys straightened out in Washington than I thought it would," Jontz said in his re-election announcement.
Both races drew nationwide attention, as the media pondered once again how
a Democrat with such progressive tendencies could survive in such a normally

Republican congressional district. A Monticello shoe repairman might have had the answer. According to Alex Martin, four pairs of Jontz's size 9D shoes had rotated into his store—one pair a week during election season—from 1983 to 1988. "He buys a quality shoe, even wingtips," Martin said of Jontz. "But they get really bad. He abuses them." Martin did all the work on the shoes free of charge, indicating it was part of his contribution to good government. "If you want to talk to him about something, he's there," Martin said of Jontz. "And what's more important than that?"[29]

Both of Jontz's re-election efforts spotlighted his ability to turn negatives into positives. "He was very, very politically savvy," Sugar remembered about Jontz, "not in a sense that he manipulated voters, I don't mean it that way. What I mean is, he knew the people he cared about and he learned their issues very deeply. And he sincerely fought for their interests. And he fought for the interests of his district." That ability came in handy during his race against Williams, who had received help in September 1988 from former President Gerald Ford. The Michigan Republican appeared at a $125 per ticket fund-raiser for Williams at the Radisson Hotel in Indianapolis, where he described Jontz as a big-spending liberal whose progressive views were out of touch with people in the district. "It's very difficult for me to see how someone as liberal as the incumbent in the 5th District can represent the voters," said Ford. Williams attempted to highlight the differences between her and Jontz during an interview with *USA Today*. A reporter asked each candidate to name their political hero. Williams selected former New Jersey congresswoman Millicent Fenwick, a former model and *Vogue* editor who also served as an ambassador to the United Nations Food and Agriculture Organization. "It's a good lesson for a woman that as you get older you don't lose your usefulness to society or your mind," said Williams. For his political hero, Jontz choose a former Hoosier state representative, labor leader, and five-time Socialist Party presidential candidate Eugene V. Debs. "He stood for compassion and fairness, and he was tireless in their pursuit," said Jontz. "He is a product of the Midwest and the working class."[30]

Williams slammed Jontz for picking a socialist leader, saying that by doing so he had shown "his true colors, and I'll let anyone make an assumption that they wish." Jontz protested the guilt by association, pointing out that another one of his heroes was nineteenth-century Whig Party statesman Henry Clay, but it did not make him a Whig. "What I admire about Gene Debs is not the party label he ran under, but the sort of man that he was," Jontz explained to a reporter from the *Indianapolis Star*. "One of the things that he was quite willing to do was speak and act his convictions. I think we need more of that in public life today. I think we've got too many people who follow the polls instead of leading the country." The Debs controversy failed to have much impact on the election, as Jontz, who had donned a Domino's Pizza delivery-man uniform to deliver pizzas during a Crown Point campaign swing, cruised to victory, capturing 56.3 percent of the vote (116,240) to 43.7 percent for Williams (90,163). Celebrating his victory election night at United Steelworkers of America Local 2958 in Kokomo, Jontz, clad in his lucky jacket from high school, told a cheering crowd, "This coat got me through another election."[31]

The founder of IG Technologies, a manufacturer of rare-earth permanent magnets, Johnson proved to be a much tougher opponent than Williams, as he spent hundreds of thousands of dollars of his own fortune to help fund his campaign. The issue of rich versus poor often came up, with Jontz using a television advertisement that focused on his opponent's opposition to raising tax rates on those with incomes of more than $200,120. "It isn't that Mr. Johnson is rich," Jontz told an *Indianapolis Star* reporter. "I don't hold that against him. But his position on issues protects the interests of people who are rich at the expense of people who are middle income." Johnson countered by noting that as a businessman, he, and not Jontz, knew how to meet a payroll and balance a budget, as well as lamenting the onerous regulations on business passed by Congress. "The only reason I became wealthy was, I sold my business," said Johnson. "The only reason I sold my business was, it was the only way to ensure that those jobs would stay there." He also attempted to downplay Jontz's well-known penchant for serving his constituents, pointing out the so-called ombudsman function of a congressman was not in the U.S. Constitution. "The official name is 'member of the House of Representatives'—not 'errand boy,'" said Johnson. "If you find a congressman emphasizing his ombudsman function, he probably is trying to obscure his voting record from the electorate."[32]

Both men did all they could to connect with voters, including participating in parades in communities throughout the district. A runner, Johnson sprinted from one side of the street to the other to shake hands and tout his candidacy. As for Jontz, he depended upon a mode of transportation that had worked wonders for him in the past—bicycles. For the 1990 race, the Jontz campaign kicked their effort into high gear, establishing a far-reaching effort to ensure Jontz's participation in seven Fourth of July parades. The

One of the enduring rituals of Jontz's time in Congress was his appearance via a Schwinn bicycle at a variety of events in his district, including a parade in Burlington, Indiana, during his 1990s campaign against challenger John Johnson.

candidate's day started at 8 a.m. at a truck stop at the intersection of US Route 24 and Interstate 65. From there, his staff drove the congressman to Hebron, where a bicycle was waiting for him. From Hebron, Jontz rushed to an airplane to fly him to Akron, where a second bicycle awaited him for the 11 a.m. parade and his plane flew on to Peru. After the Akron parade, Jontz drove to Twelve Mile before going on to the Peru airport for a flight to Marion for a nearby parade in Gas City. Five minutes ahead of schedule after Gas City, Jontz decided to add a stop in Wolcott, so he flew to Monticello while a car took his bicycle to Wolcott. He rode in the Wolcott parade for twenty minutes while his driver made his way through back streets to meet him at the end of the parade route to take him to Crown Point. Unfortunately for the candidate, the chain on his bicycle malfunctioned. According to a newspaper account, members of Jontz's staff spied a coaster-brake bicycle in the crowd and negotiated a trade—t-shirts for the entire family if the congressman could borrow the bike. Slapping campaign posters on the borrowed bike, the staff took it and Jontz to the final parade in Cedar Lake at 5 p.m.[33]

With only four days to go before the November 6, 1990, election, a poll funded by the Johnson campaign and the National Republican Congressional Committee showed the Republican trailing the incumbent by a slim one-point margin, 40 percent to 39 percent, with the remaining 21 percent declaring themselves as undecided. "We were in trouble," staff member Altman said of the Jontz re-election effort, "but John Johnson wasn't experienced enough to see that and to know that he was making gains and he pulled the funding [for advertisements]." During the race, Jontz had not had the time during the last week to campaign as much as he had previously because Congress had been in session ironing out budget differences with President George H. W. Bush to help reduce a deficit. Jontz did make it back in time to help stem the tide, winning re-election with 53.1 percent of the vote (81,373) to Johnson's 46.9 percent (71,750). "I think the rich versus poor really stuck, even though I made that money myself," Johnson said after his loss. In addition, he blamed his loss in part on Bush's budget deal with Congress in which the president had gone back on his "no new taxes" pledge he had made at accepting the presidential nomination at the 1988 Republican National Convention ("Read my lips: no new taxes."), and the unfair perception that he was arrogant. "What I believe doesn't matter," Johnson said. "Perception is more important." According to Indiana pollster Brian Vargus, "what finally did it was, he [Jontz] finally got back to the district. He did what he had always done—he just campaigned like crazy." Mike Pannos, chairman of the Indiana Democratic Party, reflected that it was easy for Jontz to "give Johnson the tag of being someone willing to help wealthy Americans. Johnson is not someone in touch with working people."[34]

The 1990 campaign that returned Jontz for a third term in office also marked the emergence of an issue that promised to dominate the congressman's final two years in office. In March 1900 Jontz had entered into a controversy far outside of his Indiana district by introducing the Ancient Forest Protection Act, a bill designed to help save thousands of acres of public old-growth forests in the Pacific Northwest. "The visitor who flies over our public lands in the Pacific Northwest is shocked by the transformation of the landscape into a patchwork of clearcut and remnant forest," Jontz said. "A national treasure, these Ancient Forests are no less scientifically valuable or ecologically unique than the Grand Canyon, Yellowstone, or the Everglades. Yet we as taxpayers, the owners of this precious resource, are allowing it to be liquidated with seeming indifference." The legislation, and Jontz, drew wild acclaim from environmental groups such as the Sierra Club, the National

Wildlife Federation, and the National Audubon Society, as well as equal condemnation from the congressional delegations from Oregon and Washington (some of whom called him "Congressman Dunce") and timber workers in those states who burned Jontz in effigy to express their anger about the possible loss of their jobs. The stage had been set for the toughest battle of Jontz's long environmental career.[35]

6

Fighting the Good Fight

The economic fortunes of the community of Hoquiam, Washington, whose name comes from a Native American word meaning "hungry for wood," has risen and fallen on one commodity—timber. From its location on Grays Harbor, the town has been a magnet for lumberman since A. M. Simpson, a San Francisco businessman, and his agent, George H. Emerson, known as the "Father of Hoquiam," established the first mill on land purchased in 1811. Since that time, more than three hundred mills have operated in the area. In the spring of 1990, with national environmental legislation in Congress threatening to slow or possibly halt logging, and a U.S. district judge blocking timber sales to save the habitat of the northern spotted owl, residents reacted by taking their cause to the streets. Signs appeared on the windows of homes with the slogans "This Family Supported by Timber Dollars" and bumper stickers on cars and trucks read "Hug a logger and you'll never go back to trees" and "I Love Spotted Owls: Baked, Broiled, or Fried."

On April 28, 1990, more than 1,500 protestors gathered for an Olympic Peninsula Family Solidarity Rally. "The reason we are here is we're mad as hell and we're not going to take it anymore," said Jim Carlson, owner of the J and J Shake Company, a manufacturer of wood shingles. The protestors, all wearing yellow armbands and chanting "families first, owls last," marched to Riverside Bridge on Highway 101 spanning the Hoquiam River, where they blocked traffic for several hours. One of the highlights of the demonstration, however, involved tossing a stuffed caricature of a congressman from the Midwest— Indiana's Jim Jontz—into a flaming pit and watching it turn to ashes. "May he burn in hell," said Bill Pickell, Washington Contract Loggers Association general manager, as the crowd cheered.[1]

Indiana congressman Jim Jontz receives a warm welcome during a visit to Ashland, Oregon, during the height of the controversy about his ancient forest legislation.

To timber-dependent communities across Washington, Oregon (the country's leading timber-producing state), and northern California, Jontz, the sponsor of a bill to help protect the ancient forests, along with the diminutive, eighteen-inch-tall spotted owl, became handy symbols of resentment in the early 1990s as the timber industry battled with environmentalists about the fate of old-growth forests—a diverse ecosystem that a 1952 U.S. Forest Service study had erroneously labeled "biological deserts." With private reserves of these forests exhausted, since the 1980s timber companies had been leasing sections of the ancient forests owned and managed primarily by the Forest Service—a practice that often resulted in losses estimated by one economist to be as much as $5.6 billion over a ten-year period. Logs from old-growth forests were particularly prized by timber companies because of their fine grain and being free of knots, and were used primarily for paneling, molding, and door and window trim. Redwoods were turned into decks and picnic tables, while incense cedar wood lined closets to repel insects and sitka spruces were turned into guitars.[2]

Jontz became a hero for those trying to turn a national spotlight on an issue that heretofore had been a regional concern handled by the members of the Pacific Northwest's congressional delegation. "I did not create the division of opinion on this issue with the Northwest. I may be a lightning rod now," said Jontz, "but I know it is necessary for Congress to resolve this issue. There must be spokespeople for regional interests and national interests. And it's my job to be the spokesperson for national interests." Believing that for too long the government had been favoring the interests of logging companies, he called for a more balanced approach "between the interests of the [timber] industry and the interests of the public." Jontz pointed out that the ancient forests on federal lands in the Pacific Northwest were owned "by all the citizens of the United States, by the people of Detroit [Michigan] as much as

The results of clear-cutting in the Gifford Pinchot National Forest in southwest Washington. Established by Congress in 1982, the forest includes the Mount Saint Helens National Volcanic Monument.

the people of Darrington [Washington]." Although he said he took no joy in causing problems for those who made the livelihood on timber, it was "either pay later or pay now."

To environmentalists in the Pacific Northwest and around the country, logging in the 2.3 million acres of ecologically significant old-growth forests that were left out of the 20 million that once existed threatened to destroy an ecosystem that had been around for centuries and had sheltered such threatened species as the northern spotted owl, the peregrine falcon, the brown pelican, the Aleutian Canada goose, the northern bald eagle, and the Oregon silverspot butterfly. Clear-cutting, removing all the trees in a designated area and burning the debris left behind, decimated the landscape. A heavy rain could wash away the topsoil and despoil nearby streams that were home to the large trout beloved by sportsmen. If timber concerns were allowed to continue clear-cutting in these cathedral-like woods, what would be left behind would be a ruined landscape that one Forest Service ranger likened to the blackened remnants after the first nuclear blast at Alamogordo, New Mexico, and a politician from Wyoming called "a shocking desecration that has to be seen to be believed."[3]

Every year, according to the National Audubon Society, timber firms chopped down enough old-growth trees to fill a truck convoy stretching for 20,000 miles. The remaining 10 percent of the original ancient forest was even being cut at a rate faster than what was occurring in the Brazilian rain forest. "The ability of the ancient forests to function as a system will be gone a long time before the last tree is cut," warned Jontz. "The forest has to be of adequate size to withstand the natural processes of fire, of wind, of disease. That's the critical concept." Nobody as yet, he noted, had gotten around the fact that it took four hundred years to grow a four-hundred-year-old tree.[4]

Timber companies and their employees attempted to frame the argument as placing the interest of an animal—the spotted owl—over that of hard-hardworking American families: owls versus jobs. If the environmentalists and their allies had their way, timber interests argued, an entire industry would be devastated in just a few years, leaving behind ruined families and ruined lives. A joint Forest Service and Bureau of Land Management study outlined a host of calamities that might befall communities if timber sales on public lands were slowed or stopped. These included "increased rates of domestic disputes, divorce, acts of violence, delinquency, vandalism, suicide, [and] alcoholism." Environmentalists were called by another name, "preservationists," in timber country, and they were accused of trying to keep the forests the way they were forever. As a worker at a Ford dealership in Douglas County, Oregon, noted: "We survived without the dinosaur. What's the big deal about the owl?" Milton Herbert, the owner of Herbert Lumber in Riddle, Oregon, spoke for many in the area when he expressed puzzlement over the push to preserve the old-growth areas. "They're trying to stop time, and that's one thing we can't do," Herbert said. "Bugs, fire or man are going to harvest the trees; they don't live forever."[5]

Jontz had been introduced to the beauties of old-growth forests in the Pacific Northwest through his interest in a natural area much closer to home—the Hoosier National Forest, located in the hills of south central Indiana. Upon taking office during his first term in the U.S. House of Representatives in 1987, Jontz received an assignment to serve on the Agriculture Committee, a logical place for a congressman with extensive agricultural interests in his district. In addition, he landed a position on the committee's

Forests, Family Farms, and Energy Subcommittee, a body that oversaw the Forest Service. Jontz noted that from his days as a student at Indiana University he had been interested in the fate of the Hoosier National Forest and other wooded areas in the state. "Indiana has a wood products industry. . . . We even have 12,000 acres of wilderness," Jontz pointed out. "We are still the nation's leading producer of quality hardwood veneer. I've been involved in forest issues for a long time."[6]

A northern spotted owl. In addition to loss of its old-growth forest habitat, the spotted owl also faces threats from a rising population of barred owls.

In 1987 Jontz received an invitation from Bob Smith, a Republican congressman from Oregon's Second Congressional District who also served on the forestry subcommittee, to attend an oversight hearing in his district to bring him up to speed on the need for continued timber sales from public lands. "I discovered there was a civil war going on," Jontz recalled, "but you wouldn't have known it from the Northwest [congressional] delegation or from the national environmental groups at the time." Andy Kerr worked in Oregon to help protect the ancient forests as conservation director for the Oregon Natural Resources Council. Raised in Creswell, Oregon, a logging community, Kerr was described by *Time* magazine as "the Ralph Nader of the old-growth preservation movement." He became public enemy number one with the logging industry, with some timber men commenting he resembled a spotted owl in appearance—an accusation that Kerr responded to with the reply: "That really ruffles my feathers." Kerr recalled that Smith seemed to believe that since Jontz was from the Midwest, he might see the Pacific Northwest forests as just another crop to harvest like corn or soybeans. "It turned out not to be the case, much to Bob Smith's regret," said Kerr.[7]

Spotted owl and marbled Murrelet habitat in an Oregon coastal forest (top) and old-growth Douglas firs at the Mount Hood National Forest located east of Portland, Oregon (above).

Before Forest Service officials took Jontz and other visitors on a helicopter tour along the Rogue River near the Siskiyou National Forest in southwestestern Oregon, Kerr advised the congressman to have the pilot fly higher than usual so he could see for himself the devastating results of clear-cutting in the area. "I was surprised at the impact on the landscape of the management practices in the national forests and BLM lands," Jontz told a reporter. Later, during an appearance at a forest activist conference in Oregon, he noted that he had been so impressed by the unspoiled beauty of the landscape he had decided to do all he could to help protect the area. "I said, 'Like hell they're going to cut this,'" Jontz remembered. As a longtime supporter of the environment, Jontz, on an intellectual basis, saw the rationale for protecting old-growth forests, said Kerr, but he developed an emotional connection as well. "He fell in love with these forests," Kerr noted. Dan Stotter, who worked as a legislative assistant in Jontz's office on environmental and legal issues, said that being in natural areas had a "therapeutic quality" for his boss from the usual relentless and stressful pace he set for himself in office. "It really had a calming quality for him," said Stotter, who remembered Jontz getting a big smile on his face whenever he visited the ancient forests.[8]

After his western visit, Jontz attempted to learn more about what was going on in the Pacific Northwest. One of the congressman's staff members called Brock Evans with the National Audubon Society, someone who had been working to save the remaining ancient forests for several years, and asked if Evans could visit with the congressman to brief him on the issue. "My heart leapt, with mixed emotions: surprise—that a fellow Midwesterner was even interested—and joy," Evans recalled. "He's on the right committee, maybe there still *is* hope somehow." Other meetings followed and Evans noted that the congressman from Indiana was not only a quick learner able to master complex subjects, but also someone who possessed "great political and personal courage—willing always to stand up for his convictions, ready always to fight for them, whatever the odds." Jontz returned to Oregon in 1989 to speak at a conference on reforming the Forest Service, and learned that the conservation community had "just about thrown up its hands and said, 'There's no way we can resolve this issue within the Northwest. We have to look for allies outside the Northwest. This has to be a national issue.'"[9]

The odds indeed seemed long when it came to protecting the ancient forests, but environmental groups and their activists soon discovered a winning strategy, a backdoor effort, to achieve their objective by working to gain

protection for the spotted owl through the Endangered Species Act. Signed by
President Richard Nixon on December 28, 1973, the act attempted to not only
protect species at risk of extinction, but also the ecosystems they depended
on for survival. Consequently, saving the spotted owl meant also saving the
old-growth forest that served as its habitat, as it nested in the broken tops
of dead trees found in those ecosystems. "The northern spotted owl is the
wildlife species of choice to act as a surrogate for old growth protection," noted
Andy Stahl at an environmental law conference at the University of Oregon
Law School in March 1988. "And I've often thought that thank goodness the
spotted owl evolved in the Northwest, for if it hadn't, we'd have to genetically
engineer it."[10]

When the U.S. Fish and Wildlife Service balked at listing the spotted owl
as a threatened species, the Sierra Club Legal Defense Fund sued and won a
court injunction in March 1989 from U.S. District Judge William Dwyer blocking a number of timber sales by the Forest Service. On June 23, 1990, the Fish
and Wildlife Service officially listed the spotted owl as threatened, igniting
strong protests from the timber industry. Their supporters in Congress did all
they could to subvert the rulings with riders (a provision added to a bill that
often has little to do with the original legislation) to appropriation bills that
increased logging and exempted such actions from lawsuits. One such rider
sponsored by U.S. senators Mark Hatfield from Oregon and Brock Adams
from Washington inspired Kerr to comment at the time: "The Hatfield-Adams
rider will kill spotted owls as sure as a drunken logger with a shotgun." Jontz
wrote a "Dear Colleague" letter opposing the rider that received the support
of 101 congressmen. The strong reaction from House members helped force
a compromise that released 1.1 billion board feet (a "board foot" is an inch-
thick square of wood) of old-growth timber on national forests in Oregon and
Washington. The compromise, which was worked out by Illinois Democrat
Sidney Yates, chairman of the House Appropriations Committee Interior
Subcommittee, pleased neither timber interests nor conservation groups.[11]

Environmental groups in the Pacific Northwest realized they would need
more than the ESA if they wanted to protect old-growth forests. National conservation organizations seemed reluctant, at first, to join in the fight against
logging in old-growth forests, preoccupied as they were in trying to forestall
rollbacks in environmental laws and threats to begin drilling for oil and other
resources in the Arctic National Wildlife Refuge by the Ronald Reagan administration. James Monteith, ONRC executive director, went as far as to say that

the national groups viewed the "entire western ancient forest campaign as an embarrassment." In addition, groups such as the ONRC realized they could not depend on any legislator from the affected region to back their efforts. "Asking the Oregon congressional delegation in 1990 to deal rationally with the end of ancient-forest cutting," Kerr told a *Time* magazine reporter, "is like asking the Mississippi delegation in 1960 to deal rationally with the end of segregation." Monteith, said the Oregon delegation hated Kerr's quote, but it was a "perfect illustration of the problem." Looking at whom in Congress might serve as a reliable ally on the issue, conservation groups in the Pacific Northwest and on a national level cast their eyes on Jontz. "He could be a champion in the Congress of the United States at a time when the local and national conservation community very much needed a champion," Kerr said of Jontz. The best way to fight a U.S. senator or a congressman, noted Kerr, is with another U.S. senator or congressman. National attention on an issue such as old-growth forests took some of the power away from politicians from the Pacific Northwest, "and they hated that," said Kerr, who took to introducing Jontz on several occasions as "Oregon's best congressman."[12]

There were some among Pacific Northwest conservationists, however, who wondered if Jontz was the right man to lead the fight. Monteith remembered that he had heard good things about the Indiana congressman, with people telling him Jontz knew what he was talking about and had courage. Still, after the first few times he had met Jontz, Monteith came away believing he was a nice guy with good intentions "but perhaps too nice to get anything done." After a subsequent meeting in Portland, Oregon, however, where the two men had their first serious talk about the old-growth forest issue, Monteith realized Jontz had the character needed to tackle what would be a tough and lonely battle in making logging in ancient forests a national issue. "We knew we had to create a national effort in order to eclipse [the opposition of] Northwest politicians," said Monteith. "Most politicians couldn't have done that, even if they wanted to. They would have realized it would be a lonely, tough slog, and of course that didn't bother him [Jontz] as much as it bothered a lot of others."[13]

In January 1990 Jontz visited Oregon on a fact-finding mission to gather information about timber issues. He appeared before a joint House-Senate natural resources hearing of the Washington Legislature in Olympia and warned the state legislators who attended that a growing segment of American society viewed what was happening to the old-growth forests of the Pacific

Northwest as a "national issue," as the public had real concerns about the fate of the environment. He said he and other members of Congress were aware that changes to logging in national forests would have a negative effect on the area's economy, and likened the situation to that faced by the Indiana steel industry, which saw job losses of 50 percent due to foreign competition. Those comments were met with hostility by supporters of the timber industry. Ron Adkins, president of the Oregon Lands Coalition, representing sixteen protimber industry citizens groups, objected that Jontz had failed to make any attempts to "learn about real issues from grassroots people." He noted that the Indiana lawmaker talked of "deliberately shutting down an industry when demand is high. He wants to replace multiple-use principles with a lock-it-up policy."[14]

What came next further inflamed the passions of those who supported logging on public lands in the Pacific Northwest. On April 4, 1990, Jontz announced he was introducing legislation called the Ancient Forest Protection Act, a measure that eventually had 131 cosponsors (none from the Pacific Northwest delegation). "We're trying to avoid this 'endangered species of the month' parade—we can't expect the Endangered Species act to carry all the weight," Jontz told a reporter from the *New York Times*. "We need an 'endangered ecosystems' approach." The legislation, which he introduced again the following year, had been crafted mainly by conservation groups with some input from Jontz. "There should be no misunderstanding about my bill," he said. "It is the environmentalists' bill. It was written to a large extent by environmentalists from the Northwest." He took up the cause because he believed it was an issue than needed to be addressed now before it was too late. "I obviously take no joy in causing people problems," Jontz said, "but it's either pay later or pay now." Monteith said the legislation "did not attempt to fix all of the problems in the forest," but instead was a "first step" in solving the national forest policy issues conservation groups sought to address. March Liverman of the Portland Audubon Society indicated it was not critical to have lawmakers in the Pacific Northwest support the bill. "We don't need to look toward the Northwest delegation for leadership in national forest policy," said Liverman. "These are national forests governed by national law."[15]

Before joining Jontz's staff Stotter, a 1989 graduate of the University of Oregon Law School, had started his career as an environmental lobbyist. He said that representatives of the big four environmental organizations—the

Flanked by photographs of western old-growth forests, Jontz outlines his Ancient Forest Protection Act at a news conference in Washington, D.C.

National Wildlife Federation, the Sierra Club, the Wilderness Society, and the National Audubon Society—had been meeting on a regular basis to discuss strategy on saving old-growth forests. When the measure that became the Ancient Forest Protection Act was being drafted, Jontz was viewed by the groups as the most likely person to care about the issue and to champion the act's passage through Congress. "The concept was presented to Congressman Jontz," Stotter recalled. "He really liked the concept and was actually an immediate supporter and took a leadership role in it." Monteith recalled that although they were able to gain some support from the national conservation groups, he believed Pacific Northwest supporters of Jontz's bill "never got the depth of work we should have" on the issue. It might have been "our fault," he added, as they "pushed things a little too quickly." Monteith had the feeling the national organizations "felt like we wanted too much, a sense that we were greedy, asking for too much." To the nationals, the change from past logging methods in old-growth forests was good enough, but groups such as the ONRC, Monteith noted, saw it as only a matter of time before the ancient forests would be gone for good. "It was a lonelier [fight] than it should have been," he said. "I don't know any other politician who could have stayed in there as he [Jontz] did."[16]

According to Jontz, passage of the act would set in motion a series of steps leading to "a science-based resolution of the fate of the Ancient Forests." The bill provided interim protection to all ancient forests on federal lands in Oregon, Washington, and California, as well as "associated" forests (areas necessary to retain the integrity of the ecosystem). Meanwhile, a group of scientists under the direction of the President's Council on Environmental Quality would be tasked with preparing recommendations "on how much Ancient Forest should be set aside so that the forest can sustain itself as a viable, functioning ecological system." It would then be up to Congress in subsequent legislation, said Jontz, to actually make such designations. Although his act did not include any provisions for economic aid to communities that would be hard hit by closing off old-growth forests to logging, Jontz said such help should be included with any environmental provisions passed.

In spite of claims to the contrary, Jontz said that spotted owls and environmentalists were not to blame for the lost jobs in the timber industry. Although timber harvests from federal lands in Oregon and Washington had increased by 900 million board feet between 1978 and 1988, timber-related jobs actually fell by 28,000 during that same period. "They are jobs which have been lost because of automation in the mills," he said, "and of greater importance from the standpoint of public policy options, the export of logs." Due to skyrocketing demand from markets in the Pacific Rim, especially Japan (one out of four logs cut in the Pacific Northwest were being shipped to that country), private timber owners had been exporting "enormous volumes of logs," Jontz noted, "while local mills—often without their own timber supply—must depend on public timber or are starved out of existence." A temporary ban on log exports would "more than compensate for timber supply lost from protecting ancient forests," he added. Cutting down and shipping trees from America's ancient forests to Japan, or using them for commercial purposes, would be like "chopping up antique furniture for firewood," said Jontz.[17]

Public opinion in the Pacific Northwest seemed to be on Jontz's side, as a poll conducted by the *Seattle Times* had 52 percent of its respondents in favor of banning logging in national forests and protecting the spotted owl, with 38 percent expressing opposition and 10 percent undecided. The region's timber interests and congressional delegation, however, greeted Jontz's proposal with anger and derision whenever he attempted to push his proposal through Congress. Smith, the congressman who had invited Jontz to view the ancient forests a few years before, called the act "as rash and irresponsible as any land management legislation I have seen. This bill is the work of people who believe Oregon should be one big national park where Easterners can go to visit." Other Oregon congressmen were contemptuous that someone from outside of their region dared to meddle in what they saw as a local affair. "All I will say is that I know that Indianans are experts on overcutting the forests," said Congressman Les AuCoin, "because a couple of centuries ago they completed the job in their own state, so now they are bringing their expertise to Oregon." A representative of a logging group in Oregon compared reading Jontz's act to reading "a Captain Marvel comic strip," as they were both "operating in a fantasy world." He estimated that job losses would total 56,635 if the Hoosier lawmaker proved successful with his legislation. One state lawmaker, Bill Markham, a Republican from Riddle, Oregon, went as far as to label Jontz as "Congressman Dunce."[18]

Other voices in the Pacific Northwest took a more measured approach to what Jontz was trying to accomplish. An editorial in Oregon's *Salem Statesman Journal* warned that politicians in the state should not be quick to make fun of the Indiana congressman, as he did not want to see the people of Oregon make the same mistakes that Hoosier pioneers had made. "Jontz has the perfect right to hope that Oregon, Washington and California will be smart enough not to destroy our land because, once gone, the crime can't be undone," the editorial noted, adding that politicians from the area needed to enlist Jontz and others "in helping our timber industry make a painful transition." Serving her first term in Congress as a Democratic representative from Washington, Jolene Unsoeld, who had worked on utility reform and environmental issues while serving as a respected state legislator, noted that while there were a number of people from her region who were upset with Jontz, he served a valuable role. "He's made visible a view that is held by a lot of the Congress and a lot of the United States," Unsoeld said. "He's shown us a view that will have to be taken into account in the final equation." Congressman Jim McDermott, also from Washington, saw Jontz's actions not as grandstanding for media attention, as some critics had claimed, but as the work of a "dedicated environmentalist who cares very deeply about what he is doing." The environment, said McDermott, no longer was just a local, but a national and international matter. "If you are concerned about clean air and the rain forests of Brazil," he said, "you also must be concerned about the forests in the states of Washington, Oregon and northern California."[19]

Although timber interests viewed Jontz's legislation as radical, there were some environmentalists who believed it did not go far enough. Save America's Forests, a coalition that included more than thirty organizations representing a hundred thousand members in eighteen states, sought to halt clear-cutting and road construction on all Forest Service land, as well as banning export of unprocessed logs on private lands. The organization believed such national environmental groups as the Wilderness Society, Sierra Club, National Wildlife Federation, and the National Audubon Society had not been doing enough on the issue, as they were constrained in part by being busy with a number of issues, "so they never take a strong absolute stand on any issue because they don't want to jeopardize their relationship with congressional members," noted Tim Hermach, president of the Native Forest Council in Eugene, Oregon. "Some members of Congress have asserted that Jontz's bill is only posturing—a far-out bill," said Mark Winstein, a Save America's Forests director and a former intern for Jontz. "That makes Jontz appear to be far on the left, but we think it is very centrist. We feel the country wants much more environmental preservation than even Jontz wants in his bill." Winstein added that the public "is far ahead of Congress on this." Christopher Klose, Jontz's chief of staff at that time, said Save America's Forests might have a tough time building broad-based support in Congress, something the congressman had already succeeded in doing with the large number of House members who had signed on to cosponsor the legislation. "I don't want to say they are out of the mainstream," Klose said, "but to some extent they will be perceived as being a more radical group or having a more hard-line stand about the environment than most environmental groups."[20]

The overall negative reaction to Jontz's decision to become involved in an issue outside of his Indiana district was partly a product of the normal business of Congress. Members seldom, if ever, interfered with what were seen as local matters in other districts. This deference usually came about because most members actually did not care about the issues facing other congressman in their districts, noted Kerr, a veteran of environmental legislative battles. In addition, meddling in the affairs of other districts could rebound on a congressman, who faced pushback on matters in his or her own district. House members could also face retaliation from influential committee chairmen or other congressional leaders, especially if the congressman they annoyed served on the powerful Appropriations Committee. No congressman wanted to risk the chance of having funding decreased or cut entirely for a pet project in his or her district. Stotter recalled seeing an aide to Democratic Speaker of the House Tom Foley, a supporter of timber interests, take Jontz aside to give him a private scolding that he took in stride. "I don't think he was unprepared for the flack," said Stotter. "I think he took it as part of what was going to happen; he knew it was going to happen." Kerr remembered Jontz commenting about Congress: "You get knocked down around this place about twenty times a day. You just get up and keep moving." Scott Campbell, Jontz's press secretary, noted that the congressman took a lot of heat on such controversial issues as the ancient forests, but the pressure did not bother Jontz because he believed he was doing what was right. "Look at the political landscape these days and ask yourself how many people are doing whatever it is they're doing, voting however it is they're voting, because it's the right thing to do. That's a pretty small club," said Campbell. Jontz's staff also had to endure the disdain of their colleagues on the ancient-forest issue. Stotter remembered having a member of Oregon congressman Peter DeFazio's staff complaining to him, "you people from Indiana don't know anything about the forests." Stotter quickly noted he had started living in Oregon in 1984, had gone to law school there, and had often visited the forests to hike. He later found out that the DeFazio staffer was actually from Virginia.[21]

For Tom Sugar, Jontz's chief of staff during the ancient-forest controversy, the congressman's stand on an issue of concern outside of his own district did not surprise him at all. "He always did what he thought was right," said Sugar. "One of those classic, 'I'm going to do what I think is right, and the politics will take care of themselves.' That's what most people like to say in moments like that." Jontz, however, took matters an extra step, said Sugar, believing, "I'm going to do what I think is right, and then I'm going to work like hell to make sure the politics take care of itself." To buffer possible criticism on the old-growth issue, Jontz would, for example, work even harder on matters of concern to his district, including senior-citizen and union issues. Sugar noted Jontz's actions were a way of saying to voters, "You may not fully know what I'm doing with the spotted owls, but I've got a 100 percent voting record with the AFL-CIO, and no one's going to match me about caring for working people."[22]

To Jontz, insinuating himself into the fray over the ancient forests seemed to be a logical extension of his longtime interest in conservation matters, as he noted: "I don't need to take on this issue to curry favor with environmentalists. I was one before I was in politics." As someone whose early career involved serving on the staff of the Indiana Conservation Council and working against the Big Pine Creek Dam project in Warren County, Jontz said he had been influenced by the career of an Democratic U.S. senator from Illinois, Paul Douglas. As Jontz had been with the old-growth forest issue, Douglas had been labeled as a "meddler" for involving himself front and center in the successful attempt to preserve the Indiana Dunes along the southern shore of Lake Michigan as a national park in the 1960s. "He used his influence and endured," said Jontz. By doing so, Douglas earned the designation as Indiana's third senator. "Frankly, the dunes wouldn't have been saved if people from outside of Indiana hadn't become involved," Jontz noted. "I was brought up on the idea that we wouldn't have places like the dunes except for the courage that some people showed." He also pointed out that it was a Hoosier lawmaker, William Steele Holman, who in the late nineteenth century had been one of the leaders behind the legislation (the Forest Reserve Act of 1891) helping to create national forests "to be managed for the people" of the country. He believed that an overwhelming majority of his constituents in the Fifth District appreciated "the fact that I'm willing to take the heat and stand up for what is best for the resource. Whatever the heat may be, whatever the political consequences may be, I'm doing it because I think it's the right thing to do. Today, people appreciate that." In addition, Jontz refused to be deterred in his environmental mission by detractors, however powerful they might be. "I do not intend to be intimidated," he said.[23]

For a young, politically naïve staff member such as Stotter, there seemed to be a real chance that Jontz's Ancient Forest Protection Act would make its way through Congress. "I wanted it to pass and wanted to believe it would pass," Stotter remembered. He noted that more experienced senior staff members in Congress who worked on the committees involved with such legislation told him not to expect such a happy outcome, but to at least be thankful that the issue had been placed on the national agenda. Other congressmen had joined the cause, with Bruce Vento, a Democrat from Minnesota, chairman of the House Interior Committee's National Parks and Public Lands Subcommittee, introducing his own bill in July 1990 that set aside six million acres in Oregon, Washington, and California as an "ancient forest preserve." A strong supporter of the environment, Vento said it was "hypocritical" for this country to hector South American nations to stop despoiling their rain forests

Representatives from Friends of the Earth Action present Jontz with a 1990 Friend of the Earth Award for his "outstanding leadership promoting sustainable agriculture and protecting ancient forests."

"when we are destroying the fragile ecosystems of ancient forests. We must lead by example." Jontz always believed, he informed a reporter from an Oregon newspaper, that the legislation ultimately passing Congress on old-growth forests would not be his bill. Instead, he predicted what would emerge would "reflect the involvement of different parties." For Monteith, the importance of Jontz's bill came from the fact that it pushed the issue onto the national stage and marked the first time environmentalists had an ancient-forest protection act that took the issue "from being negative and made it something positive," describing it as a "proactive" piece of legislation. "We wouldn't have gotten there with anybody else," Monteith said of Jontz's contribution.[24]

Alaskan congressman Don Young, a Republican, fired back at Jontz's measure by sending a letter to his congressional colleagues in early April 1990 indicating he intended to introduce his own legislation to turn 1.3 million acres in Indiana's Fifth Congressional District into a giant national forest (he followed through on his threat the following year). "This is a novel approach," Young wrote, "in that it would seek to recreate [*sic*] the Ancient Forests of the

Jontz viewed the attempt to frame the ancient forest issue in the Pacific Northwest as the spotted owl versus jobs as a mischaracterization. "The bigger issue," he said, "is whether the world's most magnificent forests . . . will remain on this earth as a viable, functioning ecological system."

region which have been decimated by industrial agriculture." Young also expressed concern that the pesticides and herbicides used by Hoosier farmers killed insects and polluted the land and water. "I'm concerned about his," he said. "I hope you are, too." Tourism, he insisted, would provide enough employment opportunities to cover those jobs lost through his legislation. Young noted these would be "non-polluting jobs," as contrasted with the agricultural and industrial jobs that threatened the health of those living in the Fifth District. Asked about Young's proposal, Congressman Smith said the idea was meant to be funny, but also included a serious message. "I think it reflects the level of frustration a lot of us in the West feel about someone in Indiana who obviously feels it is no skin off his nose regarding what probably will be the biggest economic dislocation the Pacific Northwest will ever experience," said Smith. U.S. Senator Slade Gorton, a Republican from Washington, suggested taking all the warehouses in Muncie, Indiana (a community not in Jontz's district) and "declare them to be historic treasures."[25]

At first, Jontz treated Young's measure as a joke, telling an *Indianapolis Star* reporter he had asked the Alaskan congressman for an autographed copy of his legislation. "We all like Don," Jontz said in a statement released by his office. "He's really a funny guy." In an April 9, 1990, letter to the editor of a newspaper in his district, the *Kokomo Tribune*, however, the Hoosier congressman carefully laid out the reasons behind his measure to protect old-growth forests. Jontz reiterated his argument that the land covered in his act was public property owned by taxpayers across the country. "These forests are not the private domain of the Congressmen from the states in which they are located," he said. "Someone has to stand up and speak for the rights of all the rest of the American people, which otherwise will be trampled." Although no Alaskan forests were covered by his legislation, Jontz noted one of the reasons behind Young's attack on him came from his effort to end selling off timber in the Tongass National Forest "for as little as 1 cent for each dollar of federal tax money invested." The chief beneficiaries of those sales were two pulp mills with "sweetheart" deals to buy the trees. "I was quite involved in the passage of the Tongass Reform Bill by the House in 1989, by the margin of 356 to 60, to end these practices," Jontz pointed out. "Mr. Young remembers." For his part, Young called Jontz and Robert J. Mrazek, a Democratic congressman from Long Island, New York, who initiated the reform act, "pimps for Eastern environmentalists."[26]

Young's facetious proposal did inspire a group of property owners living in Jontz's Fifth District to stage a one-hour protest at the congressman's Valparaiso office. About a dozen people representing the citizens' groups protested at the office, with some carrying signs reading: "Where's Jim?" Sue Showers, a member of a group called Stop Taking Our Property, an organization that had been battling efforts to expand the Indiana Dunes National Lakeshore along Salt Creek and the Little Calumet River in northwest Indiana, said of Jontz, "I hired him to go to Washington, and he's not doing his job. Instead, I find that he's out spending all his time writing legislation to introduce into another district which is all the way across the country on the Pacific coast. And I did not send him to Congress to settle arguments out there." Chris Schultz, also from STOP, expressed the concern that a legislator such as Jontz could interfere with another district and not face repercussions from voters in the Pacific Northwest. "A representative is supposed to represent people in his area," said Schultz. A member of the congressman's staff, George Wilson, noted of the protest: "Basically, they came, they said their piece and they left."[27]

If his stance on old-growth forests was not bad enough, Jontz further antagonized timber interests and their supporters in June 1991 by attempting to halt the practice of below-cost timber sales of trees from public lands by introducing his National Forest Timber Sales Cost Recovery Act. Under the legislation, below-cost timber sales would be phased out over a five-year period beginning October 1, 1991 (Wyche Fowler, a Democrat from Georgia, introduced a similar proposal in the U.S. Senate.) "In this time of record-high budget deficits, there are more important priorities for the use of taxpayer dollars than wasteful programs that hurt both the taxpayers and the environment," said

Jontz. According to an analysis done by the Wilderness Society, sale of publically owned timber was profitable in only twenty-two of the Forest Service's 120 forests, and the service lost $257 million from the sale of timber per year. A key problem, according to Jontz, was that the Forest Service did not account for all the costs involved in selling such timber from national forests, including the costs of road design, construction and maintenance of remote sites, and administrative expenses. In addition to saving taxpayers' money, another benefit of his legislation, said Jontz, would come from protecting the environment, as most below-cost timber sales were from areas that were hard to reach and necessitated the building of roads to reach the trees. According to Robert E. Wolf, a retired Congressional Research Service economist, if a private business followed the practices of the Forest Service, "they wouldn't just end up bankrupt—they'd end up in court."[28]

Jontz served as a handy punching bag both for his opponents in the administration of President George Bush and timber workers in the Pacific Northwest. At a hearing on the Ancient Forest Protection Act before the House Subcommittee on Public Lands in late April 1991, officials representing the Forest Service and BLM lambasted the legislation as "unwise" both from an ecological and socioeconomic viewpoint. John Beuter, a deputy assistant with the U.S. Department of Agriculture, said the bill provided no assurance that the old-growth forests would be protected and, regardless of its good intentions, would have high costs for the region's economy. Smith continued to offer his blunt remarks to Jontz, asking him at the start of the hearing: "I don't understand whether its mean-spiritedness or do you just not understand what's going on?" A new member of the subcommittee, Jontz refused to take the bait, focusing instead on questioning the administration witnesses and indicating a willingness to compromise in order to "grapple with the very difficult issues presented by both the need to preserve these invaluable ecosystems and the real and difficult changes in the Northwest economy."[29]

A few months after the House subcommittee hearing, in September, about eleven loggers and millworkers from the Pacific Northwest took their concerns directly to Jontz's Capitol Hill office. The Indiana congressman spent more than an hour with the group and attempted to explain the reasoning behind his legislation. He pointed out that if the ancient forests received no protection, both the trees and the jobs that went with them would be gone within a few years. The workers, however, refused to be mollified by a person they saw as responsible for the potential loss of their way of life.

*Jontz joins schoolchildren in Indiana in viewing a seven-hundred-year-old Douglas fir
from the Olympic National Forest hauled around the country by the Ancient Forest Rescue
Expedition. In 1989 the expedition traveled 8,500 miles across twenty-nine states to bring
attention to the ancient-forest issue. On April 27, 1990, the expedition visited a number of
Indiana communities, including Indianapolis, Marion, Kokomo, Logansport, Flora, Monticello, Rensselaer, and Valparaiso.*

Dick Wooten of Saint Helens, Oregon, accused Jontz, known for his common-
man approach, of having a "slick Madison Avenue way" of presenting himself,
and another worker labeled the congressman as an environmental zealot.
Jeannete Basl, who owned a timber firm in Sublimity, Oregon, refused to
shake Jontz's hand and their relationship continued to deteriorate from there.
In addition to calling his bill "a crock," Basl pointedly asked him if he had had a
wife, children, or ever had a job other than being a politician. Jontz answered
no to the first two questions, and yes to the last one. Although several times
Jontz asked her not to resort to name calling, saying he did not question her
"legitimacy to be here today," Basl responded by leaving behind a cartoon with
Jontz depicted as Pinocchio with his nose growing to the Pacific Northwest
and labeled with the words: "Jontz: Keep your nose in your own business." Perhaps accustomed to the territory thanks to his frequent town meetings back
in the Fifth District, Jontz seemed unruffled by the confrontation, noting that
listening to such heated exchanges was just "part of the job."[30]

The opposition to Jontz for his environmental efforts in the Pacific Northwest continued during his runs for re-election in the Fifth District. In 1990 his Republican opponent John Johnson said that by meddling in affairs outside of his district, Jontz risked having lumber and housing prices rise in Indiana. The criticism reached another level, however, in 1992 when Jontz faced a new GOP challenger, a Monticello, Indiana, attorney named Stephen E. Buyer (pronounced Boo-yer). A graduate of the Valparaiso University School of Law, Buyer had explored the possibility of running against Jontz in 1988, traveling to the fourteen counties in the district to meet with prominent Republicans. "I represent the values and the work ethic of the people of this district far greater than Jim Jontz," said Buyer, who gave way to the eventual Republican nominee, Pat Williams. Buyer's activity caught the attention of Jontz's staff. In his congressional papers is a copy of an advertisement by Buyer announcing the opening of his law office in Monticello. The advertisement included a photograph of Buyer and his biography. At the bottom a Jontz staff had noted that with advertisements "like this, he must be gearing up to be our next opponent."[31]

An event thousands of miles away from the Fifth District had a major effect on the 1992 congressional election, and Buyer's decision on whether or not to challenge Jontz. On August 2, 1990, more than a hundred thousand troops from Iraq, backed by eighteen thousand tanks, invaded Kuwait, taking control of the oil-rich country in just twelve hours. Saddam Hussein, Iraq's president for life, declared that Kuwait no longer existed and was now the "Nineteenth Province, an eternal part of Iraq." Over the next few months, pressure grew on Iraq to leave Kuwait, with the United Nations Security Council passing resolutions denouncing the invasion, calling for Iraq to withdraw, and establishing economic sanctions, including a trade embargo. In Operation Desert Shield, the Bush administration sent American forces to Saudi Arabia to protect friendly nations in the Persian Gulf, where they were joined by coalition troops from other countries. On November 29 the UN passed another resolution supporting "all necessary means" to force Iraq from Kuwait if Saddam had not withdrawn his troops by a January 15, 1991 deadline.[32]

Congress debated whether or not to give President Bush its authorization to use military force against Saddam. On January 12 the House voted 250 to 183 and the U.S. Senate voted 52 to 47 for such authorization. Jontz was one of those who voted against the war resolution. Opinions on whether or not to go to war in the Persian Gulf, or to give the economic sanctions more time to

force Saddam out of Kuwait, differed widely in the Fifth District. In the days
leading up to the vote in Congress Jontz said letters and telephone calls to
his Washington, D.C., office supported his position of continuing the international economic embargo against Iraq. "I believe there is still a possibility that
sanctions and diplomacy can work," said Jontz, "and I don't want to unnec-
essarily risk American lives and drain our treasury if our allies are unwilling
to shoulder their responsibility." The Indiana congressman criticized allied
countries such as Japan and Germany for not contributing more financially to
the effort in the Gulf. "There are a lot of nations out there who are willing to
stand and hold our coat, but that doesn't cut it," he noted. Jontz pointed out
that Saudi Arabia had realized some $9 billion in profits from higher oil prices
since the invasion of Kuwait, but had contributed less than a billion dollars to
help pay for the coalition effort to protect it from a possible invasion and to
evict Iraq from Kuwait. Jontz did stress that once a decision had been made
to go to war, America had to present a united front. "If we fight," he said, "we
must support our troops 100 percent."[33]

At 7 p.m. Eastern Standard Time on January 16, the U.S. Air Force initiated Operation Desert Storm by striking key targets in the heart of Iraq. Air
attacks continued over the next few weeks before the start of the land war on
February 24. In just a hundred hours after the start of the ground operation,
a ceasefire was declared. On February 27 Bush declared, "Our objectives are
met." Kuwait had been liberated and Saddam's forces had been bloodied at
a cost of just 148 American troops killed and 458 wounded. Rick Atkinson,
a *Washington Post* reporter who covered the war, noted that when it came to
"military objectives conquered, allied casualties minimized and popular support on the home front sustained, the war appeared to be that rarest of prizes
in the age of relativity: an absolute victory." Returning veterans of the Gulf
War were treated as conquering heroes and parades were held in their honor in
communities throughout the country, offering a stark contrast to the greeting
received by Vietnam War veterans so many years before.[34]

One of those returning Gulf War veterans was Buyer, who had served
overseas as an army reserve captain and spent five months on active duty in
the Persian Gulf as a legal counsel for the Twenty-second Theater Army as well
as interrogating Iraqi prisoners of war for suspected war crimes. In October
1991 Buyer announced he would be running against Jontz, becoming one
of the first Gulf War veterans to seek political office. "When Buyer returned
from the war," said Brian Vargus of Indiana University's Public Opinion

Laboratory, "the Republican brass must have seen him as a godsend." While serving overseas, Buyer had produced eleven installments of a "Gulf War Diary" that were printed in the *Monticello Herald Journal.* Buyer also built name recognition by talking about his experiences in the war before veterans' groups and Republican gatherings. He expressed resentment over Jontz's vote against the war, but still greeting troops as they returned to Grissom Air Force Base. "One day the American people will forgive him, but I don't think they'll forget—I won't," said Buyer, who before his service had served as vice chairman of the White County Republican Party and worked as a Indiana deputy attorney general. To counter Jontz's noted shoe-leather campaign style, Buyer kicked off his campaign by slinging his combat boots over his shoulder as he spoke at meetings and wearing his uniform at events honoring veterans throughout the district. He told audiences that anyone could "wear out a pair of shoes, but it takes a special person to wear out a pair of combat boots." Buyer went as far as to say that Jontz cared more for spotted owls than for veterans; a charge Jontz angrily dismissed. "I don't take a back seat to anyone on patriotism," he told an *Indianapolis Star* reporter. When Democrats turned around and charged that Buyer was wrapping himself in the flag, Buyer had a ready response: "Sure am. Feels good."[35]

Jontz and Buyer did have one thing in common—they both used the services of Alex Martin, owner of Martin's Shoe and Leather Repair in Monticello. Martin tried to be fair minded when a *Star* reporter asked him for his assessment of the two candidates, noting, "Both are super individuals. I think highly of both of them." A U.S. Air Force veteran, Martin added that he was no expert on politics and tended to vote for the individual instead of a particular member of a political party. He also did not share where his vote would go in the November election. "Both are very good friends," Martin said of the two candidates.[36]

The ancient-forest issue played a role during the Fifth District congressional campaign, with Buyer making a tour of the Pacific Northwest's timber country and having a fund-raiser at the headquarters of Pacific Lumber and Shipping Company in March 1992. Individuals and political action committees associated with the timber interests donated approximately $50,000 to the Buyer campaign. "Jim Jontz is perverting the Democratic system," said Buyer. "He's destroying the lives of people he doesn't represent and who can't fight back by voting him out of office." As well as money, those opposing Jontz also contributed their time in an effort to defeat him. A group of eighteen

Pacific Northwest residents took time off from their union jobs in the timber industry to travel to Indiana to personally campaign against Jontz, handing out flyers at malls and appearing on radio shows in an attempt to convince fellow union members and voters in the Fifth District to stop supporting the Democratic congressman. The trip was paid for by Forest Families in the Balance, a PAC only created, according to Jontz, as a way to contribute toward his defeat in the November election. "The timber industry has taken over his [Buyer's] race lock, stock, and barrel," said Howard Wolfson, Jontz's spokesman. "The 5th District race has now become a battle between Jim Jontz and the timber industry." Although Jontz later called the visit by the timber workers "a sideshow," his old ally, Jack Williams of United Auto Workers Local 685 in Kokomo, had bitter memories of his union brethren. "They call themselves labor but they weren't brave enough to come see us, to sit down and talk things over," Williams recalled. "Instead they were off with the Republicans, doing their dirty work."[37]

Jontz's connection with the ancient-forest issue also had an indirect effect on his re-election campaign that might have hurt his chances. Mike Busch, a Jontz legislative assistant, noted that his boss's attention had started to drift toward his true love—the environment. There were two or three weekends in 1991 and 1992 that Jontz had not come back for visits to his Indiana district. Instead, as Busch noted, the congressman traveled to the Pacific Northwest or made field trips for his House committee work. When Busch reminded Jontz that this was not how he had won previous elections, Jontz responded by saying that after six years in office it would be alright if he missed a few weekends. Busch was worried, however, as he saw Buyer as a superior candidate to the Republicans they had faced in the past, appearing to be someone the GOP could rally behind. Although Jontz remained dedicated to supporting veterans and senior citizens, Busch said when he talked with him about his trips to the Pacific Northwest there was a "passion" he did not display on other issues. "There was a spark—his eyes lit up and even if he was tired and wanted to take a nap, if you asked him about his trip west, boom, he would be right up," said Busch.[38]

In addition to raising the ire of the timber industry, Jontz might have made another powerful enemy, this time the pharmaceutical industry, thanks to a congressional field hearing on the rising costs of prescription drugs he and Congressman Jerry Costello of Illinois held for the House Select Committee on Aging and the Subcommittee on Housing and Consumer Interests on September 28 in Logansport. Those attending the hearing included area citizens, health-care professionals and representatives from the health insurance and prescription drug industries, including Indianapolis's Eli Lilly and Company. At the hearing, Jontz and Costello distributed statistics indicating that drug costs had risen more than three times the rate of inflation since 1980, with prescription drugs increasing at an even greater rate than overall health costs. Julie Newland, manager of public affairs for Lilly, pointed to the high costs of research and development for new drugs as a contributing factor. "This business is very competitive and very risky," said Newland. "Out of the 100,000 possible compounds that the industry investigates, only 10 will make it to the market. Of that number, only two return a profit." Jontz, a supporter of national health-care reform that included a cap on prescription drug costs, agreed that pharmaceutical companies needed to "make a fair profit," but added there seemed to be "no good reason why the cost of prescription drugs has risen so much."[39]

In late October as Election Day neared, Lilly's political action committee approved a $5,000 contribution to Buyer, marking the first time it had been involved in a Fifth District race involving Jontz. The incumbent congressman said the contribution was payback for his questioning of the drug company at the hearing. "They took great offense to these questions and now have decided because of my interest in trying to get control on costs of drugs so average citizens can afford them, then they'll give the maximum contribution at the last minute, hoping it won't be noticed," said Jontz. Newland said the company's employees did not share Jontz's views on health-care reform and were put off by what she called his rude, insensitive line of questioning at the hearing, saying he attempted to paint the company's workers as a "black-hatted cabal of heartless people." Jontz said the donation raised questions in his mind on whether Buyer, if elected to office, would represent the interests of consumers or be beholden to the drug firms.[40]

A host of other issues also worked against Jontz in the 1992 election. While Bush tried to fend off Democratic presidential nominee Bill Clinton, a third candidate, Texas billionaire H. Ross Perot, appeared on the scene running as an independent and skillfully using television appearances on talks shows and buying infomercials to promote his possible candidacy. Although he was an on again, off again, and then on again, presidential candidate, Perot and his running mate, Vice Admiral James Stockdale, appeared on the ballot in all fifty states on behalf of the Reform Party. He lambasted the work of

Congress and appealed to voters, sick of "politics as usual," as the antipolitician. In a speech before the National Press Club in Washington, D.C., on March 18, 1992, he declared: "This city has become a town filled with sound bites, shell games, handlers, media stuntmen who posture, create images, talk, shoot off Roman candles, but don't ever accomplish anything. We need deeds, not words, in this city." In addition, hurting Bush's re-election chances would gain for Perot a measure of revenge for having his plans to free supposed American soldiers still held in North Vietnam quashed by the president. "If [Perot] denies Bush the presidency, he'll be on top of the world," noted one Perot aide. "He hates George Bush."[41]

Perot's message that the political system was broken seemed true to a public who had been treated to national news stories about scandals on Capitol Hill. The most damaging to the image of politicians came from revelations about special perks enjoyed by congressman subsidized by taxpayers, including everything from fixing parking tickets to free haircuts and reduced entrance rates at national parks. In November 1991 Jontz sent a letter to Speaker of the House Foley seeking a review of all the privileges and benefits members received and the elimination of those not needed to conduct business. "What people are requesting is for me—and us—to take whatever action is necessary so that all members of Congress meet the highest standard of conduct," said Jontz. He even called for the elimination of benefits that did not cost taxpayers money, saying that his constituents were upset that congressmen enjoyed privileges "that average citizens do not. Their anger is in response to the symbolism of what we do, not just the costs of a particular benefit."[42]

The most serious problem that came to light, however, and the one that caused the greatest backlash, involved the way in which House members conducted their financial affairs through the institution's "bank," run by its sergeant at arms and into which congressmen's salaries were deposited. If a member overdrew his or her account, the amount would be covered by other members' deposits, for which they received no interest. As biographers of Foley noted, the bank existed as "an archaic legacy of the mid-1800s, and whatever similarities it bore to a typical community bank were more misleading than instructive." Still, the public failed to grasp these distinctions as the media pounced on the story of numerous current and former congressmen—303 in all as reported by the House Ethics Committee—"bouncing" checks. Although a special counsel, Malcolm R. Wilkey, a former federal prosecutor, investigated and found "limited" criminal conduct on behalf of House members. The damage was done, however, as the most egregious offenders received banner headlines in newspapers across the country, including such examples as Louis Stokes, a Democrat of Ohio, who had 551 overdrafts over a thirty-nine-month period from July 1, 1988, to October 3, 1991. Even GOP minority whip Newt Gingrich, a Republican from Georgia, who had been one of the leaders in insisting that the names of check bouncers be released to the public, had to confess he had written twenty-two bad checks on insufficient funds.[43]

In March 1992 Jontz issued a statement outlining the reason behind the ethics committee finding that he had been overdrawn on seven checks he had written on the House bank, and challenging four of them because the bank had failed to credit a $5,000 deposit he had made. "I don't think there should be separate rules for Members of Congress—we ought to live with the same rules everyone else does," said Jontz, who paid $50 to the U.S. Treasury for each check he overdrew. "Other people pay service charges when they over-draw their accounts, and Members of Congress should too." He noted he had voted for full disclosure of all members alleged to have written checks with inadequate funds and the number of checks they wrote because he believed "the American people have a right to come to their own conclusions about whether or not a Member of Congress abused the system." Jontz had even gone further, he said, including voting for a failed measure that would have allowed a complete audit of the records of every House member who overdrew his or her account, as well as disclosing the total amounts of the overdrawn checks. The explanations were not enough for Buyer, who jumped on the issue, demanding: "How can we trust them managing our country if they can't handle their own checkbooks?"[44]

The public outrage about the House banking scandal and other special perks contributed to a sense of gloom on Capitol Hill for many. In an April 12, 1992, the *Indianapolis Star* quoted Republican Indiana congressman John Myers as saying that the morale in Congress was a the lowest level he had ever seen in his twenty-five years in office. "You work hard," Myers said, "but people back home think you are just a bunch of bums, money grabbers and everything else." Jontz expressed frustration about the public's lack of knowledge about what a congressman did on a day-to-day basis, as the media seemed unwilling to report on issues of real substance. "The public has no confidence anything can be accomplished down here," he noted. "One of the reasons is the focus of the media is on one tiny fraction of what is going on here."

Although Jontz acknowledged that Congress needed to work harder, there were a number of members "trying to push things forward. I think people at home are interested, but the work we were elected to do does not seem to be of any importance [in the media]." Incumbency, he went on to predict, would not be the benefit it had been in previous elections. "If anything," he said, "it's an obstacle to overcome. It's not an asset the way it used to be." That fact hit home during a campaign stop Jontz made at an automotive parts plant in Wabash, Indiana. When he offered a woman worker his literature, she refused and told the congressman, "We're going to vote all the incumbents out." Another worker rushed past and called out over her shoulder to Jontz that she sometimes thought "you people are as bad as the people who run this place." Jontz kept his sense of humor, responding: "I'm not that bad."[45]

The reaction against Congress puzzled others in Washington as well. Tom Kenworthy, a national environmental reporter for the *Washington Post* who had covered Capitol Hill for five years, had regularly bashed Congress and had been one of the media hordes hounding former House Speaker Jim Wright to leave office and agreed that reforms to the institution were long overdue. Still, he urged voters in an article for the newspaper titled "Keep the Bums In!" to be selective about voting out incumbents and not randomly act as a "reflexive stab at the House bank 'scandal.'" Kenworthy said there were dozens of "bright, hard-working, serious-minded members who go to work every day and try to serve their own particular version of the public interest," citing as examples Don Edwards of California, John Dingell of Michigan, Robert Michel of Illinois, and Jontz. Kenworthy had traveled with Jontz in the Fifth District and been impressed on how hard he worked on behalf of his constituents. The reporter called upon those who viewed politicians as lazy and overpaid to do what he did and go to Kokomo to witness Jontz "enjoy his four-day weekend. I did once—and never again." He noted he and the Hoosier congressman had started their day at 6:15 in the morning and by ten o'clock that night "Jontz was still racing across his rural district in a ratty old Chevette so he wouldn't miss a meeting with eight members of a Junior Chamber of Commerce to brief them on a road construction project. That's his idea of fun."[46]

Late in the campaign, Buyer and Indiana Republicans attempted to turn a good deed Jontz had started when he first took office—a scholarship fund for students in the Fifth District financed by the congressional pay raises he had turned down—into a negative. Both Buyer and Rex Early, state GOP chairman, charged that Jontz had misled the public, since he had received pay

Steve Buyer, the Republican who defeated Jontz in the 1992 congressional race. In 2002 his district was renumbered as the Fourth Congressional District. Buyer announced his retirement from Congress on January 29, 2010.

increases totaling $155,000 over the years and had distributed only a portion of that amount to students (Early said Jontz had given out $15,000 in scholarships, while Buyer set the amount at $23,000). "Jim Jontz has distorted what he has done to the extent that somebody needs to call attention to it," Early said during a visit to Fulton County Republican Headquarters in Rochester, Indiana. The charges were labeled as a "last-ditch, low-blow, mudslinging attempt" by the Jontz campaign. According to Wolfson, the congressman had contributed $50,424.86 to his scholarship fund and $23,500 had been given to students. "The rest is in the bank drawing interest so it can grow, just like any other endowment," said Wolfson. He noted that Jontz had donated all of his raise from his first term in Congress to the fund, as well as part of the money from each additional salary increase, and that Early's figures did not take into account one thing: "Jim has to pay taxes on the pay raise just like anyone else."[47]

As the November 1992 election neared, Jontz attempted to follow the same pattern he had followed to success in previous elections—working from sunup to sundown. He had a harder road to travel, however, as the Fifth District had undergone redistricting and had expanded to include portions or all of twenty counties, including some areas where voters had never before heard of Jontz. Just a week before the election, on October 31, a reporter from the *Northwest Times* followed the congressman as he started his day at 6:15 a.m. at a pickle factory, Pilgrim Farms, in Plymouth, Indiana, as the city and all of Marshall County were part of the new sections of his district. To help ward off the cold on that chilly morning, Jontz wore a plaid coat from his high school days that he had worn for luck on every election night since his first win in

1974. "Every time my mom sees me wearing it on TV she tells me to get a new coat," he joked. At the gates to the pickle factory, Jontz shook hands with workers and distributed a flyer protesting the movement of American jobs overseas. From there, he moved on to greet voters at the Alibi Restaurant in La Paz and visited Democratic headquarters in Plymouth before conducting door-to-door canvassing in the community. "The pattern of patter is different from the plant gate," the reported noted of Jontz's work. "After introducing himself and offering his brochures, Jontz often asks the resident's name, sometimes asks their dog's name and if the resident has any concerns to tell him." The congressman was able to visit approximately seventy-five houses in a matter of a few hours, with someone being home to greet him about half the time.[48]

While Jontz had been able to count on a loyal base of volunteers in each of his elections, in the 1992 race there seemed to be a schism between some longtime workers and a new group of environmental activists who came to the state to work on behalf of the champion of ancient forests. Jim Britell, who had worked with the Kalmiopsis Audubon Society to save old-growth forests in Oregon, brought to Indiana forest activists from all over the country to support Jontz's candidacy. Organized as a separate entity from Jontz's regular campaign, the group raised money to complete two house-to-house canvasses of the district (visiting a hundred thousand houses in one month), as well as paying for flyers and maintaining two residences to house the volunteers. The environmentalists mixed with Jontz's staff like oil and water, with Britell calling the congressman's staff "bullies and tryants" and forbade them "to talk or even be in the presence of any campaign volunteers and would not allow any of his office staff even to set foot in any of the two houses we maintained for volunteers."

Britell also expressed frustration with the candidate, especially his refusal to use new technology and targeting and strategic information. For example, Britell said Jontz decided not to use portable telephones in the campaign for fear that constituents might see him talking on the phone while in a car "and see him as 'snooty' or above them." Also, the candidate turned aside voter lists to help target motivated voters in an area, particularly Democrats who had not voted. "Why knock on a door of an unregistered voter or a motivated Republican?" asked Britell. Jontz, however, did what he did on all of his other campaigns—try to knock on every door that could be knocked on. "If we went to a street we knocked on every door," Britell remembered. "Drove me crazy."

He went on to note that the congressman was "impossible to persuade once he got an idea and he was oblivious to calls to be realistic in policy or tactics and that was his strength and his downfall."[49]

Brian Mayes, who had volunteered on each of Jontz's congressional campaigns, believed that in 1992 Jontz, in part because of his activism on behalf of the ancient forests in the Pacific Northwest, had failed to "remain symbolically connected to the everyday concerns of ordinary citizens." Although his work to keep public lands from being destroyed might be a laudable goal for some voters, the issue had "little resonance for the farmers and factory workers of Indiana." Mayes noted that the campaign staff derided the distribution of an "environmental canvass piece" to educate voters in some areas of the district on preservation of the forests and blasting Buyer for accepting money for a "dirty dozen" timber companies. The staff referred to the literature as "a net minus" and the "smell the bark" piece, he added. Jontz, said Mayes, had come to symbolize many things to many people, and, in the end, the "pressure to live up to his own image may have led him to pursue his environmental quest as a means of preserving his own identity."[50]

Mayes also acknowledged tension existed in the Jontz campaign between longtime volunteers such as himself and the environmentalists who had come to the Hoosier State. He said he arrived in Indiana in late October or early November to work on Jontz's behalf for what would be his fourth campaign. Back in 1990 he had been referred to as the campaign's "institutional memory," so Mayes was put off by being taken for a walk and interviewed by one of the environmentalists. "I remember going out to canvass with a mix of the enviros and the staff," Mayes recalled. "One of the enviros had a large 'Vote Green' button, which I thought stupid both in terms of message and frankly it made it look like our candidate's name was 'Green.' I remember a staff person saying to me in frustration, 'This guy can't read a map,' which was completely true." Mayes did note there were a large number of well intentioned people who worked their hearts out for Jontz during the election, but the campaign needed a "firm hand at the top to control this (my old friend Scott Campbell who managed in 1990 could maybe have pulled this off), and this was utterly lacking."[51]

All of the hard work for which Jontz was famous was not enough to stave off defeat, as Buyer captured the Fifth District seat with 51 percent (112,492) of the vote to 49 percent (107,973) for Jontz. It marked the first time the Democrat had ever lost a run for public office and came on the same night when his party's leader, Clinton, edged out Bush in the presidential contest.

For years, said Sugar, the congressman and his staff had been beating their heads against the wall trying to deal with Republican presidents. He recalled how terrible he and other supporters of the congressman felt standing at their headquarters in Monticello, Indiana, watching on television as a Democrat won the White House, only to realize they would not be involved in working with the new administration. "It was hard to believe it could happen," said Sugar. Jontz kept his good humor on what would be his first loss in a long political career. When told when he arrived at about 10:30 p.m. at Cass County Democratic Headquarters that returns were coming in later than usual, he joked, "I brought a sleeping bag."[52]

The thirty-three-year-old Buyer, who spent the last month before the election campaigning with walking pneumonia, said he saw the momentum shift toward him on October 18 at a fund-raising hog roast at the Cass County 4-H Fairgrounds in Logansport. "When Joni [his wife] and I walked in there," Buyer said, "we got a standing ovation from 400 people and you just had the feeling it was going to happen." Tom Weatherwax, a GOP state senator from Logansport, credited Republican unity throughout the district with helping Buyer beat the incumbent Democrat, as the rookie candidate received the support of previous candidates who had lost to Jontz, including Jack Guy, Jim Butcher, Pat Williams, John Johnson, as well as former congressman Bud Hillis. The former candidates had a brainstorming session, noted Brandt Hershman, Buyer's press aide, and passed on what they had learned during their campaigns to Buyer. "He had better support and networking at the grass-roots level," Weatherwax said of Buyer, "and I really think that's what did it." Buyer also received aid from the National Republican Campaign Committee, which gave him the maximum contribution, $50,000, in an attempt to finally capture the Fifth District from Jontz. Congressman Guy Vander Jagt of Michigan said Buyer was able to convey the message to voters that if they wanted "to make a change in the House, they have to change their congressman." Another group celebrating Jontz's defeat was the timber industry in the Pacific Northwest. "If the people of the Northwest can cheer one thing out of this election, it is that they won't have to put up with Jim Jontz for another minute," said Dave Redmond, a spokesman for Oregon congressman Smith. "He embodied a lot of what people in the Northwest have come to fear and loathe from the most radical elements of the environmental movement."[53]

Learning of Jontz's loss, Lake County Democratic party chairman Robert A. Pastrick expressed little surprise at the loss in a normally Republic district:

"He [Jontz] hung from his knuckles for a long time." The candidate himself seemed sanguine about the outcome, saying that while 93 percent of incumbents were returned to office, only three Democratic House members served districts that had more Republicans than the Fifth District. "We talked about the right issues," Jontz said the morning after his defeat and midnight call to congratulate the victor, "but we were just overwhelmed by the desire of the voters to see some changes in the individuals who would represent them." He noted that if he had thought the race would be easy, he would not have started campaigning as early as he did, last March. Although Jontz was quick to discount the effect his stand on old-growth forests had in his loss, Jack Williams said it might have been a factor, especially the money timber interests donated to Buyer's campaign. Jontz's usual base of labor support failed to come through in Howard County, the biggest county in the district, with Jontz losing to Buyer by 2,442 votes out of 33,828 cast; it marked the first time he had failed to win the county in his congressional races. "If the rank and file had been there, Jontz would have pulled out Howard County," Williams said. Britell noted he will never forget seeing returns come in from precincts in Kokomo that needed to have Jontz winning over Buyer 60 percent to 40 percent actually coming in at 55 percent to 45 percent. "As soon as we saw that we knew it was all over and then the whole devastation of that election started coming in and we were so desolate," he recalled. Mayes noted that one of Jontz's environmental advocates said after the congressman's defeat that the trees were "sentient beings and they are on Jim's side," a statement for which Mayes had the rueful rejoinder: "Unfortunately, they don't vote."[54]

Buyer's close ties to White County, he graduated from North White High School in Monon, Indiana, damaged Jontz's re-election chances, as the Democrat had developed that normally Republican area into a solid base of votes in previous campaigns. In 1992 Buyer captured White County, winning 5,099 votes to 5,032 for Jontz. He might have also been hurt in his home area because he had spent the last two weeks of the campaign concentrating on two new counties in the Fifth District, Marshall and Kosciusko, and that took time away from other parts of the district. Buyer captured twelve of the twenty counties in the district, including Cass County, which Jontz had won in all of his previous contests. The congressman had a feeling he might lose the race. "To be honest," he said, "I had the same feeling in 1990," when he edged out Johnson. "I felt less anxious about this election," Jontz added. "I had prepared myself mentally [for a loss]." Reflecting on his effort, he said he had no regrets about the campaign. "A lot of people said a Democrat couldn't get elected in the 5th District, and a lot said a Democrat couldn't survive after being elected," said Jontz, but he had proved them wrong.[55]

Late on election night, when he knew he had been defeated, Jontz asked Tom Sugar, his chief of staff, to take him back to the Chrysler plant in Kokomo he had visited after he won his first race for Congress in 1986. Early the next morning, Jontz, joined once again by Williams and Sugar, was at the automotive factory gates to thank the workers for their years of support. As the workers filed into the factory, Jontz reached out his hand and told them: "Thank you for the opportunity. It was my honor to represent you." Sugar said that some of the workers refused to shake hands with Jontz. He remembered thinking at the time that these were men Jontz and his staff had fought for throughout their years in office, never refusing to support their issues, and now they had been convinced by popular advertising and "front-porch homilies" by Perot that they were no good. But, now liberated from seeking their votes, the former congressman responded a couple of times to having his hand refused: "Oh, come on now, be a man, shake my hand." Sugar said he was proud of his boss "for not just rolling over and taking it. He had given his life to their causes." Looking back on that morning, Sugar added that he hoped those union workers who avoided Jontz are embarrassed to this day about how they behaved. "In politics," said Sugar, "you have to bite your tongue a lot, not that morning, and he didn't, and that's how it ended."[56]

The night after the election, Jontz, his congressional staff, and campaign team had a farewell dinner at Solly's Restaurant in Reynolds, Indiana. Mayes remembered that he and several other Jontz supporters broke down in tears at the gathering. Jontz thanked everyone for all of their hard work on his behalf. Kathy Altman, the congressman's district director for his offices in Indiana, remembered that Jontz noted how fortunate he felt for holding his congressional seat for three terms, especially given the Republican tilt of the district. Altman also said Jontz told her that while in Congress he had voted the way he thought he should have voted for six years, and was grateful for that, as not many politicians had that opportunity while in office. "That gave him a great deal of satisfaction," said Altman. Later, while helping move files out of his office at the Longworth House Office Building in Washington, D.C., Jontz reflected to a reporter from the *Indianapolis Star* that he had learned about the volatility of the voting republic and how vulnerable politicians could be in his first race for office in 1974 when he barely edged out Indiana House majority leader Jack Guy. "I've been skating on thin ice," Jontz observed. "A lot of people didn't think I was going to last more than one term in the state legislature. So I have been living on borrowed time for years." Reminiscing on this time as a congressman, Jontz, when asked to pick his finest moment in office, decided to select not a victory like the passage of a bill, but when he voted in favor of a failed bill allowing senior citizens additional access to home-health services. "It wasn't something I wrote or made a great contribution to," he said, "but I can't describe the pride I had in supporting it, because it was right." There would be other projects Jontz supported because he believed it was the right thing to do in the years to come.[57]

7

Long May You Run

During the fall of 1994 Hoosiers watching their favorite television programs were greeted with a lesson in world geography of sorts compliments of a would-be U.S. senator driving a battered, red Chevrolet pickup whose odometer edged over the hundred-thousand-mile mark. The intrepid traveler, Jim Jontz, the Democratic nominee against Republican incumbent Richard Lugar, traveled the world without ever leaving the state. As he explained in the advertisement, Jontz began his journey because he was curious when he heard that Lugar had helped obtain billions of dollars in aid from the federal government for Moscow. Hoping to learn more, Jontz hopped into his trusty truck and drove to Moscow, Indiana, where a local resident told him, "Nope, haven't seen a cent." The answers were the same at his other stops in Lebanon, Peru, Brazil, Mexico, and Scotland. "You must be kidding," a man in Peru responded when Jontz told him about $50 million being allocated for Peru (unfortunately for those in the community, the country in South America, not for them). The commercial ended with Jontz saying that while Lugar had taken care of every other place around the world but his home state, he would "take care of Indiana first."[1]

The tongue-in-cheek message was a highlight in a quixotic campaign that saw Jontz fight the biggest odds in his political career as he tried to deny Lugar a record-setting fourth term in office, breaking a jinx that had brought down such prominent Indiana political figures as James Watson, Homer Capehart, Vance Hartke, and Birch Bayh. The race also marked a return to politics for Jontz just a short time after he had tackled his party's own president, Bill Clinton, in a grassroots fight against passage of the North American Free Trade Agreement among the United States, Mexico, and Canada. The battle saw Jontz organize groups that he had fought for and tried to bring together for common cause during his three terms as a congressman—labor unions and conservationists. "Workers and environmentalists are affected by the same corporate powers," noted Jontz. "We're all part of the global economy that isn't friendly to our interests."[2]

Following his loss to Steve Buyer in 1992, Jontz had been rumored to be in line for a possible position somewhere in the Clinton administration, thereby switching from the legislative to the executive branch of government. In December 1992, as he packed up his belongings from his Washington, D.C., office, Jontz fielded questions from newspaper reporters by indicating a wait-and-see attitude. Although he said that the "process isn't focused on my level of position at this point," Jontz indicated there could be the potential for jobs in the Agriculture or Interior departments, both agencies in which he believed he could make significant contributions. "It depends on what the administration wants to do in those areas, if they want to make some changes," Jontz said. The call, however, never came. Asked about why Jontz never received an offer to join the Clinton team, Tom Sugar, his former chief of staff, bitterly noted that the ex-congressman was denied a position because the timber interests and logging unions "started burning up the FAX machines in Washington" with messages protesting giving their old foe any consideration for a job.[3]

Without his legislative post, Jontz seemed adrift for a time. After all, it was the first time in eighteen years he had been out of office. Longtime Jontz aide Kathy Altman remembered him referring to himself for a time as "a recovering congressman." The looming fight on NAFTA, however, soon had him back in the fray, and may have had some on the Clinton staff wishing they had done more to find Jontz a position with the administration. First negotiated during President George H. W. Bush's administration, and signed by Bush on December 17, 1992, the agreement, which had to be ratified by a simple majority in the House and Senate, was designed to end tariffs and trade barriers from the Yucatán in the south to the Yukon in the north. The agreement had been an issue during the 1992 presidential election, as Reform Party candidate Ross Perot had warned voters to listen for the "giant sucking sound" of American jobs being vacuumed away south to Mexico if Congress enacted NAFTA. Other groups also opposed the agreement, as labor unions worried about jobs moving overseas, environmentalists pointed to Mexico's poor track record on protecting the environment, and consumer organizations fretted about the possibility of American food and safety laws being threatened.[4]

Images captured from Jim Jontz's campaign commercial for the 1994 U.S. Senate race making light of his opponent, Republican Richard Lugar, and his role in securing foreign aid instead of concentrating on matters in Indiana.

During his time as a congressman, Jontz had been adamantly opposed to NAFTA. To his way of thinking, passage of the pact would translate into lost jobs for workers in Indiana's Fifth Congressional District. "It's a terrible deal for America's working families," he said. "It's also a bad deal for many small manufacturers who will be unable to compete with the large corporations that can relocate to Mexico." In March 1991 United Technologies announced that it was closing its automotive parts plant in Wabash, Indiana, costing 243 employees their jobs. Noting that United Technologies had sixteen manufacturing facilities in Mexico, Jontz said the consequences of passing NAFTA would be "even more investment and jobs going south of the border." Because the automotive parts industry provided Hoosiers with tens of thousands of jobs, Indiana, said Jontz, would be especially vulnerable. "Trading Indiana jobs for Mexican imports is not my idea of free trade," he said.[5]

With his organizing skills and ties to unions and enviornmentalists, Jontz made the perfect choice to become director of the Citizens Trade Campaign, a coalition of approximately sixty labor, consumer, environmental, family farm, religious, and civic groups organized to defeat NAFTA. Scott Paul, a former Jontz staff member who served as a deputy director for the CTC, said Jontz was a "perfect fit" for the position and he brought his own style of grassroots politics to the NAFTA fight and it ended up being a very effective strategy. "Jim was a master at herding stray cats, which was a lot of his job at CTC at the outset," recalled Paul. "Disparate groups united around an issue, but coming at it from different perspectives." Jontz, who had moved from his former home in Monticello to his late grandparents' home in Silver Lake, Indiana, after his 1992 defeat, said his new job was not "that different from what I used to do. I'm directing a campaign, I'm working with the grassroots instead of the legislative end. I'm working with a varied, broad group, and I'm working with a staff."[6]

What was different in this case, and what befuddled and angered progressive Democrats such as Jontz and groups such as labor unions and environmentalists that had a long history of supporting the party, was their opponent in the NAFTA fight—a Democratic president in Clinton who viewed the agreement as good for the country. For liberals in the party, NAFTA represented what they had been fighting against for a number of years during the Republican presidential administrations of Ronald Reagan and Bush. The trade pact received opposition from such progressive stalwarts as consumer advocate Ralph Nader, the Reverend Jesse Jackson (who quipped "NAFTA is a shafta"),

President Bill Clinton made passage of the North American Free Trade Agreement—eliminating many trade barriers among the United States, Canada, and Mexico—one of his priorities during his first administration. Upon signing the legislation, Clinton said it would "permit us to create an economic order in the world that will promote more growth, more equality, better preservation of the environment, and a greater possibility of world peace."

House Majority Leader Richard Gephardt of Missouri, and House Minority Whip David Bonior of Michigan. "They are flabbergasted that Bill Clinton, who they worked to elect," said Jontz, "would now carry water for the policies of the past, and, frankly, this enrages local activists who thought they were getting something else." That unrest made the trade agreement a dangerous issue for the Democrats, he added, because the "activists at the local level, who are the ones on whom the party depends, are not happy."[7]

In addition to opening fissures within the Democratic Party, NAFTA created some strange alliances among groups. In Congress, Clinton found himself trying to find enough votes to secure passage from his nemesis, minority whip Newt Gingrich of Georgia, as his administration needed the votes of three-quarters of the GOP members to go along with one-third of the House's Democrats. Clinton also called upon ex-presidents Bush, Gerald Ford, and Jimmy Carter to join him at a September 14 ceremony at the White House to express their support for NAFTA's passage. Anti-NAFTA Democrats were on the same side for now as Perot and his nationwide organization, United We Stand. Perot claimed the real purpose of NAFTA was not to promote trade, but to "protect U.S. and foreign corporations that want to locate their factories in Mexico, exploit low-wage Mexican workers and ship products into the rich U.S. markets." Also on hand to lend his verbal fusillade to the occasion was conservative activist Pat Buchanan, who criticized his fellow Republicans for supporting the agreement. Buchanan called NAFTA an "insider's deal for the buyout of American liberty," and praised Perot as "an American patriot" for his determined opposition to the treaty.[8]

The Clinton administration had attempted to ease the concerns of its former allies, especially labor unions and environmentalists, by negotiating side agreements with Mexico on such issues as workers' rights, child labor, minimum wages, health and safety concerns, and pollution. Mickey Kantor, U.S. trade representative, said the new agreements had fixed the "major flaws" with NAFTA—an opinion not shared by the trade pact's critics. At an August 13 press conference at the National Press Club in Washington, D.C., Jontz, joined by a number of heads of national unions, blasted the supplemental accords negotiated by Kantor. Jontz said:

> These side deals aren't half a loaf. In fact, they aren't even half a slice. NAFTA is fundamentally an agreement to protect investors, to encourage them to go to Mexico to take advantage of low wages and lax environmental standards and enforcement. And nothing in the side agreements announced this morning will fundamentally change that. NAFTA is still a bad agreement for workers. It's still a bad agreement for the environment, it's still a bad agreement for family farmers, it's still a bad agreement for consumers.[9]

From the CTC's small one-room office in Washington, D.C., Jontz and his staff of six people and a yearly budget of $400,000 tried to run a campaign against the resources the Clinton White House could muster and the millions of dollars available to such business groups supporting the agreement as USA-NAFTA. "They're Goliath and we're David," Jontz noted. Unable to personally lobby his former House colleagues for one year due to ethics rules (Paul handled that assignment), Jontz relied on a network of state and regional captains to help plan events to raise public awareness of the issue and to meet one on one with representatives' staffs back in their districts. Jontz described the vote on the agreement as a "career-defining" moment for congressmen. "Every factory that closes in their district they will have to explain if they vote for NAFTA," he warned. A lot of his work, Jontz told a reporter from the *New York Times*, involved serving as an adviser to local groups opposed to NAFTA and rounding up speakers for demonstrations. "Our campaign is the base of the Democratic Party," he said. "People see this very much about whether they're going to have control over their communities or leave it to corporate board rooms." When the Clinton administration organized a giant trade fair on the south lawn to highlight the products of companies set to benefit from NAFTA, the CTC helped set up an exhibition showing examples of products and jobs that would be lost if the agreement passed. When congressmen went on a four-day recess in November shortly before the House vote on NAFTA, the CTC was busy targeting its efforts on sixty to seventy congressional districts. "We have phone banks going," said Jontz. "We are planning district visits with lawmakers and anti-NAFTA demonstrations."[10]

The fierce backlash from groups on which he could normally count on rankled Clinton, who accused labor unions and their allies of using "roughshod, muscle-bound tactics" to get their way. Jontz brushed aside Clinton's complaints. He instead termed what the anti-NAFTA forces were doing as "tough love" for the president. Public opinion on the issue, however, began to be swayed toward the Clinton administration's case through a carefully managed public relations campaign that included national television advertisements by former Chrysler chairman Lee Iacocca, who claimed NAFTA had nothing "to do with the jobs we've lost to Japan and Timbucktoo." A November 9 debate on the CNN television program *Larry King Live* between Perot and Vice President Al Gore also helped turn the tide to NAFTA's favor, as Gore exposed Perot to the viewing audience as "shallow, opinionated, poorly informed, egocentric and erratic." Ken Cole of USA-NAFTA saw the television debate as a turning point. "When I saw the debate," said Cole, "I knew we were going to win. This is ours. They were going to start running [away from Perot]."[11]

Clinton also used his stature as president to twist the arms of reluctant congressman, personally talking to two hundred of them and securing their votes with political favors. Some House members were genuinely agonizing about their vote, Jontz observed, others tried to convince the president to accommodate their constituents' concerns about parts of the trade agreement, and some saw an opportunity to grab all they could for their districts. "I know one member who sent the White House a list of eight things he wants in exchange for his vote," said Jontz as the congressional vote neared. He quipped that if the administration "could sell part of the White House lawn to get the votes, they would do it." Paul described the situation as a "classic case of people versus power." Clinton defended his actions, noting it was not like his administration had given lawmakers "backrubs or whorehouses or money. We were trying to make policy accommodations in exchange for enough votes, and they were trying to look out for the folks back home. That's what the voters hired us to do." It worked; on November 17 NAFTA passed the House of Representatives by a 234 to 200 vote, and three days later the U.S. Senate ratified the treaty by a 61 to 38 margin.[12]

Paul remembered that Jontz did not appear to be disappointed about being on the losing end in the effort to stop NAFTA. "He stood up to big interests and made it a huge fight," said Paul, who today still works on trade issues as executive director of the Alliance for American Manufacturing. "He helped create a new progressive coalition to address globalization. It was (and remains today) the biggest fight ever on a trade matter in modern times." The battle seemed to reenergize Jontz's spirits, and he discovered that he still had the desire to make a political difference, perhaps even run again for office back in Indiana. "I gave that responsibility 110 percent," he said of his fight against NAFTA. "When the vote concluded, I was then able to give some thought to what would be next for Jim Jontz and look at the options for 1994." Jontz considered several possibilities for his future, including staying in Washington as the CTC director, helping the organization monitor NAFTA's effect and keeping "an eye on these multinational corporations." He also pondered whether or not to return to Indiana to try and recapture his Fifth District congressional seat from Buyer, or, in what any political observer would term the ultimate long shot, win the Democratic Party's nomination for U.S. Senate and take on Lugar in the fall election. "I've still got another race or two in me," Jontz said. "I'm rested up—really also fired up about what's going on in the country today." The heated debate on NAFTA had made him realize how difficult it was "for the average American to be heard. I knew that before, but it's reinforced my belief that the little guy doesn't have very many people speaking for him or her in Washington. It's important that that change."[13]

Lugar, the former mayor of Indianapolis and an Eagle Scout like Jontz, had served in the U.S. Senate since 1977. In his last re-election contest in 1988, he had won 68.2 percent of the vote against his Democratic opponent, Jack Wickes. Lugar lost only one portion of the state, Lake County, and even captured three other areas—South Bend, Evansville, and Terre Haute—that usually supported the Democratic Party. During his time in the Senate, Lugar had earned the respect of his colleagues as a voice they should listen to on agricultural and international issues. He won national attention for his work with Democrat Sam Nunn of Georgia, chairman of the Senate Armed Services Committee, to dismantle nuclear weapons in former republics in the Soviet Union. Lugar's supporters had begun work on the 1994 campaign years before, raising $2 million before the Democratic Party had rounded up a candidate to run against him. Asked why Hoosier voters should select him for another six-year term in office, Lugar told a reporter from the *Indianapolis Star*: "First of all, they know me. I have got a reputation of public service and service with purpose and integrity. That is meaningful to many people making a choice for high federal office. Beyond that, I hope they like me as a person. They see the same possibilities I see for my continued service."[14]

Compared to Lugar's healthy campaign war chest, Jontz had a long road to travel, as he still owed $30,000 from his last congressional race. Just days before the primary election, the Democrat had less than $60,000 for the general election. "He's the money candidate," Jontz said of Lugar. "That's not to say I won't raise money, but a lot of what we do will be small donors." In addition to trailing in the money race, Jontz also had name-recognition problems in many areas of the state, particularly in southern Indiana. That problem was highlighted during the May Democratic primary when Jontz managed only a 10-percentage point win (55 to 45) over a fringe candidate, John W. Taylor of Evansville, a follower of political extremist Lyndon LaRouche. Jontz dismissed the results, noting that Taylor did as well as he did not because there were a great number of LaRouche supporters, but "rather because many voters don't know either of us." Political pollster Brian Vargus of Indiana University–Purdue University at Indianapolis said the results were a bit of a mystery to him, and attributed it to "some kind of disaffection from the boll-weevil or anti-union vote. I suspect a lot of people don't know who this guy [Taylor] is. It's got to be an anti-Jontz vote."[15]

Economic issues formed the backbone of Jontz's effort to unseat Lugar. At the start of his campaign, he wrote a forty-page paper outlining the declining value of work. "People used to believe that if you did what you were supposed to—if you worked hard—you would be okay," Jontz said. "People don't believe that anymore. And they're worried." As he traveled the state, often driving himself to events in his truck, the ex-congressman tried to paint Lugar as a "Washington insider and an Indiana outsider," out of touch with average Hoosiers and sitting on the sidelines as the developing global economy threatened the U.S. economy. "Jobs are America's number one foreign policy concern," Jontz said. "No one in the country was better positioned [than Lugar] to see the growing strength of competition . . . and to signal the American people and Congress that we needed a new strategy to face global competition. Certainly what happened in Indiana demonstrates the consequences of failing to respond." He cited statistics showing that over a ten-year period from 1979 to 1989, an average family living in Indiana saw its income drop by more than $3,000, and that for 80 percent of Americans hourly wages declined from 1979 to 1991. While Jontz said the Clinton administration had done some good things for the economy, the recovery did not mean that all Americans were better off than they had been, as fewer than half of the jobs created were full-time, private-sector jobs, and these positions paid less and offered fewer benefits. Lugar's team discounted Jontz's economic stands as old fashioned tax-and-spend liberalism. Jontz did not shy away from the liberal label, if being a liberal meant "someone who cares about people and believes in protecting the environment and taxpayers."[16]

A golden retriever did, for a time, help to buttress Jontz's point about Lugar being out of touch with his home state. In a political advertisement, the Lugar campaign showed the senator, dressed in a flannel shirt, strolling through the approximately six hundred-acre farm he owned in southwestern Marion County. During the commercial, Lugar was seen bending down to scratch behind the ears what appeared to be his dog. The dog, however, was a stand in; Lugar's own golden retriever, Magnum, remained at home in Virginia. "The dog is a campaign volunteer," noted Martin W. Morris, Lugar's chief of staff. "It is not his dog." Morris added that it was deemed too expensive to fly Magnum to Indiana for the commercial's filming. Democrats pounced on the discrepancy, with Joel Leonard, Jontz's campaign manager, calling it "symbolic of him [Lugar] not being a Hoosier anymore." A frustrated Morris pointed out that the nuclear explosion that was in the commercial was also "not our nuclear explosion." Jontz also tried to capitalize on the issue with a last-minute advertisement of his own before Election Day that showed a mime twisting a long yellow balloon into the shape of a dog as a voiceover said Lugar was so out of touch he had to borrow a dog to make a commercial about his life in Indiana. "I wanted to get the message across with humor," Jontz noted. "There are so many differences between Jim Jontz and Dick Lugar that we should be able to have a discussion of the issues without the discussion getting out of hand." *Indianapolis Star* political reporter Mary Beth Schneider decried the scorched-earth style of most of the political advertisements in the 1994 campaign, but had kind words for the Senate race. She said most candidates as far behind in the polls as Jontz "would have been chucking the mud from Day One. Jontz attacked, but on issues and . . . with civility and humor."[17]

As he had with all of his previous campaigns, Jontz practiced a personal style of politics. Although he realized he could not knock on every door as he had done in the past, the self-described "Roads Scholar" vowed to knock on as many as possible to introduce himself and his program to voters. "I know this sort of personal attention works, has an impact," said Jontz. "I just wish there were more hours in the day." He traveled extensively, visiting county fairs, holding town meetings, and appearing in fourteen Fourth of July parades, always spending as little as possible to hoard funds to use for advertising, "We've got to do more with less, no doubt about it," said Jontz, who noted his campaign spent money on yard signs and brochures, but decided to skip buying bumper stickers to promote his candidacy. "I have people on my staff telling me I shouldn't travel at all, that I should spend all my time on the

Jontz on the campaign trail in the 1994 U.S. Senate race. In addition to hitting Lugar for his support of NAFTA, Jontz also called for a reorganization of spending priorities, noting that the federal government spent $100 billion a year on the North Atlantic Treaty Organization and only $25 billion a year on education.

phone raising money," Jontz told a reporter from the *Indianapolis News*. "I tell them that isn't politics. Politics is about getting out and talking to people." Those talks sometimes translated into financial help for the underdog candidate. After a speech he made before a convention of building and trade union members in Bloomington, where he made sure to point out Lugar's antiunion voting record, the workers passed the hat around the room and collected more than $4,000 in contributions for Jontz.[18]

Although the Jontz campaign had hoped for a series of debates around the state between their candidate and Lugar, only one such event was held on October 24 at the DePauw University Center for Contemporary Media in Greencastle. Answering questions from a media panel and some sent in by average Hoosiers, the two men stuck to the themes they had been exploring for the past several months. Lugar touted the gains made in the economy,

Jontz and Lugar shake hands at the candidates only debate at DePauw University in Greencastle, Indiana, on October 24, 1994. Sponsored by the League of Women Voters, the debate excluded the two others running for the Senate—Libertarian Party candidate Barbara Bourland and Indiana New Alliance/Patriot Party candidate Mary Catherine Barton.

while Jontz tried to reinforce his view that the senator had become out of touch with his Indiana constituents. After Lugar had commented on a *New York Times* article claiming two million jobs had been created in 1993, with 72 percent being high-paying jobs, Jontz pounced on the opportunity, saying to his opponent: "Don't tell us what your read in the *New York Times*. Tell us what you see here in Indiana." He went on to say that the new jobs being created in Indiana during the Clinton presidency paid $9,000 less per year than the old jobs they replaced, "but the problem today for so many Americans is they're working but not making a living." Both candidates expressed satisfaction with their performances during the one-hour debate, with Lugar noting, "I think I did pretty well tonight," and Jontz pointing out the two men were able to "give voters a clear choice." Although a few exchanges between the two turned testy, the debate remained cordial for the most part, with Lugar even commenting that he had recommended Jontz for a job with the Department of Agriculture after the congressman lost his re-election attempt in 1992. Jontz's barbs during the debate did get under Lugar's skin a bit, as he noted his opponent had been "less kind" to him than he anticipated. Asked later if he would still recommend Jontz for a job, Lugar laughed and told the media, "Well, I'd have to think about it." Jontz said after the debate that he "was grateful for the support the senator gave me."[19]

Behind both in the polls and in money raised, Jontz planned a final, desperate push for votes as he embarked on an attempt to visit all of the state's ninety-two counties in the ninety-two hours before Election Day. While Lugar spent time visiting schools in the Indianapolis area, Jontz began his whirlwind state tour at 10 p.m. Friday, November 4, in Michigan City, and hoped to be in Rising Sun at 6 a.m. on Tuesday, November 8, to cast his ballot before continuing his travels throughout the day. "There's something very poetic about starting out in Rising Sun," said Jontz in a car-telephone interview with a reporter from the *Bloomington Herald-Times*. "I've been in every county several times during the campaign. This is a means of reinforcing my focus on what's happening in Indiana and listening to the concerns of the average citizens." Already on his sixth driver, Jontz said he took catnaps during the trip to rest between stops. "As far as I know, no political candidate has tried to visit all 92 counties [during a campaign] before, so we'll be making history—win, lose or draw," he said. "This is the final push and I'm hanging in there."[20]

Jontz's last-ditch attempt failed to turn the tide and there was no storybook finish to his final political campaign. Lugar broke Indiana's fourth-term jinx for its U.S. senators and cruised to an easy victory, capturing 67.4 percent of the vote (1,039,625) to 30.5 percent for Jontz (470,799)—an impressive victory that fueled belief the senator might be a GOP presidential candidate in 1996. "We fought hard, but it wasn't enough," Jontz said. The 1994 election proved to be disastrous for other Hoosier Democrats as well, as incumbents Jill Long and Frank McCloskey lost their re-election attempts. Nationally, Republicans, capitalizing on the unpopularity of the Clinton administration during its first two years in office after bruising fights with Congress on health care and gun control, won a majority of seats in the U.S. House of Representatives for the first time in forty years and also captured the U.S. Senate. "On November 8 we got the living daylights beat out of us," Clinton later said. He added that Gingrich, the new Speaker of the House, had "proved a better politician than I was."[21]

The appalling results for the Democrats in the 1994 election had consequences for Jontz's career over and above the loss he suffered in the U.S.

Senate race. With the GOP's historic victory, Republicans set about to fill the promises their party had made in its "Contract with America," including a balanced budget, welfare reform, term limits for members of Congress, and tax cuts. GOP conservatives also set about introducing legislation seriously threatening a host of environmental measures, including clean air and water laws, wetlands, and particularly the Endangered Species Act. Passed with bipartisan support in 1973, the act, overseen by the U.S. Fish and Wildlife Service and the National Oceanic and Atmospheric Administration, had saved hundreds of species from extinction over the years. Under the act, no one could "harass, harm, pursue, hunt, shoot, wound, kill, trap, capture or collect" protected wildlife. Conservatives with the antienvironment "Wise Use" movement (property-right advocates, developers, ranchers, and their congressional allies) upset with excessive government regulations had circulated bogus horror stories about the ESA, including a man fined for killing a grizzly bear attacking him, spotted owls mating atop a Kmart store in southern Oregon, and a salamander responsible for flooding homes in California. "Wise Use" supporters viewed environmentalists as "Green Nazis" and "watermelons," green on the outside and red (Communist) on the inside, but used similar grassroots organizing techniques as conservationists to promote their cause. Those who attended "Wise Use" rallies in western states had a simple solution for those worried about federal authorities tracking them down for violating the ESA by harming threatened wildlife—"Shoot, Shovel, and Shut Up!"[22]

To help protect the ESA, Jontz moved back to Washington, D.C., in January 1995 to become director of the Endangered Species Coalition, an alliance of more than two hundred environmental groups of all sizes working together to help preserve the ESA from harmful changes by Congress. The National Audubon Society served as the coalition's sponsor, giving it office space and paying its staff. Jontz had experience in handling ESA issues during his time as a congressman. During his 1992 re-election campaign, he said the act had become an issue when Hoosier farmers raised fears that they could not tear down their barns if they needed to if an Indiana brown bat took up residence inside one. "When we checked with the Fish and Wildlife Service," Jontz recalled, "we were told that . . . they knew of no case where a farmer had this particular problem. I think that is the point in many cases with the ESA. There has been much misinformation about the ESA. And that has been unfortunate, because the experience of the ESA has been very positive in many cases." He noted that opponents of the act used phony anecdotes "as a crutch because the science community won't support their arguments. In the big picture most people understand this Endangered Species Act is the best law we have to protect the ecosystems we all depend on."[23]

As a former state legislator and congressman, Jontz, noted environmental activist Andy Kerr, brought to the coalition's directorship a political perspective that was often lacking in the conservation community. He had the ability, said Kerr, to frame issues, force debate, hire good staff, cajole, raise money, and, most important, inspire people. Jontz led, "where most others merely manage," Kerr added. Jontz ran a grassroots campaign to defend the ESA, communicating with activists around the country who used the information provided by the coalition to lobby their representatives in Congress. Roger Featherstone, a coalition staff member who had pushed for Jontz to be hired as the group's director, remembered during their time together he faced Jontz's ire only once. "I'd been in charge of setting up visits for Jim with activists during one of his road trips and had failed miserably," Featherstone remembered. "I learned the hard way that Jim just couldn't stand wasting time and that any spare minute that wasn't filled on the road (or just about anywhere) was wasted." Featherstone also discovered that Jontz traveled light, eschewing a suitcase as an unnecessary encumbrance. "A three- or four-day trip only required his battered leather brief bag and a suit," Featherstone said. "Jim sometimes multitasked during boring conference sessions by nodding off, although I rarely saw him miss the point of the discussion or go off track. He was usually too polite to butt in during a lively discussion—until frustration took over."[24]

Jontz had been leading the coalition for only a few months when a crisis threatened his new position. To help bring in additional support to save the ESA from its congressional critics, the coalition's major funder, the Pew Charitable Trusts, asked Jontz to come up with a intensive media campaign to go along with his grassroots approach, and wanted him to consider using the Environmental Information Center, which Pew also funded, to direct the operation. Along with the center's director, Phil Clapp, Jontz came up with a $600,000 budget for the effort to be covered by Pew with an additional $400,000 from other foundations, but the two men could not seem to see eye to eye on matters. When the coalition's steering committee in August sided with Jontz, Pew pulled its financial backing along with other foundations, forcing the committee to side with Clapp over Jontz. "Money was the deciding factor," Jontz said, and he and the other coalition staff

were fired by the Society the Friday before Labor Day. According to
Featherstone, Jontz faced the disaster with stoicism. "I took it kind of personal," said Featherstone, "while Jim just moved on. Jim and I are classic
Midwesterners. Protestant work ethic, no emotion allowed in public, stiff
upper lip, the whole nine yards. We both believed that we should forgive, but
never forget."[25]

Fortunately, for some of the coalition's staff, including Jontz, Featherstone, and Kerry Allen, another environmental group, the Defenders of
Wildlife, saw their worth and offered them office space and served as fiscal
agent for a new organization, the GrassRoots Environmental Effectiveness
Network. GREEN worked to provide information and offer assistance to
activists around the country striving to protect wildlife and the environment.
While Featherstone served as the organization's director, Jontz worked half
time as executive director of the Western Ancient Forest Campaign (later
known as the American Lands Alliance), which had been organized in 1991 to
build a national constituency to save old-growth forests in the Pacific Northwest, and half time for GREEN. "Jim's work week was about 100 hours, so that
half time from him was more production than most achieve fulltime," Featherstone noted. Shortly after GREEN had started its operations, Featherstone
learned how seriously Jontz took the issues he cared about. Jontz had refused
the business cards offered to him by Defenders because they had not been
printed in a union shop. On a trip to Madison, Wisconsin, Featherstone went
to a union print shop he knew and had the proper cards made. "I had grown
up on a dairy farm," said Featherstone, "so unions were not in my culture,
but after that, I think anything GREEN printed was union made." The group
produced a daily newsletter, *GREENLines*, written by Jontz and distributed by
Featherstone because he had the expertise when it came to computers and the
Internet. "Jim was always in a good mood, always industrious," Featherstone
recalled. "Always the sound of typing, of Jim on the phone—often both. His
wit and humor and memory for corny jokes or quotes was readily apparent
when someone dropped by his desk or met him in the break room." The two
men worked so late at night that they often missed the last Metro ride of the
evening and had to share a taxi to take them to their homes. "We did [it] so
often enough that we found the perfect spot (only one zone and equidistant
between his house and mine) for a cab to drop us off without wasting much
money," said Featherstone. He noted that Jontz lived a Spartan life and never
really volunteered much personal information to his colleagues. "I think that

to him, it had no bearing on what was important—the work of paying the rent by saving the planet," said Featherstone.[26]

The conservation community needed all the industrious sprit it could muster, as the Republicans in Congress did not share its devotion to environmental laws such as the ESA, especially one House member who Jontz had faced off against before—Congressman Don Young of Alaska. With the GOP takeover, Young had been named as the new chairman of the House Resources Committee (he had removed the word "Natural" from the committee's name). His allegiance to timber, mining, and the oil industries could be ascertained by visiting his office, which was adorned with a bear head and skin; the remains of a wolf, boar, and elk; and a large piece of the Trans-Alaska Pipeline. In September 1995 Young, with fellow Republican Richard Pombo, a California rancher, introduced a bill—House Resolution 2275—to substantially scale back the ESA's ability to protect endangered plants, animals, and fish, as well as providing compensation for private property owners for the loss of the use of their land due to species protection. A similar measure had been introduced in the U.S. Senate by Republican Slade Gorton of Washington. "People are terrified they are going to find an endangered species on their property and are destroying habitat before it becomes inhabited by these species," said Pombo. "This bill creates incentives to encourage property owners to host endangered species. It is better for both species and people than the current act." The measure was in part a response to a recent U.S. Supreme Court decision backing a rule by the Fish and Wildlife Service that "harm" under the ESA included significantly modifying an animal's habitat enough to injure or kill a protected species. The Young-Pombo bill defined harm as "direct action" against a species.[27]

Environmental organizations were quick to respond to the Young-Pombo legislation, which seemed to fly in the face of a recent National Academy of Sciences study that had found habitat protection to be critical to the survival of threatened or endangered species. Although it had originally been banned from doing any work on the ESA, one of GREEN's first jobs, noted Featherstone, involved putting together a field campaign to stop the House bill because of the group's expertise with that side of Congress, while Clapp's well-funded organization tackled the Senate. Once again, Jontz and his views on the ESA were heard in numerous newspaper articles on the controversy. He told reporters that the new legislation would roll back the progress made in saving species and ecosystems under the act for the past twenty-two years.

"Young and Pombo will take away from the American people one of the strongest conservation laws in the world," Jontz added. He also noted that interests that opposed the act—timber and mining companies and utilities—had always wanted to see the act weakened or eliminated. Experts at the Environmental Defense Fund noted that if the changes in the ESA were approved, protection would be hindered for such species as the bald eagle, sea turtle, whooping crane, and Rocky Mountain gray wolf. Jontz and the coalition had plenty of support for its campaign, as Democrats and moderate Republicans in the House worked to either modify or eliminate the most stringent aspects of the proposed legislation. The measure also faced opposition from the new House leader, Gingrich, who seemed reluctant to move ahead. "Gingrich has a bit of crinkle in his conservative ideology, and it is the environment," noted John Shanahan, an analyst with the conservative Heritage Foundation. "He is proud of his roots and for having marched in the first Earth Day." Members of Congress from the East, Midwest, and even the South, said Jontz, were beginning to "realize that Mr. Young and Mr. Pombo aren't very representative of the concerns in their districts."[28]

Disparate groups also came together to rally behind the ESA, which had enjoyed overwhelming public support since its passage. Even GOP pollsters discovered the public held strong views about defending the environment, with one finding 72 percent of those polled deemed the environment so important it should be protected "regardless of the cost," and another study finding 55 percent of all Republicans did not trust their own party when it came to preserving the environment. Religious groups and those involved in the medical profession took direct action to help save the ESA. A group called the Evangelical Environmental Network launched an advertising campaign that used Bible verses and portrayed the act as a modern-day version of Noah's Ark. "This is God's world and these are his creatures," noted Reverend Stan LeQuire, the network's director. To counteract the spurious claims of harm done by the ESA, physicians pointed to the benefits offered by nature, especially rare plants that could hold the cure to diseases. Keven Browngoehl, a pediatrician from a Philadelphia suburb, touted the story of his three-year-old patient Jackie Buckley, who had been diagnosed with leukemia. Browngoehl noted that Buckley was in remission thanks in part to Vincristine, a drug originally derived from the rosy periwinkle plant in Madagascar, and added that a third of all the drugs prescribed in the country came from plants or other natural products. One editorial spread the story of how the life of Senate

Majority Leader Bob Dole, Republican of Kansas, had been saved by a species of infection-fighting soil bacterium when he had been severely wounded as a soldier in World War II. A frustrated Young, who had called environmentalists "waffle-stomping, Harvard-graduating, intellectual bunch of idiots," saw the writing on the wall and realized his legislation had a slim chance of being enacted. Young said he should have listened to the advice of Congressman Doc Hastings, a Republican from Washington, who had urged him to repeal the ESA "right quick before anybody realized what had happened."[29]

As Jontz continued to work to successfully save the ESA from evisceration (the Young-Pombo bill failed to make its way through the legislative process), another environmental crisis, this one involving his longtime interest in the ancient forests of the Pacific Northwest, drew him to commit an act of civil disobedience. The fate of old-growth forests had seemed to be settled after President Clinton had organized a forest summit in April 1993 in Portland, Oregon, with environmentalists and logging interests to craft a plan suitable for both parties. The ensuing Northwest Forest Plan restricted the amount of lumber to be cut from some twenty-four million acres of federal land in Washington, Oregon, and northern California to protect the habitat of the endangered northern spotted owl, salmon, and other species, as well as promising a sustainable amount of timber for the logging industry and more than a billion dollars in economic aids to communities affected by the restrictions. The plan received approval from U.S. District Judge William Dwyer of Seattle, who had issued an injunction banning logging in the region. Brock Evans, at the time with the National Audubon Society, said that in one sweeping stroke the plan had reduced annual logging rates downward across the board by about 85 percent from what they had been. "Most of us who had actually participated in the daily struggles thought we had 'won'—won as much as the political system of the times allowed . . . and then some," Evans recalled.[30]

Unfortunately, Clinton's bold plan for the Pacific Northwest was derailed by the GOP-controlled House. Western lawmakers had huddled with industry supporters to once again open up ancient forests to logging. A "salvage rider" to a must-pass appropriations bill that included funding for disaster relief for victims of the bombing of the federal building in Oklahoma City and reductions in spending, finally signed by Clinton in July 1995 after an initial presidential veto, allowed for one year the removal on public lands controlled by the Forest Service and U.S. Bureau of Land Management of any "dead, damaged or down" trees and exempted such logging from most environmental laws as the National Forest Management Act, the National Environmental Policy Act, and the ESA, as well as court rulings and public appeals. Sponsored by Congressman Charles Taylor, a Republican from South Carolina, in the House and Gorton in the Senate, the rider, which had been produced by the timber industry and had not been debated openly in Congress, ushered in an era of what environmentalists called "logging without laws." Timber companies were being allowed by the U.S. Forest Service to harvest healthy trees along with ones damaged by fire, disease, or insects. U.S. Senator Bill Bradley, a Democrat from New Jersey, said the measure essentially gave the Forest Service carte blanche to cut down as salvage "all trees made of wood." The adoption of Clinton's forest plan, noted Adam Berger of the Sierra Club Legal Defense Fund, while it had not pleased everyone, did signal "the end to a very painful period." The salvage rider had reopened old wounds, Berger said, creating "a very divisive and unnecessary step backward." Jontz termed the situation "a disaster," as everything that had been learned about logging in the West "had been thrown out the window. This is the old style, clear-cuts the Forest Service said they'd never do again. It's the destruction of fish, the pollution of waterways, the imperilment of wildlife, the liquidation of the last and best of our forests." He later lambasted the broadened definition of what constituted salvage, saying under their terms "you could sell your desk," and seemed to include anything that was "dead or dying or associated with dead wood."[31]

With their access to a legal remedy blocked and facing a hostile Republican Congress, environmentalists turned to civil disobedience. Activists ranging in fervor from the radical environmental advocacy group Earth First! to officials from national conservation organizations, from hardcore activists to grandmothers, sat in trees and blocked forest roads denying access by loggers to the timber they wanted throughout the West, with protests organized in Idaho, Montana, Colorado, New Mexico, and especially Oregon. The actions of what Jontz called a Congress that cared "very little for the environment" pushed him to join those who were in danger of being arrested to save the forests they loved. "Everything I worked for in the Congress, and everything we accomplished to protect the last of these great forests is now at risk," said Jontz, who saw protesting the logging going on as his duty and a way to show the public the salvage rider's terrible effects. By risking arrest, activists were putting "a human face on the issue," he said. Because environmentalists could not appeal the sales through the courts, Jontz pointed out, their only route was "the court of public opinion. The Earth is our home. These cathedral groves

COURTESY MARY LEE TURK

Jontz (at left) and Brock Evans (right) are handcuffed and wait to be dragged off during an October 1995 protest at the Siskiyou National Forest in Oregon.

don't grow back in a day and [are] part of the complex natural system we don't understand. I am the conservative in these debates saying we should be careful. This is a moral issue. It is spiritual."[32]

On Monday, October 30, Jontz, wearing on his business suit his congressional lapel pin, was one of three hundred people gathered to protest the Sugarloaf timber sale at the Siskiyou National Forest in southwestern Oregon. "There is nothing to do to stop Sugarloaf," Jontz said of that timber sale, but there was still time to "insist Congress stop the assault on our environmental laws." Along with the ex-congressman, others acting out that day against the 9.5 million board feet of timber being harvested by the Boise Cascade Corporation included Evans, Charlie Ogle of the Sierra Club, and Mike Roselle, cofounder of Earth First! According to Evans's account of the arrest, he and Jontz were in a group of about a hundred protestors who marched down a remote logging road to a barrier erected by the timber company. As the group sang protest songs, including "We Shall Overcome," Josephine County sheriff deputies and Forest Service officers appeared and ordered the group to move, but they refused and just sang louder, Evans remembered. "A CNN television crew showed up, and the timber people backed away from arresting us immediately—bad publicity," he said. "They knew, as we did, that this time the TV image would be of the 'suits' [being arrested]—especially that of a former congressman!"

Law enforcement at the site decided to wait the protestors out and retreated behind a bend in the road behind which stood the forest to be cut down. When television crews said if there was to be no action they would probably have to leave, Jontz decided to force the issue. "He did a most courageous thing—so typical of him, and his commitment," Evans recalled. "He stood up, walked around the gate, and up the road. The sheriffs then had to approach him, had to stop *this* trespass. Still in plain view, as the law officers approached him, Jim fell limp—as we had been trained to do—and the officers dragged him off, around that bend." Evans and the others followed suit and were hauled away one by one as the television crews captured it on tape for a nationwide viewing audience. "Now the whole nation knew what was really at stake in their forests. I like to think of that arrest (and many others like it) as the beginning of the end for that atrocious and wrongful 'logging without laws rider,' which was soon after strongly attacked in the media, [and] allowed to lapse the following year," said Evans.

Brian Vincent, a veteran of environmental protests who worked with Jontz at the WAFC, had always respected the law enforcement personnel he dealt with during a variety of protests over the years, and realized the difficult spot many of them were in when it came to dealing with these types of protests. He remembered Sugarloaf, however, as "probably the most frightening action I've been a part of, and I've been in some actions that have been pretty nerve-racking." Vincent, Jontz, Evans, and others involved that day might have been tipped off that they faced a possible tough time when noticing the patches on the uniforms of the county officers had on them a logging truck. Those arrested were dragged away out of view of the media, handcuffed, and chained together. One of the first arrested, Vincent remembered an officer screaming at him to get down on his knees while pointing a shotgun at his head; he quickly complied with the order. They were chained together for many hours, and Vincent remembered one young protester, twelve or thirteen years old, had to go to the bathroom and the officers made her urinate in front of everybody. "I thought they treated Brock and Jim more harshly than anyone else," said Vincent, perhaps because of their prominence in the environmental community. Evans remembered being "heaved bodily" into the back of a pickup before being chained to his fellow protesters, and noted thirteen hours passed as "our captors hauled us, about eight at a time, younger ones first, down to the Josephine County Jail, sixty miles away, in a little police van. By the time they got to the 'older men,' Jim and I were among the very few left. We were hauled into the van too, persuaded our guards to at least let our hands be cuffed in front, not in back."[33]

Those arrested for trespassing arrived at the county jail in Grants Pass, Oregon, the county seat of Josephine County, about two in the morning. After undergoing initial processing, the protesters were herded together into an upstairs holding cell. They sought sleep wherever they could find it, with Evans using his shoes as a pillow as he stretched out on the cold, cement floor. "But not Jim," said Evans. "He walked about that 'tank,' engaging each one of us in turn, talking, reminiscing, making sure we were all okay—by his example, ensuring that no one else need be afraid, either. So typical of Jim was this quiet, unassuming courage, no matter what the situation. The best and most inspiring kind of courage, I have always thought." Vincent had been "pretty rattled by the experience," but had been calmed by the inspirational support offered by both Evans and Jontz. "A lot of people looked up to Jim—for good reasons," Vincent said. "He kept people's spirits up." Upon their release from jail later that morning, the protesters were greeted by a cheering crowd of supporters who had kept a vigil outside. Roselle told reporters this protest was significant because it had received support from national environmental groups. "When we talked about these issues before, the national environmental groups would run for cover," he said. "Now they are getting arrested with us." A spokesman for the timber industry, Barry Polsky of the American Forest and Paper Association, called the demonstrations "more of a nuisance than anything. . . . These harvests are necessary because private forests cannot support the American public's demand for wood and paper."[34]

On January 18, 1996, Jontz repeated his direct action against cutting in old-growth forests when he and approximately twenty-five demonstrators were arrested for trespassing as they protested the logging by private timber companies of approximately 204,000 trees, mostly Douglas firs, at the Umpqua National Forest near Roseburg, Oregon. Jontz, Ogle, and other activists, who were issued citations and released after walking onto the porch of an off-limits ranger station, argued that the logging threatened to allow sediment to pollute waterways where cutthroat and steelhead trout and coho salmon lived. "People are compelled to take personal action because, as citizens, we

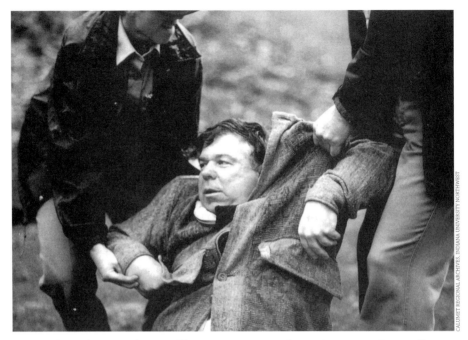

Jontz is dragged away and arrested by U.S. Forest Service law enforcement officers Kelly Wright and Dale Walker for participating in a 1996 protest at the Umpqua National Forest near Roseburg, Oregon. One forest activist remembered Jontz as someone willing "to put his body on the line" to protest the logging of ancient forests, but also someone "willing to negotiate and to compromise without abandoning his principles, the forests, or the workers."

have no recourse" under the new law, Jontz said after his arrest. Speaking to the protesters, Jontz noted that repealing the rider and saving threatened species was a matter of justice calling environmentalists to bear witness much as Martin Luther King Jr. had done for the civil rights movement. "The only thing that is possibly fair is to save the five percent of ancient forests that remain," said Jontz.[35]

In addition to his acts of civil disobedience, Jontz used the skills he had learned during a lifetime in politics to derail the salvage rider through both the legislative process and executive branch action. In December 1995 Jontz persuaded Elizabeth Furse, a Democrat from Oregon, to introduce a bill in the House to repeal the salvage rider and reinstate all applicable environmental laws (a similar bill was introduced in the Senate by Bradley and Barbara Boxer, a Democrat from California). "We were told over and over again that the [law] was an emergency measure to remove dead and dying trees to protect the health of our forests," said Furse. "But instead, it is being used to clear-cut healthy forests, some as old as 500 years." She said she did not oppose logging, as long as it was conducted in compliance with environmental laws. "State and private citizens must comply with state forest laws," Furse told a House task force considering the issue. "Why cannot the Federal Government do the same on Federal Lands?" Gorton, who had worked in the Senate to free up timber sales, slammed Furse's proposal, saying it demonstrated the "total indifference some members feel to the thousands of families throughout the Northwest who have been unemployed for years on end." The Washington senator said the salvage rider was about one thing and one thing only—jobs. Republican leaders in the House stonewalled efforts to bring Furse's rider repeal up for a vote, but her effort to kill funding for the salvage logging came within two votes of passing.[36]

Those working against the salvage rider had better luck in slowing logging by pressuring the Clinton administration. At a conference at Southern Oregon College in February 1996, Jontz had told the three hundred in attendance that those in the environmental community needed to make the White House "feel a lot more pain. This is President Clinton's forest rider. He signed it into law. He knew better—or perhaps he got some bad advice." Clinton had come to rue the day he approved the legislation, especially the "unintended and unwarranted consequence of the way the timber rider has been carried out." Vice President Gore called the rider's passage the administration's "biggest mistake." To keep the pressure up, Jontz asked his staff at the WAFC to document all of the timber sales in roadless areas on public lands in the salvage rider. These areas served as critical habitat for animals such as lynx, grizzly bears, salmon, trout and other species requiring large tracts of undisturbed wilderness. "The unprotected roadless areas of our National Forests provide quality drinking water, outstanding fish and wildlife habitat and unique recreation opportunities for millions of Americans," noted Jontz, who added it was time the Forest Service to stop logging these ecosystems and protect them for future generations. At first, recalled Steve Holmer, WAFC's campaign coordinator, the staff thought Jontz "was crazy because this was a massive project that involved documenting over 150 pending roadless sales." Using its grassroots network of forest monitors across the country, however, the organization was able to put together a report it could use to sway officials in Washington to take some action. On July 2 Dan Glickman, Secretary of Agriculture, the department that oversaw the Forest Service, issued a directive to tighten restrictions on timber sales under the salvage rider to make sure those trees harvested were actually due to emergency situations such as to combat insect infestations or for fire control. In addition, his order prohibited salvage logging in roadless areas and reduced road building on public lands. Although environmentalists were wary about the administration's true intentions, the timber industry protested Glickman's action, with an industry spokesman saying the ruling would bring salvage logging around the country to a "screeching halt."[37]

Environmentalists also won victories in 1998 when the Clinton administration instituted a moratorium on building new logging roads on about thirty-three million acres of national forests, and saw the defeat of a bill by Congressman Bob Smith, Republican from Oregon and chairman of the House Agriculture Committee. Called the Forest Recovery and Protection Act, Smith's legislation came under fire from conservation groups that saw its call to cut dead and dying timber to help with fire and disease control as a Trojan horse for more logging on public lands by timber firms. The bill allowed logging in roadless areas, streamside riparian areas, and old-growth forests. An emboldened Clinton administration opposed Smith's bill, threatening a veto if it passed. Glickman told the congressman in a letter it was unacceptable, particularly because it expanded forest restoration programs then in place to also include commercial logging. "The administration strongly opposes the bill's funding mechanism, which turns an existing restoration-type fund—the Roads and Trails Fund—into a commercial timber harvesting program, that would include salvage and thinning of timber in entire forests," wrote Glickman.[38]

For several weeks, according to Holmer, Jontz camped out in the offices of Congressman Sherwood Boehlert, a moderate Republican from upstate New York who had been a major figure in acid rain provisions in the 1990 Clean Air Act amendments, to "pursue and amendment strategy to moderate this bad logging bill." Fortunately for the bill's opponents, Western lawmakers overreached when the bill came up for a vote on March 27. "When the floor debate took place, we were prepared to see Representative Boehlert's moderating amendment pass, but then the Smith logging bill to also be approved," said Holmer. "However, during the floor debate, Representatives [Helen] Chenoweth and [J. D.] Hayworth offered an unexpected amendment to ensure the logging bill also applied to roadless areas. This wasn't part of the deal, and Representative Boehlert stood to oppose their amendment." When Hayworth referred during the debate to Boehlert as "the devil," Holmer added, the New

York representative spoke out forcefully against both the roadless amendment and the bill itself. Democrats and moderate Republicans from the East Coast banded together to send the Smith bill down to defeat by a 201 to 181 vote. "Their greed so overwhelmed them that they couldn't help themselves," noted Mike Francis, forest director for the Wilderness Society, "and they offered the amendment that brought about their own destruction." An elated Ken Rait, conservation director for the Oregon Natural Resources Council, said Smith tried to "peddle a logging industry bill as a forest health initiative, but Congress wasn't buying it."[39]

The battle over old-growth forests continues to this day. As Kerr noted in a 2011 interview, "to this day, ancient forests of the Pacific Northwest are not protected by statute." For Jontz, however, his interests soon turned to the issues he had tackled while fighting against NAFTA, especially curbing the worst excesses of global corporations when it came to average working people. "People power," he noted, "not corporate power." The economy had evolved over the years to become dominated by giant companies that dwarfed even the size and power of some countries and they had an agenda they aggressively pursued to "make anything they want, anywhere they want to, and sell it anywhere they want for as much money as they can," said Jontz. To counterbalance corporations' attempts to move their operations overseas, rollback environmental safeguards, and grab tax concessions that threatened a community's ability to have enough funds to education their children, Jontz worked once again to unite in common cause two groups he had been a champion for throughout his career—union members and environmentalists. "Workers and environmentalists are affected by the same corporate powers," Jontz noted. "We're all part of a global economy that isn't friendly to our interests." It would turn out, however, to be Jontz's final battleground.[40]

8

The Last Hurrah

The streets of downtown Seattle, Washington, were treated to a rare sight in the early afternoon of Monday, November 29, 1999. As delegates settled in for the start of meetings at the Third Ministerial Conference of the World Trade Organization, the entity that works to deregulate international trade, they could see from their hotel windows a large crowd of protesters marching toward the Washington State Convention and Trade Center and rallying behind the slogan to "Make Trade Clean, Green and Fair!" Mixed in with union members, environmentalists, street theater performers, and other activists were approximately 240 people clad in cardboard costumes representing endangered sea turtles—the creation of Seattle activist Ben White, who came up with the idea while soaking in his bathtub. A WTO tribunal had ruled that the United States' Endangered Species Act, which had required shrimp boats to use nets with devices to help sea turtles escape being caught in them, constituted an unfair trade practice. Before the march started, White told those who wore the costumes, "Comport yourself as a turtle. Turtles are ancient repositories of wisdom. They never fight back. We're representing them. We owe it to the turtles to be their voice." The turtles were a hit, uniting in a common cause union members (blue) and environmentalists (green). One longshoreman hoisted a sign during the protest reading, "Teamsters and Turtles Together at Last!" Nancy Pennington, a Seattle animal rights supporter, was one of those who helped make the turtle outfits and donned one for the WTO protests. "I think they were very effective," said Pennington. "We made a statement without hurting anyone. . . . People didn't react in a negative way. But I think it was still a forceful statement about what the WTO is doing to the environment by superseding national laws."[1]

Antiglobalization protesters managed to shut down the WTO meetings on Tuesday, November 30, as thousands took to the streets in what came to be known as the Battle in Seattle. Police responded to the demonstration with force, using pepper spray and tear gas and shooting some of those who had come from around the world to have their voices heard with rubber bullets. Peaceful for the most part (a small group of black-clad anarchists did smash windows and deface the stores of such corporate giants as McDonalds, the Gap, and Nike), the demonstration had made a little-known organization (the WTO) a household word. The upheaval also inspired further protests in subsequent years against such groups as the World Bank and the International Monetary Fund, as well as demonstrations at the Republican and Democratic national conventions in 2000 and 2004. "Before Seattle, we were dead in the water on trade," George Becker, president of the United Steelworkers of America, told a *Time* magazine reporter. "The big companies had their way completely. Now we've raised the profile of this issue, and we're not going back."[2]

Months before the WTO meetings, Jim Jontz and leaders of other environmental groups had warned what might happen if the organization expedited efforts to ease trade in forest products or weakened environmental laws when it met in Seattle. "Our forests don't need more logging," Jontz told reporters after a three-day meeting of environmentalists from around the world in June 1999 in Leavenworth, Washington. "In fact, they need stronger protection." He later predicted that if tariffs were lowered, demand would rise for forest products such as plywood from Indonesia and other low-cost producing nations. "This is the last place in the world where you want to increase logging," Jontz said of Indonesia, citing its lax environmental regulations and the threat increased logging posed to tropical rainforests.[3]

For Jontz, who found refuge from the chaos on the streets of Seattle on the couch at the home of a friend's sister, the demonstrations were a watershed for union and environmental activists. "We saw all of a sudden what the potential was if we combined our efforts," he noted. The demonstrations had shown people that the issue was not about fair trade, Jontz added, but the threat posed by multinational corporations. "The promise of Seattle—that a progressive alliance of 'Teamsters and turtles' could sidetrack the WTO and replace a corporate-driven economic agenda with a global economy in which people and the environment come first—can still be realized," Jontz said. "In fact, it must be achieved if citizens globally are to have any chance to protect what they value most."[4]

Scenes from the protests in Seattle, Washington, from November 29 to December 3, 1999—members of the International Brotherhood of Teamsters on a protest march (top), police in riot gear surround two protestors (right), and a closer view of the turtle costumes worn by activists at demonstrations (bottom).

To help create "a world where nature is protected, workers are respected, and corporate greed is rejected," Jontz, who had moved to Portland, Oregon, in 1999 (living first in a house on Sauvie Island along the Columbia River and later in an apartment on North East Russell Street), left the American Lands Alliance to become executive director of the Alliance for Sustainable Jobs and the Environment. The ASJE had been formed before the WTO meeting in Seattle when environmentalists from such groups as the Sierra Club, Friends of the Earth, and Jontz's American Lands Alliance joined with teacher, public employee, postal, steel, and food union members to fight a common foe—the Maxxam Corporation and its CEO Charles Hurwitz. On May 19 environmental and labor leaders confronted Hurwitz in Houston, Texas, to demand that his corporation, which included Kaiser Aluminum that had locked out steelworkers in five cities and Pacific Lumber that had clear-cut ancient redwood trees in the Headwaters Forest in Humboldt County in Northern California, be held accountable for its unfair labor practices and damages to the environment. Grassroots environmental activists and rank-and-file union members, noted David Foster, then director of United Steelworkers District 11, quickly realized they had more in common than they had differences and began to work together to push "a vision of overall labor and environmental collaboration in the global economy." In its "Houston Principles," the ASJE pledged to seek stricter enforcement of labor laws and advocate for new measures to guarantee working people the right to form unions and bargain collectively; demand that global trade agreements include enforceable environmental and labor standards; and make workplaces, communities, and the planet safer by reducing waste and greenhouse gas emissions. "Our mission is to tear down the corporate-drive myth that jobs and a healthy environment don't mix," said David R. Brower, former director of the Sierra Club, a beloved figure in the ecology movement, and a key force behind the ASJE's formation.[5]

In his efforts on behalf of the ASJE, Jontz maintained his usual busy schedule. He could be found back home in Indiana, speaking to union members in South Bend about the dangers of new free-trade agreements such as the proposed Free Trade Area of the Americas (an attempt at creating what he called a North American Free Trade Agreement "for the whole hemisphere"), as well as appearing in Evansville to accuse the AK Steel plant in Rockport of "discharging million of pounds of toxics just miles upstream of where Evansville gets its drinking water." In his new home in Portland, Jontz and the ASJE campaigned against a steel mill that had locked out members of the United

Steelworkers of America, filing suit against the company for violations of the Clean Air Act and trying to ensure it could not get a piece of contracts for a public transportation project in the community. Time and time again he spoke to public interest groups working on issues he cared about. At a meeting of Indiana's Citizens Action Coalition (Jontz was a lifetime CAC board member), he called upon activists to build their power and strength to convince politicians "that if they're going to save our workers, the environment, and our family farms, they cannot vote for a global corporate economic agenda and sacrifice all of the things we care about in the name of corporate profits. That's really what this is all about." Confronted with the argument that groups such as the ASJE's statements sounded isolationist, Jontz said the organization was not out to halt global commerce, but instead sought trade agreements with real "teeth" in them to protect the rights of everyday workers and the environment.[6]

Foster, today director of the BlueGreen Alliance, a national partnership of labor unions and environmental organizations, noted that in its early days the ASJE struggled with figuring out how to be both a rank-and-file membership organization, but also win institutional support from both the labor and environmental movements. The organization, he noted, fought to maintain the vibrant grassroots activism that had been engendered by its fight with the Maxxam Corporation on the Headwaters Forest issue and the Kaiser Aluminum union lockout, and to establish institutional support from national labor and environmental institutions. Dan Leahy, a faculty member at Evergreen State College in Olympia, Washington, who eventually took over as ASJE director, recalled that it was barely an organization in any formal way. "Jontz to me," said Leahy, "was a master of moving within this non-formal arena to keep the possibilities of different alliances going."[7]

In addition to traveling around the country speaking to meetings and conferences spreading the word about the ASJE's mission and trying to find financial backing for the group, Jontz took a nonpaying position representing one of the nation's leading liberal lobbying organizations—Americans for Democratic Action. Founded in 1947 by such progressive icons as Eleanor Roosevelt, Reinhold Niebuhr, Arthur Schlesinger Jr., John Kenneth Galbraith, and Walter Reuther to reconstruct a "liberal movement free of totalitarian influence from either the Left or the Right," the ADA had over the years lobbied on behalf of civil rights, antipoverty programs, national health care, increases to the minimum wage, and limitations on political contributions. As Reuther told the

Former Indiana congressman Jim Jontz leads a 2003 workshop. Even when leading discussions, Jontz always had time for old friends, sometimes stopping his speeches to greet them if they walked into a room.

conference at which the organization was formed, its watchword "must not be back to the New Deal but forward from the New Deal."[8]

Elected by its members to serve as ADA's national president in 1998, Jontz contrasted the economic realities of 1947 with those dealt with by average citizens as he took office as president. He noted that the economy near the start of the twenty-first century was dominated by giant companies with a specific agenda. "They want to make anything they want, anywhere they want to, and sell it anywhere they want for as much money as they can," he told the ADA members at the group's fifty-first annual convention in Washington, D.C., on June 13, 1998. Jontz added that companies would "move factories overseas, support authoritarian regimes, lobby to roll back those pesky worker and environmental safeguards here in the U.S. because of competition off shore. They will extract tax concessions from local and state governments, making it impossible for cities and states to raise the revenue they need to educate our kids." Part of the ADA's mission during his four years as president, and his subsequent service as president emeritus, would be to let people know "it isn't labor unions or the environmentalists or the welfare recipients who are causing this giant race to the bottom of lower wages and lower environmental safeguards. . . . This is the agenda of the multinational corporations."[9]

Amy Isaacs, ADA's national director, who had suggested Jontz for the president position, had met him when he was first running for Congress in 1986 and a friend of hers who had worked with state legislators said Jontz would be someone to watch in the years to come. Isaacs was impressed by Jontz's willingness to take on difficult issues, even given the tough district he served, his ability to articulate his goals and ideas, and his abilities "to look at a problem and find ways to solve it that were sometimes unusual." The role of the president in the ADA depended upon the person, said Isaacs. She described Jontz as "extremely effective" during his two years in office, as he attended all the meetings, participated in all decisions and discussions, helped to formulate policy and come up with program ideas, and aided in fund-raising. "The organization has always been strongest when we've had active and involved presidents and he was the perfect example of that," said Isaacs. In essence, she said, he became an adjunct staff member for ADA.[10]

A change in presidential administrations in 2000 from Democrat Bill Clinton to Republican George W. Bush only intensified Jontz's efforts to spread the word about the dangers to American laborers from unfettered international trade agreements and the importance of unions to the fight for social justice. Unions were necessary, he said, not only because of what bad employers did to workers, but also because unions were a "prerequisite to workers being treated fairly in the workplace, good employers or bad." He told an ADA conference in May 2000 that American society could not have social or economic justice unless unions were strong. "We are not going to win our battles over health care, over housing, over education, we are not going to achieve *any* of the causes for which we are fighting, without unions," said Jontz, who became ADA president emeritus in 2000. As part of his work with the ADA, Jontz set out about a year before the important Iowa caucuses to convince those Democrats seeking their party's presidential nomination to take on Bush in the 2004 election to support rules in future trade pacts that served the "values and interests of workers, consumers, and the environment—not just investors and multinational corporations."[11]

The ADA's Regime Change 2004 project, which Jontz headed, attempted to convince potential presidential candidates to oppose trade deals such as NAFTA and organizations such as the WTO. With nine Democratic candidates vying for their party's presidential nomination, Jontz saw a unique opportunity to push against the global trade agenda, especially when it came to a move by multinational corporations to protect their investments in the service economy, including education, health care, public services, construction, transportation, water supply, waste disposal, and electricity generation. Businesses seek to use new trade agreements to pursue privatization and deregulation, he said, by "moving these issues from the public policy arena to a trade regime where decisions are made like commercial disputes; i.e., by lawyers behind closed doors, where our power can't reach." Of course, Jontz knew that some of the candidates would attempt to dodge the issue, because as long as they could "court Microsoft and Boeing and GE [General Electric], while all along telling us how much they support the interests of workers and the environment, they will." The time had come, he said, for voters to ask themselves if the country's next president would continue to pursue a "failed NAFTA model for global integration, or develop a new model that better protects the interests of workers, the environment, and human rights?"[12]

Jontz displayed the same dogged determination in pursuing candidates as he had during his own campaigns. On a trip to Mason City, Iowa, he attempted to track down any labor leader who might ask U.S. Senator John Kerry of Massachusetts, one of the Democratic frontrunners for the presidential nomination, a question about trade at a televised town meeting hosted by U.S. Senator Tom Harkin of Iowa. Although a couple of "bigger fish" were unavailable, Jontz did find a union president for a cement factory in Mason City. "I camped out at a bar near his house, and left a series of messages on his home phone . . . and his cell phone," he said. "Finally, I found him and persuaded him to let me buy his dinner at the bar." Although the union man was at first reluctant to be the "point guy" to ask Kerry about trade, he relented and asked the question at the town meeting. "Kerry gave such a lousy answer," said Jontz, "it depressed us both." Fortuitously, because all the other candidates were ready with answers that were satisfactory to the ADA, Jontz was able to focus his efforts on Kerry, "and before long, we saw a 'new' John Kerry on the stump. The week before the Iowa caucus, we got a statement from him on trade that met all of our basic requests."[13]

Roger Featherstone, Jontz's former colleague with the Endangered Species Coalition, remembered running into him during this time at the Minneapolis airport. Featherstone was on his way back to Washington, D.C., from a trip to Anchorage, Alaska, while Jontz was "on a hellish schedule in the Midwest and Northeast trying to make the candidates address blue-green issues as part of their campaigns." Featherstone did not know how many cities Jontz had on his itinerary, but recalled that Jontz mentioned he had never before had traveled so much. The chance meeting also offered Featherstone an opportunity to learn more about his environmental comrade. "The baseball season was winding down toward the World Series and Jim was distracted by a game on an airport television screen," said Featherstone. "I realized that after all the time

I had known Jim and how much time we worked side by side, I had no idea he was a baseball fanatic."[14]

With Kerry's nomination as the Democratic presidential challenger to Bush in 2004, Jontz redoubled his efforts to hold the Republican president responsible for job losses and a weak economy by spreading the message in key states. Beginning in late July, the ADA hired ten organizers in eight states to start community-based education campaigns in fifty communities that had been affected by trade-related jobs losses. Using the theme "Stop Outsourcing Our Future," organizers held town meetings in such cities as Mansfield, Ohio (thirteen meetings were held in Ohio cities alone); Beloit, Wisconsin; Muscatine, Iowa; and Saint Joseph, Missouri. "There were fewer election-related resources in these communities, the lure of the GOP on social issues was stronger, and the loss of manufacturing jobs from trade was more visible," explained Jontz, who noted that they also supported community leaders in building a local infrastructure for networking and education. The ADA's Regime Change project attempted to reveal that the Bush administration's trade policies had not only encouraged companies to move their jobs overseas, but also undermined wages and benefits for workers at home. "We offered not just small-bore policy ideas, but a vision of a world where government becomes 'an instrument of fairness' by replacing the failed NAFTA model with new trade rules that end the 'race to the bottom,' and insure that workers share the benefits of global commerce," said Jontz.

Following Kerry's loss to Bush in the fall election, Jontz reflected that in hindsight, the ADA's campaign had been "much too modest" to obtain the votes needed for a Democratic victory. There were some successes in targeted areas. In Maine's Second Congressional District, the Regime Change project conducted six town meetings and a media tour, making it the group's most concentrated effort. "Perhaps we helped Kerry win this district—and one electoral vote—where job losses from trade are highly visible," Jontz said, "and where Congressman Mike Michaud strongly reinforced our message about the links between Bush trade policy and local mill closings." In Iowa, Kerry won six of the seven communities the ADA targeted in a "Stop Trading Away Iowa" campaign, and in the seventh, Marshalltown, Kerry actually improved the vote total of Al Gore during the 2000 presidential election. "However, we lacked the time and resources to connect with the number of undecided voters who could have moved Ohio, Iowa, or any other state, from red to blue," Jontz said, concluding that organizers should have been in place doing their work three years before Election Day, not three months before.[15]

The work Jontz did in the 2004 Democratic presidential primaries and election did lead to one of his most enduring legacies as a political activist—the ADA's Working Families Win project (Jontz became its director and a paid ADA staff member with health benefits). Don Kusler, then ADA's communications director, called the project an empowerment program centering on issues that united, rather than divided, people. Usually, these were people who had never before been involved with politics or policy issues, noted Kusler, who today is WFW's project director. Under the program, the ADA targeted eleven House races in seven states held by Republican representatives that Jontz believed could be turned into wins for proworker candidates in the 2006 congressional election (WFW was also involved in U.S. Senate races in Ohio and Pennsylvania). Officially nonpartisan, the project sought to change the political behavior of swing voters in small and mid-sized communities in battleground states through educational efforts—what Jontz referred to as a volunteer driven, pocketbook based "neighbor to neighbor" persuasion campaign—on such issues as raising the minimum wage, implementing fair trade, and pushing for universal health care. "It wasn't talking at people," said Kusler, "it was talking with people." For the 2006 effort, WFW organizers knocked on forty thousand doors, held twenty-two town hall meetings on worker issues, sponsored twenty-six candidate forums, organized four hundred house meetings to recruit volunteers, and made more than sixty thousand get-out-the-vote contacts through either e-mail or telephone calls.[16]

Working alongside Jontz in the WFW program was a former Democratic congressional candidate, Christine A. Cegelis. In 2004 Cegelis had run a spirited, if losing, campaign against Republican incumbent Henry Hyde in Illinois's Sixth Congressional District. She tried again in 2006, but lost in the Democratic primary to L. Tammy Duckworth. Cegelis met Jontz through the Chicago chapter of the ADA, and the two got together during one of his visits to the city. "It was clear that we shared common goals and Jim worked really hard to help me in my second run for Congress," Cegelis recalled. "He spent a lot of time talking up my candidacy to labor and others in an effort to help me get through the primary." Jontz offered her advice and also introduced her to several members of Congress, including Ohio congresswoman Marcy Kaptur. On Primary Election Day he came to the Illinois district to knock on doors on

Cegelis's behalf. "He said that was what he liked to do best," she noted, as he enjoyed the face-to-face contact with voters.[17]

After Cegelis lost in the Democratic primary, Jontz got in touch with her and told her he needed a national coordinator and "general IT [information technology] guru" for the WFW program. Lead organizers were also hired for each of the targeted districts. Cegelis kept in direct contact with these organizers, charting their contacts—telephone calls, knocking on doors, town meetings, and house meetings—via a central computer database. The program concentrated on districts where there were very slim margins between the two political parties, targeting about three thousand voters in each. Through research, Cegelis noted, they knew that it took multiple contacts with a voter to get them to hear the WFW message, which, in the end, was spread by approximately forty workers across the country supported by between fifty and 250 volunteers in each district (48 percent of those volunteers were new to electoral politics). Most of the WFW organizers were young people just out of college, and Jontz attempted whenever possible to hire organizers who had ties to the district for which they were responsible. Such connections were helpful, Kusler noted, because there is always a gap between the start of organizing and gaining trust. Having organizers with local connections helped to narrow "that trust gap and allows for the organizing to begin as soon as possible and for trust to begin as soon as possible," said Kusler.[18]

Although Jontz knew the importance of technology in this kind of work, he did not want direct involvement in that part of the operation. "The organizers and I always laughed and sometimes cried about Jim's lack of technical savvy," said Cegelis. "Though we were only a few months apart in age we were miles apart in our use of technology. He even refused to carry a cell phone and opted to look for pay phones wherever he went to make his calls. His computer never had a wireless connection." Still, Cegelis and Jontz made a good team, as she managed to bring the project up to speed using the technology of the day, while he had connections with activists and organizers across the country and a lifetime of organizing skills to draw upon. "Since he traveled extensively, he had contacts everywhere," Burkett McInturff, one of the field organizers, said of Jontz. McInturff noted that Jontz served as the "ideas guy" for the WFW program, serving as an inspiration for everyone involved due to how much he brought to the table in terms of understanding and explaining complex issues, and always being willing to talk when organizers encountered problems or had questions. Cegelis remains amazed to this day at Jontz's ability to "work a room like nobody's business," always able to converse easily with anyone he met.[19]

One of the WFW organizers working for Jontz was a fellow Hoosier, Mike Englert, who was a volunteer for Jontz's 1992 congressional race against Steve Buyer while he was a student at Indiana University in Bloomington. An environmental activist himself—he had been involved in a tree-sitting protest against the building of an apartment complex in Brown's Woods on the city's west side—Englert had run for Monroe County commissioner in 2004 and Jontz did a joint fund-raiser for him and Andy Mahler, a fellow Hoosier environmentalists who was running for a similar position in Orange County. After losing the election, Englert moved to Wisconsin and was surprised to receive a telephone call in July 2006 from Jontz asking if he might be interested in a position with the WFW program. The organizer responsible for Minnesota's Sixth Congressional District race, an area in the northern suburbs of the Twin Cities of Minneapolis-Saint Paul, had "burned out" and Jontz was looking for her replacement. "It was pretty much a no brainer for me," said Englert, who quit the job he had and accepted the offer of the person he considered a hero. "It was an honor to work for him."

The WFW effort made a difference. "Of the eleven districts," recalled Cegelis, "seven of them flipped and two were so very close that they were heart breakers." In addition, Democrat Sherrod Brown won the U.S. Senate race in Ohio; Robert Casey Jr. captured a seat in the Senate from Pennsylvania; and voter turnout increased by 15 percent in the targeted areas. Unfortunately for Englert, his district was not one of the success stories, as Republican Michele Bachmann won her first race for Congress over Democratic-Farmer-Labor candidate Patty Wetterling. For the future, Jontz planned to organize the WFW program to persuade presidential candidates to endorse a working families platform in such key states as Iowa, New Hampshire, and South Carolina, as well as to strengthen the project's capacity so it could have a neighbor-to-neighbor effort on pocketbook issues in the 2008 presidential race for such battleground states as Ohio, Wisconsin, Pennsylvania, Iowa, and New Hampshire. He also wanted to sustain and increase WFW's volunteer base in communities around the country.[20]

Jontz did not have the opportunity to see the program he nurtured and led continue to grow. The intense work pace he maintained had finally caught up with him. According to his sister, Mary Lee Turk, in the winter of 2005 Jontz was on the road for WFW when he fell ill and received a misdiagnosis of diverticulitis during a visit to an emergency room. He became ill again that spring and received the bad news from his doctor—he had colon cancer. During a six-hour operation, doctors discovered that the cancer had spread throughout his abdominal cavity, with some on his stomach, some on the abdominal wall, and some on his liver. "I remember hearing that the doctors were glad they saved both of his kidneys," said Turk. Although Jontz embarked on an aggressive round of chemotherapy treatments, he never stopped working. Cegelis believed Jontz knew he was dying, as she remembered him telling her he would not be alive to see another presidential election. "He never really discussed his spiritual life with me," she said, "but I think that when he knew that he was dying, he basically went all out to do the most he could, and I am almost 100 percent sure that Working Families Win came out of [his question], 'How could I have the greatest effect in the short amount of time I have left?'"[21]

Turk first saw her brother after his cancer diagnosis during the Thanksgiving holiday in 2005. When she first saw him, Turk could tell the chemotherapy was taking a toll on him, as he was "doing things a little slower, he had lost weight, and his stature was a bit stooped, but it was the same Jim." During the holiday that year in Chicago he maintained two family traditions. At Thanksgiving, Jontz recited—from memory and with the proper inflection and great Hoosier twang—two classic Indiana poems, "Ain't God Good to Indiana:" by William Herschell, a longtime *Indianapolis News* reporter, and "When the Frost is on the Punkin" by James Whitcomb Riley, the Hoosier Poet. For Christmas, he presented to his mother, Polly Jontz Lennon; sister; and nieces, Katie, Beth, and Emily, his "usual relatively random gifts," often items he had picked up from craft fairs. "He still had his great laugh and sense of humor," Turk recalled, "and he still buried himself in papers he was reading at every free moment." Those traditions continued again the following year, with Jontz coming to Chicago to see his sister complete with gifts he obtained while on a trip to Hong Kong, where he had joined thousands of other protesters at the WTO's Sixth Ministerial Conference. "He brought us back some funny signs (where the Chinese didn't translate into English very well) as Christmas presents," she said.[22]

Scott Paul, who had worked in Jontz's congressional office and also fought against NAFTA with him at the Citizens Trade Campaign, had kept in touch with him over the years. Paul remembered that Jontz never failed to give him

Jontz poses with his beloved red Chevrolet pickup outside of his home in Portland, Oregon. The truck's rear is festooned with bumper stickers touting the causes in which Jontz believed in, including labor and the environment.

a call whenever he passed through Paul's hometown of Rensselaer, Indiana, while "on his way to Chicago or Indianapolis and [he] stopped at the Dairy Queen near I-65, where we made many stops together while I served on his congressional staff, and where he knew I worked one summer long ago." On May 28, 2006, Jontz attended Paul's wedding to Ilisa Halpern at the Woodend Nature Sanctuary operated by the Audubon Naturalist Society in Chevy Chase, Maryland. In early August Paul's wife had business in Portland, so he spent the day with Jontz, who still had his old red Chevrolet pickup, complete with a host of bumper stickers touting environmental, labor, and other causes. The two men drove around the city and went for a hike on Sauvie Island, where they picked wild blackberries. "One thing I know about Jim," said Paul, "he had a closer connection to nature than nearly anything else. The time and commitment he gave to preserving nature gave him a great deal of satisfaction and fulfillment." Although being treated for his cancer, Jontz, said Paul, "looked well and was still very active with ADA and other ventures." Learning that Jontz's condition had worsened in the spring of 2007, Paul called and spoke to him. Jontz recounted during the conversation that he had arrived at the Audubon property early on the day of Paul's wedding at Woodend and "had gone for a hike alone in the woods. In a deeply personal reflection, he told me he had said 'goodbye' to the trees and felt at peace. It was very emotional,"[23] said Paul.

In spite of his illness, Jontz had attempted to be his old self while at home in Portland, reporting for jury duty and attending a vigil for fairness for hospital workers fighting to form a union, noted his friend Lynn-Marie Crider. "He took public transit to the vigil and walked the route, though he staggered through the final blocks and finished behind the rest; a friend and I drove him home," said Crider. Jontz's condition deteriorated and, in March 2007, he telephoned his family that he was not doing well. Turk suggested to her mother that the two of them and any of her daughters that were free should travel to Portland to share a weekend with him. Before they could leave on their flight from Chicago, Jontz called them to let them know he had been admitted to the Kaiser Sunnyside Medical Center outside of Portland (Jontz had comprehensive health insurance with Kaiser Permanente through his position with the ADA). When his family members saw him, he appeared to be very jaundiced, and "it was clear that his liver was not functioning well," said Turk. "He told us that they [Jontz's doctors] had told him there was nothing they could do for him now." Turk's daughter, Katie, had accompanied her mother on the trip, and she engaged her uncle in a conversation about the history of labor in America. "That was the last real classic Jim conversation I heard," Turk recalled. "He was incredibly knowledgeable and she knew just what questions to ask him. I think they both thoroughly enjoyed the conversation." Jontz knew he only had a short time to live, and he told his mother he had already said good-bye to the forests he loved and worked so hard to protect. He also mused that although he never had children of his own, he had served as a mentor to quite a few young people—a statement seconded by friends such as Cegelis. "He took some young people [in WFW] and gave them a vision they've been able to carry on," she noted. "He cared deeply about people and deeply about the environment. He managed to inspire people to make that their life's work."[24]

News of Jontz's serious illness had begun to spread among those who had worked with him or knew him during his career. They responded by sending him cards, letters, e-mails, as well as calling him to offer their support. Among the callers were the man he ran against in 1994, U.S. senator Richard Lugar;

Jontz clad in his blue union jacket. John Cardwell, a noted Indiana public policy expert, said Jontz had the unique ability to "discuss international economics and environmental externalities with executives, farmers, factory workers, and schoolchildren."

former U.S. senator Birch Bayh of Indiana; U.S. senator Dick Durbin of Illinois; and Congressman Steve Buyer, the man who had beaten Jontz for his seat in Congress. Paul, Tom Buis, and Tom Sugar of his congressional staff visited him in the hospital. When he walked into his room, Sugar noticed that Jontz had not given up the fight for the causes he believed in, as he was involved in a telephone conference call. Paul called it "an extraordinary thing to see." Jontz began to cry when he saw his old political comrades in arms, but remained in good spirits for the rest of their visit. Sugar, who served as chief of staff for U.S. senator Evan Bayh, had grown frustrated with public service and was thinking about doing something else, even consider-ing becoming a lobbyist. "Jim in that moment could have said something judgmental," Sugar said, but instead offered: "Well, that's a lot of money, I'm sure you'll make the right choice." Although Sugar said he does not measure his life on Jontz, he called it "a moment full of grace." The three men went on to spend most of their time swapping stories with Jontz about their days together in Congress.

Even at the end of his life, Jontz continued to work on behalf of the causes he believed in. Kusler noted at the time that every moment Jontz was awake and "able to work on whatever cause it is, he is doing that. Even at this point in his life, that hasn't changed." While still in the hospital, Jontz talked on the telephone with Richard Trumka, then secretary-treasurer of the Ameri-can Federation of Labor and Congress of Industrial Organizations, to convince the national trade union to fund the WFW program. "I helped get Jim set up for the call and he used every bit of his strength and drive to make that phone call," remembered Turk. "He was cogent, clear, and convincing (at least to me)." (Some months later, the union came through with a financial contribution for the project.) After he finished his conversation with Trumka, Jontz told his sister he had one more task to accomplish. He had promised to write a letter of recommendation to the New York University School of Law for McInturff, one of the organizers who had worked for him in WFW. "At that point," Turk said, "Jim could not type the letter himself or operate his computer, so he dictated it to me and I typed it on my laptop. I read it back to him and he told me what words and sentences to change until he was satisfied with it. He wanted it to be good." Turk bought a printer at an office supply store near the hospital and printed out the letter, which Jontz signed. "He asked me several times if I got the letter sent," she added. "It was very important to him to follow through on his promise." McInturff, who was accepted by NYU for admittance to its law school, said because of the school's privacy policy he never had the opportunity to read what Jontz wrote about him. "It's amazing he got it done," McInturff said.[25]

Isaacs noted that in addition to the conversation with Trumka, Jontz participated in another, even more courageous conference call with WFW organizers, informing them that he had only a short time to live and urging them to continue their efforts on behalf of working families as the program would and should continue after he was gone. Of course, the organizers were pleased to hear the news that their work would go on, but were distraught to hear about Jontz's terminal illness. "To me," said Isaacs, "that call was maybe the only real profile in courage—I mean, I've seen other people take gutsy stands—but this one was so far and away beyond that, that I can't begin to tell you how wonderful it was, but also how inspiring it was. That he could put so much ahead of himself at a time like that."[26]

Brian Vincent, who had worked with Jontz at the Western Ancient Forest Campaign and had been arrested with him protesting the Sugerloaf timber sale in Oregon, had learned his friend had terminal cancer via e-mail. Stunned by the news, Vincent organized a letter of tribute to Jontz signed by more than two hundred people from across the country whose lives Jontz had touched, including politicians, environmentalists, union officials, newspaper reporters, friends, and former constituents. The letter read:

It is with great sadness that we learned of your struggle with cancer. We hope you are aware of the many people rooting for you.

We wanted to take this moment to tell you just how much we appreciate, love, and respect you. Your spirit, leadership, and perseverance have inspired us to continue our collective efforts to protect this glorious, yet fragile, planet. There is no doubt you have stirred our souls, transformed our lives, and uplifted our hearts. When we heard you speak eloquently on the House floor about the needs to save our last ancient forests, we were moved to take action. Those of us who were with you that somber day at Sugarloaf will never forget the courage you displayed as police dragged you away. Others who walked the quaint neighborhoods of Indiana's fifth congressional district with you during your campaigns were deeply touched by your tireless commitment to union workers, Vietnam veterans, and working families. We all smile when we think of you, with your sleeves rolled up and tie askew, your mind whirring with brilliant ideas, huddled with activists to map out strategies to protect sacred spaces and vanishing species. You have always been our beacon, shining light on the way forward. You are without question one of the greatest leaders the environmental movement has ever known.

In many ways you remind us of Jefferson Smith, the hero in Frank Capra's classic film, *Mr. Smith Goes to Washington*. Like Mr. Smith, you entered politics to fight a dam project. At the age of 23, you took on the powerful House majority leader and won. Later you brought your populist campaign to the U.S. Congress to challenge the establishment. Just as Jefferson Smith had done, you waged the hard, difficult battles, remained true to your convictions, and spoke with an idealism and purity that is so rare in politics. What amazed us all was how you never gave up. When the odds looked grim and when others may have conceded defeat, you mustered the strength to boldly carry on.

This splendid Earth is richer for the presence of Jim Jontz. Your legacy is one that will live on through the plaintive howl of the wolf, the grace of a trumpeter swan in flight, the sweet smell of an alpine meadow in bloom, the muscular stride of the grizzly. Like an ancient Douglas fir, you are a towering figure who has and will continue to awe and inspire us. Thank you, Jim, for the simple, yet precious, gifts you have given this world. Our lives are forever blessed because of you. As you fight a more personal battle now, please know that our thoughts and prayers are with you.[27]

Discharged from the hospital during the start of the week of April 9, Jontz went into hospice care back at his apartment, which was equipped with a hospital bed and around-the-clock nursing assistance. Turk and Lennon were with him for a few days, but they both had to get back home (Turk worked as a tax attorney and this was the busiest time in the year for her profession). "Jim waved goodbye with his fingers. That was the last time he saw mom. We really thought he would have another week or so," Turk recalled. Jontz was not alone; his Portland friends had arranged a schedule so that one of them would be with him at all times. Vincent sat in a chair by Jontz's bedside all day and into the evening on Friday, April 13—a night Vincent called the most emotionally wrenching experience of his life. "Jim was a fighter obviously,"

Upon Jontz's death in 2007, his friend and colleague Scott Paul wrote that his former boss in his life "made a difference to an extraordinary number of people," including those who lived in Warren County who wanted a dam stopped, "family farmers who struggled to make ends meet, Vietnam veterans who desperately sought readjustment counseling" and "every American who wanted to preserve our nation's great forests and natural areas for future generations."

he said. "I think what was most difficult about being with him on his dying day, literally, is he did not go quietly in the night . . . he fought. He would pass away, there would be this big long silence, then . . . another breath would come back into him. He did not want to go. I think he felt he still had things to accomplish."[28]

Turk had planned to return to Portland on Sunday, April 15, but received a call from Jontz's friend, Rick Brown, on Friday evening indicating Jontz was not doing well. She flew out to Portland on Saturday morning, April 14, and arrived at about 11 a.m. Pacific Time. "When I got to the apartment," Turk said, "I was escorted to Jim's bedside. He had just died. Rick Brown told me that he told Jim I was coming and that Jim knew that. . . . Rick believes that Jim was still there with us as I came to his bedside. I will never really know. I was close." A half an hour after Jontz's death, Turk received a telephone call on her cell phone; she had given her number out to people who wanted to talk to her brother. Turk said a woman's voice on the phone said, "Hi, this is Carole King, the singer. I understand this is the number to talk to Jim Jontz." I said, yes, it was, but Jim had just died." (Jontz had met King, the American singer/songwriter best known for her album *Tapestry*, through his environmental work.)

Tributes poured in from across the political spectrum upon the news of Jontz's death. Lugar released a statement noting he had talked to his former opponent on April 10 and had expressed to him the senator's appreciation for "his passion, service, strength and deep concern for the environment." Lugar also thanked Jontz for the positive tone he had struck in the 1994 U.S. Senate campaign, which had enabled the candidates to "focus on the issues that each of us felt important." The former congressman, he concluded, had been a source of great inspiration to many and had helped to launch the careers of numerous "outstanding individuals and made a profound impact in each of his endeavors." Mitch Harper, a Republican from Allen County who served alongside Jontz in the Indiana House of Representatives, spoke for many when he described him as "an honest Hoosier original." Memorial services were held in Jontz's honor in Washington, D.C.; at Mount Hood National Forest in Portland; and at the Indiana Statehouse in Indianapolis. At the Statehouse ceremony, Buyer, who served nine terms in Congress, remembered how when Jontz campaigned he routinely helped people in his district mow their lawns or carry groceries from their cars to their homes—something voters also expected him to do. "He had a certain charm and grace, even with those who disagreed" Buyer said of Jontz. "His was a life lived well."[29]

Jontz returned to the state of his birth following his death, as his body was cremated and his mother and sister scattered his ashes among the woods at Crown Hill Cemetery in Indianapolis. Along with a stone plaque with his name and dates of birth and death, there is a native Indiana tree planted on the edge of the woods in his memory. The commitment Jontz showed to the environmentalists, students, the elderly, veterans, and others who sought a hand up, not a handout, resonates today with the people who knew him best—those who worked alongside him and continue today to fight the good fight for the causes he believed in. Reminiscing about his friend while sitting in his Zionsville, Indiana, office, where he works as senior vice president for the nonprofit Complete College America, Sugar sighed and noted it had been a long time since he had been as inspired as he had been during his days working with Jontz. During his life Sugar had shaken hands with presidents and had been backstage at the Democratic National Convention, but "this boy from Kokomo" had never been as "impressed as much by anyone as I was [by] Jim Jontz"—someone who was not perfect, Sugar added, but was prepared to "risk it all every day for what he believed in." He felt lucky to have had as his first real job a boss who was so idealistic and hardworking. "He did operate like a man on borrowed time," Sugar noted. "And I think that was the story of Jim's adult life. No matter what job he occupied, he always acted like he was on borrowed time. Tremendous impatience, but [an] impatience that is targeted in a positive way. Not an impatience that creates outbursts and anger, but impatience for finding a way around the obstacle or through it." In the end, in many ways, said Sugar, Jontz gave his life "for everyone else. He lived a life that was bigger than his own."[30]

Notes

Chapter 1

1. See, John Maxwell, "Fall Creek Gorge Nature Preserve: Hit the Potholes of Warren County," *Outdoor Indiana* (May/June 2010): 38–39; Catherine Caufield, "A Reporter at Large: The Ancient Forest," *The New Yorker* (May 14, 1990): 48.

2. Author interview with Mary Lee Turk, April 27, 2010.

3. Grace Witwer, "This Boy-Next-Door Legislator Gives a 'Damn about Dams,'" *Indiana Daily Student*, March 15, 1975.

4. Americans for Democratic Action conference, June 13, 1998, C-Span Video Library, http://www.c-spanvideo.org/program/Americansfor.

5. George Stuteville, "Movin' On: Defeated Jontz Knew He Was Living on Borrowed Time," *Indianapolis Star*, December 16, 1992.

6. Mike Thoele, "Hoosier Fights for Northwest Forests," *Eugene Register-Guard*, June 3, 1990; Doug McDaniel, "Forest Bill Puts Jontz in Middle of Controversy," *Indianapolis Star*, June 24, 1990.

7. Andrea Holecek, "Jontz Goes Out on a Limb to Save Public Forests," *Northwest Times*, August 6, 1990; Dan Carpenter, "Rep. Jontz Is Rare Official to See Forest for the Trees," *Indianapolis Star*, August 2, 1990; author interview with Phillip Perdue, January 12, 2010.

8. S. P. Dinnen, "Jontz and the Fight over U.S. Forests," *Indianapolis Star*, January 6, 1993; Steven Higgs, "Jontz Urges Move beyond Endangered Species Act," *Bloomington Herald-Times*, January 30, 1993.

9. Brock Evans, "Remembering Jim Jontz," June 2007, in "Soul of a Hero: A People's Tribute to Jim Jontz," prepared by Brian Vincent, unpublished collection of tributes to Jontz, copy in author's collection; John Osborn, "Tribute to Jim Jontz," ibid.

10. Thoele, "Hoosier Fights for Northwest Forests;" David Rohn, "Indiana's Political Roadrunner," *Indianapolis Star*, January 18, 1994.

11. Debra Noell, "Jontz: A Day in the Life of White County's First Congressman," *Monticello Herald Journal*, December 9, 1987.

12. Turk interview; author interview with Polly Jontz Lennon, April 22, 2010; Stuteville, "Movin' On."

13. Dick Durbin, "Remembering Congressman Jim Jontz," *Congressional Record*, April 17, 2007.

14. David Kitchell, "Best Congressman on Two Wheels," *Terre Haute Tribune–Star*, April 19, 2007; Noell, "Jontz: A Day in the Life of White County's First Congressman"; author interview with Tom Buis, August 26, 2010. Kitchell noted that when Jontz stopped at coffee shops to chat with his constituents, he would occasional buy them coffee. "Most of the time, they bought his," wrote Kitchell. "Best Congressman on Two Wheels."

15. Witwer, "This Boy-Next-Door Legislator Gives a 'Damn about Dams'"; author interview with Tom Sugar, April 30, 2010.

16. Sugar interview; Perdue interview.

17. Author interview with Kathy Altman, May 12, 2010; Perdue interview; and author interview with Scott Paul, August 6, 2010.

18. Author interview with Scott Campbell, May 6, 2010.

19. Author interview with Christopher Klose, May 6, 2010.

20. Author interview with Elaine Caldwell Emmi, May 13, 2010; author interview with Amy Isaacs, October 4, 2011; author interview with Andy Kerr, July 18, 2001.

21. See, Brian Mayes, "About Jim Jontz," *Ecclectica*, http://ecclectica.ca/issues/mayes_be .cc.asp/; author interview with Mayes, May 12, 2010; Mayes, "Running to the Reagan Fight," *The Newspaper*, University of Toronto, November 19, 1986.

22. Altman interview; Roger Featherstone, "Remembering Jim," in "Soul of a Hero"; author interview with Bart Chilton, July 29, 2011.

23. Lynn-Marie Crider, "Reflections about My Friend Jim," in "Soul of a Hero."

24. Sugar interview; Campbell interview.

25. Evans, "Remembering Jim Jontz."

Chapter 2

1. Author interview with Kathy Altman, May 12, 2010.

2. Patrick Siddons, "'Unbelieveable': Jim Jontz, Possibly Youngest Member of House, Recalls His Close Victory," *Louisville Courier-Journal*, January 12, 1975.

3. Author interview with Mary Lee Turk, April 27, 2010.

4. Betsy Harris, "What's Past Is Her Future," *Indianapolis Star*, July 31, 1995.

5. James H. Madison, "Economy," in David J. Bodenhamer and Robert G. Barrows, eds., *The Encyclopedia of Indianapolis* (Bloomington and Indianapolis: Indiana University Press, 1994), 61–71,

6. Turk interview.

7. Author interview with David Corbin, June 16, 2011.

8. Doug McDaniel, "Forest Bill Puts Jontz in Middle of Controversy," *Indianapolis Star*, June 24, 1990.

9. "Jim Jontz, 1951–2011: Eagle Scout, State Legislator, Congressman, Conservationist, Advocate for Working Families," unpublished tribute in author's collection; Turk interview.

10. Corbin interview.

11. Author interview with Polly Jontz Lennon, April 22, 2010; Letter of Recommendation from Jacquelyn Pavey for Jim Jontz, June 3, 1965, Jim Jontz Papers, Calumet Regional Archives, Indiana University Northwest, Gary, IN (hereafter cited as Jontz Papers).

12. Corbin interview; Lennon interview.

13. Turk interview; Application for Eagle Scout, Boy Scouts of America Central Indiana Council, Jontz Papers; Lennon interview; author interview with Pat Puckett, October 25, 2011.

14. Jim Jontz, "The Law of Nature," in *Etchings in Thoughts: An Anthology of Student Composition from North Central High School, 1969–1970*, Jontz Papers.

15. "Draft Remarks for Speech to Frontier High School Career Day," November 29, 1989, ibid.

16. Turk interview.

17. Author interview with Fred Martin, June 30, 2011; Fred Martin, "Entrance Requirements," March 27, 2011, sermon, http://www.efcbemidji.org/443869.ihtml.

18. Author interview with Larry Peck, June 14, 2011; author interview with Kent Shields, June 21, 2011.

19. Lennon interview; Corbin interview.

20. Peck interview; Shields interview; William F. Gulde, *Hopes, Dreams, and Books: The Story of North Central High School, 1956–2004* (Indianapolis: Par Digital Imaging, 2004): 58–61.

21. Gulde, *Hopes, Dreams, and Books*, 81–89.

22. Scholastic Aptitude Test score results, Jontz Papers; Corbin interview; Richard Stock e-mail to author, June 14, 2011.

23. Peck interview; Corbin interview.

24. Grace Witwer, "This Boy-Next-Door Legislator Gives a 'Dam about Dams,'" *Indiana Daily Student*, March 15, 1975.

25. Mary Ann Wynkoop, "Dissent in the Heartland: The Student Protest Movement at Indiana University, Bloomington, Indiana, 1965–1970" (PhD diss., Indiana University, Bloomington, June 1992), 221.

26. See Benjamin Kline, *First Along the River: A Brief History of the U.S. Environmental Movement* (San Francisco: Acada Books, 1997), 77–78; Thomas R. Wellock, *Preserving the Nation: The Conservation and Environmental Movements, 1870–2000* (Wheeling, IL: Harland Davidson, 2007), 161–66.

27. Wellock, *Preserving the Nation*, 172–73.

28. William Mullen, "In a Time of Trouble 40 Years Ago, Apollo 8 Lifted Spirits," *Chicago Tribune*, December 18, 2008.

29. Anne Kibbler, "Environment Back on the Agenda," *Bloomington Herald-Times*, April 22, 1990; Constitution of the Committee to Publicize Crisis Biology, Indiana University Archives, Bloomington, IN; Mike Griffin, "Biologists to Fight Pollution," *Indiana Daily Student*, September 16, 1969.

30. Author interview with Rod Crafts, June 2, 2011.

31. Bill Christofferson, *The Man from Clear Lake: Earth Day Founder Senator Gaylord Nelson* (Madison: University of Wisconsin Press, 2004), 302–4, 312.

32. See, Ken Ferries and Linda Herman, "IU Environmental Fair," *Indiana Daily Student*, April 23, 1970; Sue Bischoff, "Nelson Pleased by Turnout, Originality," ibid., April 23, 1970; Wynkoop, "Dissent in the Heartland," 214; author interview with John Goss, July 22, 2011.

33. Author interview with Bob Rodenkirk, April 29, 2010.

34. Author interview with Tim Harmon, June 3, 2011; Goss interview.

35. Rodenkirk interview.

36. See Tim Harmon, "First Crisis Meeting to Discuss Recycling"; Harmon,"Recycling Project has Small, Solvable Snags"; Harold P. Schlechtweg, "Recycling Major Concern," undated *Indiana Daily Student* articles, Jontz Papers.

37. Mike Kinerk, "Grayson Hits 'Disaster Lobby,'" *Indiana Daily Student,* November 11, 1971; Harmon interview.

38. "This Boy-Next-Door Legislator Gives a 'Damn about Dams,'" and Goss interview.

39. Rodenkirk interview.

40. Author interview with B. Patrick Bauer, August 15, 2011. See also Justin E. Walsh, *The Centennial History of the Indiana General Assembly, 1816–1978* (Indianapolis: The Select Committee on the Centennial History of the Indiana General Assembly in cooperation with the Indiana Historical Bureau, 1987), 640–41.

41. Ray Miller, "Attitude Big Problem in Pollution: Jontz," *Indiana Daily Student*, July 18, 1972.

42. Jim Jontz, "Corps Unsuccessful in Image Change," ibid.; undated column drafts in Jontz Papers.

43. Jontz, "'Sinkhole' Gets Down to Basics," *Indiana Daily Student*, April 7, 1972.

44. Goss interview; "Crisis Biology May Join InPIRG," *Indiana Daily Student*, May 4, 1972.

45. Author interview with Elaine Caldwell Emmi, May 13, 2010.

46. "Study Shows Pollution Controls Could Save Billions: Jontz," *Indianapolis Star*, July 12, 1972.

47. *Indiana Conservationist* columns, Jontz Papers.

Chapter 3

1. William Watt, *Bowen: The Years as Governor* (Indianapolis: Bierce Associates, 1981), 111–12; Leland R. Johnson, *The Falls City Engineers: A History of the Louisville District, Corps of Engineers, United States Army, 1970–1983* (Louisville, KY: United States Army Engineer District, 1984), 101.

2. George Neavoll, "Saving Scenic Streams," *Christian Science Monitor*, February 11, 1974.

3. "Big Pine Economic Benefits Wishful Thinking: Parmenter," *Attica Daily Ledger Tribune*, July 17, 1974; "Ballots Rolling in on Big Pine Question," *Williamsport Review-Republican*, July 18, 1974.

4. Norman Bess, "Fall Creek Gorge 'Protected,'" *Indianapolis News*, June 12, 1973.

5. Jim Jontz, "Dear Friends" letter, November 21, 1973, Jontz Papers, Calumet Regional Archives, Indiana University Northwest, Gary, IN (hereafter cited as Jontz Papers).

6. Author interview with Elaine Caldwell Emmi, May 13, 2010.

7. Ibid.; Patrick Siddons, "'Unbelievable:' Jim Jontz, Possibly Youngest Member of House, Recalls His Close Victory," *Louisville Courier–Journal*, January 12, 1975.

8. Emmi interview; author interview with Bill Parmenter, April 26, 2010; author interview with Laura Ann Arnold, May 10, 2010.

9. Author interview with David Dreyer, November 1, 2010.

10. Jim Jontz and David Dreyer, *Big Pine Creek: A Report on Big Pine Creek, Warren County, Indiana, and its Future* (Attica, IN: The Committee on Big Pine Creek, 1974).

11. "'General Assembly Can Stop Big Pine Dam,' Says Candidate Jontz," *Williamsport Review–Republican*, October 10, 1974.

12. Siddons, "Jim Jontz, Possibly Youngest Member of House, Recalls His Close Victory"; "Running for District 20 Representative in Primary Election," *Monticello Daily Herald-Journal*, March 18, 1974.

13. "Jim Jontz Plans Door-to-Door Effort," *Williamsport Review-Republican*, September 5, 1974; Grace Witwer, "This Boy-Next-Door Legislator Gives a 'Damn about Dams,'" *Indiana Daily Student*, March 15, 1975.

14. Emmi interview.

15. Jim Jontz, "Why I'm a Candidate for State Represenative" flyer, Jontz Papers.

16. Emmi interview.

17. "Young Democrat Hopes for Upset," *Monticello Daily Herald-Journal*, November 4, 1974; author interview with Kathy Altman, May 12, 2010.

18. "Public Big Pine Meeting Confirms 10–1 Sentiment Against Dam," *Williamsport Review-Republican*, August 1, 1974; Emmi interview.

19. "Warren County Farmers Protest Dam," *Williamsport Review-Republican*, August 8, 1974.

20. Watt, *Bowen*, 113.

21. "Jontz Makes Statement of Views," *Williamsport Review-Republican*, August 15, 1974.

22. Emmi interview.

23. "This Boy-Next-Door Legislator Gives a 'Damn about Dams'"; Emmi interview.

24. Jeff Fisher, "Jontz Tops Guy by Two Votes," *Daily Herald-Journal*, November 6, 1974.

25. Author interview with Stan Jones, May 4, 2010; Justin Walsh, *The Centennial History of the Indiana General Assembly, 1816–1978* (Indianapolis: The Select Committee on the Centennial History of the Indiana General Assembly in cooperation with the Indiana Historical Bureau, 1987), 646.

26. Jontz State Representative campaign advertisement, Jontz Papers; Emmi interview.

27. "A Humbling Day for 'Rookie' Jontz," *Marion Chronicle–Tribune*, June 12, 1991.

28. Emmi interview; Sherry Brown, "Jontz 'Lobbies' for Legislative Goals," *Lafayette Journal and Courier*, February 3, 1980.

29. Johnson, *Falls City Engineers*, 107.

30. "Big Pine Project Finally Deauthorized," *Williamsport Review-Republican*, January 12, 1990.

31. Jim Jontz, Possibly Youngest Member of House, Recalls His Close Victory"; Jones interview; "Jontz 'Lobbies' for Legislative Goals."

32. Michael Thrall e-mail to author, June 3, 2010.

33. Author interview with Terry Mumford, September 6, 2011.

34. Author interview with Marilyn Schultz, August 10, 2011; Arnold interview; "Jontz Completes Warren County Visits," *Williamsport Review-Republican*, September 23, 1976.

35. Author interview with Donlyn Meyers, September 7, 2011.

36. "Jontz Appeals to Voters in Both Parties," *Monticello Herald Journal*, May 4, 1982.

37. Doug Richardson, Associated Press, "Young Legislative Veteran Marches to Different Drummer," *Warsaw Times-Union*, April 9, 1985.

38. Jones interview; Mumford interview; Schultz interview; Bauer interview.

39. Author interview with Louie Mahern, January 25, 2011.

40. Richardson, "Young Legislative Veteran Marches to Different Drummer"; Richard D. Walton, "It's Jontz at the Mike (Oh, no! Not again!)," *Indianapolis Star*, February 13, 1984; "Jontz 'Lobbies' for Legislative Goals"; Schultz interview.

41. Walton, "It's Jontz at the Mike."

42. Ibid.; Richardson, "Young Legislative Veteran Marches to Different Drummer"; Jones interview.

43. Richardson, "Young Legislative Veteran Marches to Different Drummer."

44. "State GOP Takes Aim at Jontz," *Rensselaer Republican*, October 27, 1984.

45. Altman interview; author interview with Michael Riley, July 13, 2011.

46. Jeff Bonty, "Jontz, Wolf Take State Seats," *Monticello Herald Journal*, November 7, 1984.

47. Memo to Jim Jontz from Abandoned House Members, Jontz Papers; Jim Jontz Memorial, Remarks by Katie Wolf at Indiana Statehouse, June 23, 2007, copy in author collection.

48. Doug McDaniel, "Hillis Eyes New Pursuits after Career in Congress," *Indianapolis Star*, July 21, 1985; W. S. Wilson, "Keep Your Eyes on Jim Jontz," *Rochester Sentinel*, November 12, 1985; "Democrat Jontz Optimistic in Race for 5th District Seat," *Indianapolis News*, August 7, 1985; "State Senator Seeks Hillis' Seat in Congress," *Indianapolis Star*, August 7, 1985.

Chapter 4

1. Author interview with Tom Sugar, April 30, 2010.

2. Michael Barone and Grant Ujifusa, *The Almanac of American Politics 1986* (Washington, DC: National Journal, 1985), 461.

3. Author interview with Allen Maxwell, July 11, 2011.

4. Author interview with Laura Ann Arnold, May 10, 2010; Doug Richardson, Associated Press, "Double Duty for Legislators Seeking Congressional Berths," *Warsaw Times-Union*, February 17, 1986.

5. Author interview with Louie Mahern, January 25, 2011.

6. Author interview with Jill Long Thompson, August 9, 2011.

7. William R. Wood, "Ridlen-Butcher: Establishment vs. Religious Right," *Marion Chronicle-Tribune*, May 7, 1986.

8. Gail Townsend, "Butcher Triumphs over Ridlen," ibid., May 7, 1986; Linda Miller,

"Butcher Issues Ridlen a Defeat," *Kokomo Tribune*, May 7, 1986.

9. Author interview with Jack Williams, July 19, 2011.

10. Author interview with Michael Riley, July 13, 2011; author interview with Mike Busch, January 31, 2011.

11. Bill Craig, "The Campaign: See How Jontz Mingles with His Constituents," *Nuvo*, August 29–September 5, 1990; Riley interview; author interview with Phillip Perdue, January 12, 2010.

12. Busch interview.

13. Author interview with Christopher Klose, May 6, 2010; author interview with Kathy Altman, May 12, 2010.

14. Perdue interview.

15. Author interview with Brian Mayes, May 12, 2010, and Mayes, "Running to the Reagan Fight," *The Newspaper*, University of Toronto, November 19, 1986.

16. Busch interview; Craig, "Campaign."

17. Klose interview.

18. Chris Sautter, "Jim Jontz, the Hoosier 'Roads Scholar,' Will be Missed," *Roll Call*, May 3, 2007; Perdue interview.

19. Dave Kitchell, "Jontz: Catching Up 'One Day at a Time,'" *Logansport Pharos-Tribune*, October 2, 1986; "Actress Boosts Jontz Campaign," *Kokomo Tribune*, October 2, 1986.

20. Altman interview.

21. Maureen Groppe, "You Have to Love a Parade if You Run for U.S. Congress," *Kokomo Tribune*, July 15, 1990; Jane Prendergast, "Jontz Wears Out Shoes, and His Associates," *Marion Chronicle-Tribune*, October 17, 1988.

22. Frank Morris, "Jontz, Butcher: At Odds on Everything," *Marion Chronicle-Tribune*, September 26, 1986.

23. David J. Remondini, "Candidates Trade Views, Seek to Fill Hillis' House Seat," *Indianapolis Star*, September 9, 1986; Paula Ulrey, "Butcher, Jontz Disagree on Issues," *Wabash Plain–Dealer*, September 9, 1986.

24. "Style Contrast: Jontz, Butcher on RBF [Round Barn Festival] Stump," *Rochester Sentinel*, July 14, 1986; "Dear Neighbor" letter from Louise Jontz, Jim Jontz Papers, Calumet Regional Archives, Indiana University Northwest, Gary, IN.

25. Frank Morris, "Jontz Campaigned Until Polls Closed," *Marion Chronicle-Tribune*, November 5, 1986.

26. Maxwell interview; Bill Andree, "Jontz's Victory Disheartens GOP," *Monticello Herald Journal*, November 5, 1986; Dave Kitchell, "Jontz to Congress," *Logansport Pharos-Tribune*, November 5, 1986; Doug McDaniel, "Victory on GOP Turf Is Old Hat for Jontz," *Indianapolis Star*, November 7, 1986; Linda Miller, "Jontz Win Breaks Hold of the GOP on District," *Kokomo Tribune*, November 5, 1986; Frank Morris, "Butcher Taking Time to Smell the Roses," *Marion Chronicle-Tribune*, November 7, 1986.

27. Sugar interview.

28. Williams interview.

29. Ibid.; Sugar interview.

30. Doug McDaniel, "Jontz Learning Congress' Ways, Means," *Indianapolis Star*, December 15, 1986, and McDaniel, "Freshman Congressman Finds Advantages to Being in Majority," ibid., May 26, 1987; Maxwell interview.

Chapter 5

1. Thomas Grose, "New Congressman Gets Used to Washington Scene," *Valparaiso Vidette–Messenger*, January 7, 1987; author interview with Kathy Altman, May 12, 2010; "Jim Jontz, 1951–2007: Eagle Scout, State Legislator, Congressman, Conservationist, Advocate for Working Families," author collection; Jack Alkire, "Jontz Finds a Niche in D.C.," *Lafayette Journal and Courier*, May 10, 1987.

2. News release, "Jontz Payhike Goes to Scholarship Fund," Jim Jontz Papers, Calumet Regional Archives, Indiana University Northwest, Gary, IN (hereafter cited as Jontz Papers). Those serving on the first scholarship committee for Jontz were: Jack Williams, Kokomo, Chrysler employee and United Auto Workers official and committee chairman; David Hinkle, Walton, accountant and committee treasurer; Glenn Dillman, Flora, teacher; Robert Peterson, Rochester, attorney; Arabelle Kriegbaum, Marion, voter registration clerk; Shirely Barbour, Marion, realtor; John Whikehart, Kokomo, city director of personnel; Connie Blackketter, Rensselaer, teacher; Chester Clampitt, Atwood, printer; Charles Thornbert, Cedar Lake, retired Inland Steel employee; Ray Geyer, Peru, retired school superintendent; John Yost, Kentland, newspaper editor; Delores Aylesworth, Hebron, teacher; Reverend John Kiefer, Monterey, priest; Nancy Bell, Wabash, Chamber of Commerce director; and Jan Faker, Monticello, mother and homemaker. Ibid.

3. Undated news release, Jontz Papers.

4. Author interview with Christopher Klose, May 6, 2010.

5. "Job Has Frustration, Fulfillment," *Valparaiso Vidette-Messenger*, August 29, 1990; Robert Bryan, "Jontz Busy but Still Available," *Peru Daily Tribune*, July 3, 1987.

6. Author interview with Bart Chilton, July 29, 2011.

7. Constituent letter files, Jontz Papers.

8. Jontz 1991 letter to American Legion Post 34, Indianapolis, ibid.

9. Jontz 1991 letter to Gail Sweet, ibid.

10. Jontz 1991 letter to Terry and Linda Magers, ibid. See also Brady Campaign to Prevent Gun Violence, http://www.bradycampaign.org/legislation/backgroundchecks/bradylaw/.

11. Tom Hays, "Calls from Home Make a Difference," *Gary Post–Tribune*, May 27, 1987; "Jontz Says: Dial Your Congressman in D.C." news release, Jontz Papers.

12. Author interview with Tom Buis, August 26, 2010.

13. Altman interview; Chilton interview.

14. Author interview with Karen Davis, January 10, 2011.

15. Author interview with Marcy Kaptur, June 29, 2011.

16. Author interview with Tom Sugar, April 30, 2010.

17. Author interview with Scott Paul, August 6, 2010; Jane Prendergast, "Jontz Wears Out Shoes, and His Associates," *Marion Chronicle-Tribune*, October 17, 1988.

18. Klose interview; author interview with Mike Busch, January 31, 2011; author interview with David Bozell, March 16, 2011.

19. Bush interview; Bill Craig, "The Campaign: See How Jontz Mingles with His Constituents," *Nuvo*, August 29–September 5, 1990.

20. Craig, "Campaign."

21. Sugar interview.

22. Busch interview; Paul interview.

23. See Re-election announcement for Congress, Jontz Papers; "First Jontz-Sponsored Bill Passes," *Monticello Herald-Journal*, October 26, 1987; "Jontz' Bills Await President's Signature,"

Rensselaer Republican, January 13, 1988.

24. Buis interview.

25. See "Statement of Rep. Jim Jontz on H.R. 3037, The Veterans PTSD Treatment and Psychological Readjustment Act," Jontz Papers; Jim Jontz editorial, "The Time to Act is Now," ibid.; news release, "Congress Provides Funding for PTSD Programs, Jontz Reports," ibid.

26. Stephen Huba, "Nightmare That Didn't End with the War," *Huntington Herald-Press*, September 15, 1989; Mike Paluck, "Session Explores Disorder," *Kokomo Tribune*, September 17, 1989.

27. "Congress Provides Funding for PTSD Programs, Jontz Reports"; Paul interview.

28. Author interview with Scott Campbell, May 6, 2010.

29. Prendergast, "Jontz Wears Out Shoes, and His Associates."

30. Sugar interview; Nancy J. Winkley, "Ford Stumps for Williams," *Gary Post-Tribune*, September 22, 1988; Martha T. Moore, "Party Lines Vague in House Race in Indiana," *USA Today*, September 15, 1988.

31. Vic Caleca, "Contrasts Many in 5th District," *Indianapolis Star*, October 16, 1988; "Jontz Observes the Domino Effect," *Gary Post-Tribune*, September 4, 1988; Anne Schmitt, "Jontz Wins Second Congressional Term," *Kokomo Tribune*, November 9, 1988.

32. John R. O'Neill, "Jontz No Stranger to Close Races, Facing Tough 5th District Battle," *Indianapolis Star*, November 2, 1990; O'Neill, "5th District Race Shaping Up as Battle for Middle Ground," ibid., September 30, 1990; O'Neill, "Jontz Jaunts, and Johnson Wants to Catch Him," ibid., June 24, 1990.

33. Maureen Groppe, "You Have to Love a Parade if You Run for Congress," *Kokomo Tribune*, July 15, 1990.

34. Altman interview; Jeff Walz, "Jontz Proves Polls Wrong," *Vidette-Messenger*, November 7, 1990; Rada Indjich, "Johnson Admits Mistakes in Campaign Efforts," *Munster Times*, November 9, 1990.

35. News from Congressman Jim Jontz, "Preserving an Ancient Forest Ecosystem," Jontz Papers.

Chapter 6

"Hoquiam—Thumbnail History," HistoryLink.org, The Free Online Encyclopedia of Washington State History, http://www.historylink.org/index.cfm?DisplayPage=output.cfm&file_id=8652; "Protesters Block Road, Burn Jontz Caricature," *Washington (IN) Times-Herald*, April 30, 1990.

2. See Catherine Caufield, "The Ancient Forest," *The New Yorker*, May 14, 1990, 48; "When Chainsaws Pare the Hills of Ancient Trees," *New York Times*, November 3, 1991.

3. Ted Gup, "Owl vs. Man: Who Gives a Hoot?" *Time*, June 25, 1990, http://www.time.com/time/magazine/article/0,9171,970447,00.html.

4. Mike Thoele, "Hoosier Fights for Northwest Forests," *Eugene Register–Guard*, June 3, 1990.

5. Gup, "Owl vs. Man" In 1999 ECONorthwest, a Eugene, Oregon, economic consulting company, released a study claiming that the Pacific Northwest's economy did not suffer massive employment losses as a result of efforts to halt logging in old-growth forests and the northern spotted owl in the early 1990s. According to the study, of the 21,000 wood products jobs lost by 1996 as federal timber harvests declined, only 9,300 of those jobs were due to protection of old-growth forests. Instead, the bulk of the job declines were due to market conditions. "Mounting evidence indicates the region has prospered in part because of logging reductions," said Ernie Niemi of ECONorthwest. "Standing forests are now more valuable to the economy than logged

ones." Timber industry officials rejected the findings, suggesting most of the job growth in the region had occurred in urban areas, while small towns dependent upon logging for the economic well-being were still hurting. See "Spotted Owl Controversy Didn't Cause Overall Massive Job Losses," Associated Press, October 22, 1999, http://forests.org/archived_site/today /recent/1999/skynotfa.htm.

6. Thoele, "Hoosier Fights for Northwest Forests."

7. Kathie Durbin, *Tree Huggers: Victory, Defeat and Renewal in the Northwest Ancient Forest Campaign* (Seattle, WA: The Mountaineers, 1998), 146; David Seideman, "Environmental Terrorist in a White Collar," *Time*, June 25, 1990, http://www.time.com/time/magazine /article/0,9171,970474,00.html; author interview with Andy Kerr, July 18, 2011.

8. "Hoosier Conservationist Back in Old-Growth Fray," *Oregonian*, April 7, 1991; "Timber Workers Tree Rep. Jontz," *Gary Post-Tribune*, February 3, 1992; Kerr interview; author interview with Dan Stotter, August 9, 2011.

9. Brock Evans, "Remembering Jim Jontz" in Soul of a Hero: A People's Tribute to Jim Jontz," prepared by Brian Vincent, unpublished collection of tributes to Jontz, copy in author's collection; "Hoosier Conservationist Back in Old-Growth Fray."

10. Durbin, *Tree Huggers*, 93.

11. "Logging Showdown This Week?" *Eugene Register-Guard*, September 11, 1989; Mike Sante, "Owl is Debate Focus," *Gary Post-Tribune*, October 7, 1990.

12. Kerr interview; Seideman, "Environmental Terrorist in a White Collar"; author interview with James Monteith, October 7, 2011.

13. Monteith interview.

14. "Old Growth Called 'Treasure,'" *Ellensburg Daily Record*, January 4, 1990; "More Timber Cutbacks Predicted" *Spokane Chronicle*, January 4, 1990; Robert Sterling, "'Ancient Forest' Tour Incites Industry," *Medford (OR) Mail Tribune*, January 7, 1990.

15. "When Chainsaws Pare the Hills of Ancient Trees"; "Hoosier Conservationist Back in Old-Growth Fray"; Judith Barra Austin and Carol Bradley, "U.S. Rep. Jim Jontz: Preserving the Forest Primeval," *Lafayette Journal and Courier*, June 16, 1991; Lance Robertson, "Bill Halts Logging in Old Growth Areas," *Eugene Register–Guard*, April 6, 1990.

16. Stotter interview; Monteith interview.

17. Jim Jontz, "Preserving an Ancient Forest Ecosystem," "Statement of Rep. Jim Jontz on the Introduction of the Ancient Forest Protection Act," and "Jontz Defends Preservation of Ancient Forests in Northwest," Jontz Papers, Calumet Regional Archives, Indiana University Northwest, Gary, IN (hereafter cited as Jontz Papers).

18. Dan Morain, "Timber Tussle: Opponents Find Common Ground on Log Export Ban," *Los Angeles Times*, May 16, 1990; "Jontz Pushing for Pacific Northwest Logging Ban," *Peru Tribune*, February 1, 1991; "Bill Halts Logging in Old Growth Areas," *Eugene Register-Guard*, April 6, 1990; "Oregon Lawmakers Attack Forest Bill in Congress," *Eugene Register-Guard*, February 1, 1991.

19. "Don't Laugh at Hoosier," *Salem (OR) Statesman Journal*, April 11, 1990; Thoele, "Hoosier Fights for Northwest Forests"; "Jontz Tries to Put Focus on Forests," *Wabash Plain-Dealer*, May 8, 1990.

20. "A Tough Environmental Stand: New Coalition Says Jontz Forest Bill Too Weak," *Lafayette Journal and Courier*, September 9, 1990.

21. Stotter interview; Kerr interview; author interview with Scott Campbell, May 6, 2010.

22. Author interview with Tom Sugar, April 30, 2010.

23. "Hoosier Conservationist Back in Old-Growth Fray"; Austin and Bradley, "U.S. Rep. Jim Jontz."

24. Stotter interview; "Forest Preserve Bill Introduced," *Eugene Register-Guard*; Thoele, "Hoosier Fights for Northwest Forests"; Monteith interview.

25. "Alaskan Wants to Turn Gary into National Forest," *Munster Times*, April 10, 1990; "New Forest Planned for Northeast Indiana," news release from Congressman Don Young, Jontz Papers; "Legislator Suggests Indiana Get a Taste of Own Medicine," *Eugene Register–Guard*, April 10, 1990.

26. Doug McDaniel, "Forest Bill Puts Jontz in Middle of Controversy," *Indianapolis Star*, June 24, 1990; Jontz April 9, 1990, letter to John Wiles, editor, *Kokomo Tribune*, Jontz Papers; Timothy Egan, "Fighting for Control of America's Hinterlands," *New York Times*, November 11, 1990.

27. "Jontz Criticized for Ancient Forest Activity," *Logansport Pharos-Tribune*, February 1, 1991.

28. "Jontz's Bill Would Halt Below-Cost Timber Sales," *Monticello Herald Journal*, June 27, 1991; "Jontz Bill Would Stop Below-Cost Timber Sales on Federal Property," *Rochester Sentinel*, June 28, 1991; Donald G. McNeil Jr., "How Most of the Public Forests Are Sold to Loggers at a Loss," *Indianapolis Star*, November 3, 1991.

29. "Jontz Bill Rapped in Hearing," *Kokomo Tribune*, April 26, 1991; "Bush Administration Opposes Jontz Bill," *Valparaiso Vidette-Messenger*, April 26, 1991.

30. Judith Barra Austin, "Timber Workers Protest Jontz Preservation Bill," *Lafayette Journal and Courier*, September 24, 1991.

31. "Buyer Tests Jontz Seat for Fit," undated newspaper clipping, and Stephen E. Buyer, attorney at law advertisement, Jontz Papers.

32. See Rick Atkinson, "Murky Ending Clouds Desert Storm Legacy," *Washington Post*, http://www.washingtonpost.com/wp-srv/inatl/longterm/fogofwar/intro.htm; John Robert Greene, *The Presidency of George Bush* (Lawrence: University Press of Kansas, 2000), 112–27; Jeffrey R. Biggs and Thomas S. Foley, *Honor in the House: Speaker Tom Foley* (Pullman: Washington State University Press, 1999), 153–57.

33. Bill Andree, "Gulf Resolutions: Rep. Jontz against Military Option," *Monticello Herald Journal*, January 12, 1991; "Jontz Says He Will Vote for Sanctions Resolution," *Rochester Sentinel*, January 12, 1991; Jean Marie Brown, "Visclosky, Jontz Will Vote No on War in Gulf," *Gary Post-Tribune*, January 12, 1991.

34. Atkinson, "Murky Ending Clouds Desert Storm Legacy."

35. John Manners, "Aiming for High Office," *Money* 21 (November 1992); William Booher, "GOP Hopeful Uses Boots to Point to Feats," *Indianapolis Star*, October 13, 1991; Deborah Hanlon, "Battle Lines Drawn in Fifth District Race: Gulf War is Issue," *Crown Point Lake County Star*, November 5, 1991; "Desert Storm Veteran Ready to Challenge Jontz," *Vidette-Messenger*, October 14, 1991.

36. Booher, "GOP Hopeful Uses Boots to Point to Feats."

37. Dan Spalding, "Buyer Accepts Union Invitation to Northwest," *Warsaw Times-Union*, March 31, 1992; Maureen Groppe, "Visitors Hit Jontz Stands," *South Bend Tribune*, October 30, 1992; Terri Hughes-Lazzell, "Jontz Not as Popular with One Labor Group," *Kokomo Tribune*, April 3, 1992; David Helvarg, *The War against the Greens: The "Wise-Use" Movement, the New Right, and the Browning of America* (1994; rep., Boulder, CO: Johnson Books, 2004), 60.

38. Author interview with Mike Busch, January 31, 2011.

39. Terri Hughes-Lazzell, "Drug Costs Questioned," *Kokomo Tribune*, September 29, 1992; "Jontz Holds Hearing on the High Cost of Prescription Drugs," news release, September 29, 1992, Jontz Papers.

40. Maureen Groppe, "Did Drug Hearing Cost Jontz?" *South Bend Tribune*, November 2, 1992; Sylvia A. Smith, "Jontz Raps Buyer over $5,000 Contribution from Lilly," *Fort Wayne Journal-Gazette*, October 31, 1992.

41. "American Political System," Ross Perot Speech at National Press Club, March 18, 1992, C-Span Video Library, http://www.c-spanvideo.org/program/25063-1; Greene, *Presidency of George Bush*, 167.

42. Howard M. Smulevitz, "Jontz Asks House Speaker to Review Lawmakers' Perks," *Indianapolis Star*, November 7, 1991; Judith Barra Austin, "Jontz Urges House to Eliminate Perks," *Lafayette Journal and Courier*, November 7, 1991.

43. Biggs and Foley, *Honor in the House*, 174–79; David Hess and Ellen Warren, "House Lists 303 Names of Check Writers," *Gary Post-Tribune*, April 17, 1992.

44. "Statement of U.S. Rep. Jim Jontz on the House Bank," news release, March 18, 1992, Jontz Papers.

45. George Stuteville, "Members See House Morale Sinking," *Indianapolis Star*, April 12, 1992; Jeffrey H. Birnbaum, "Campaign '92: Indiana Revisited: Anti-Incumbent Mood Gets Rep. Jontz up Early, Gives Mr. Buyer and Issue," *Wall Street Journal*, May 1, 1992.

46. Tom Kenworthy, "Keep the Bums In! A Congress-Basher Urges the Voters to Look at the Positive Side," *Washington Post*, April 26, 1992.

47. "Early Takes a Swipe at Jim Jontz," *Rochester Sentinel*, October 29, 1992; Bob Brown, "Buyer Says Jontz Misled Voters on Scholarships," *Munster Times*, October 31, 1992. The issue of scholarships came back to plague Buyer during his final days as a congressman. In early 2010 the Citizens for Responsibility and Ethics, known as CREW, a government watchdog group, alleged that the Frontier Foundation, a nonprofit organization Buyer helped to found to raise money for scholarships for Hoosier students, had raised more than $800,000 since 2003 but had failed to award any of those funds for scholarships. Buyer's family members ran the foundation and served on its board. Nearly all of the donors to the fund were from twenty companies or trade organizations that were concerned with issues before the House Energy and Commerce Committee on which Buyer served. CREW charged that Buyer "used the charity to foot golf fundraisers at exclusive resorts where he hobnobs with corporate donors . . . who have business before him." For his part, Buyer said he had started the fund "out of the goodness of my heart, not for any type of attention whatsoever, so that is why these attacks are so bothersome to me." The goal, he added, was to "raise a sufficient sum so that we will be sustainable for decades." In late January 2010 Buyer announced he would not seek a tenth term in Congress due to an incurable autoimmune disease suffered by his wife, Joni. The House Office of Congressional Ethics dropped the CREW complaint against the Indiana congressman in late March 2010. See Sylvia A. Smith, "Buyer Ends Re-Election Bid, Says Wife Ill," *Fort Wayne Journal-Gazette*, January 30, 2010; Trent Wright, "Buyer Responds to Claims," *Monticello Herald Journal*, October 14, 2009; "Buyer Ethics Complaint Dismissed," March 29, 2010, WLFI.com, http://www.wlfi.com /dpps/news/indiana/ethics-complaint-dismissed-against-buyer2_3295297.

48. Phil Wieland, "Jontz Starts Campaigning before Dawn," *Northwest Times*, October 31, 1992.

49. Jim Britell e-mails to author, July 7, 2011.

50. Brian Mayes, "About Jim Jontz," Ecclectica, http://ecclectica.ca/issues/mayes_b.ecc.asp.

51. Brian Mayes e-mail to author, August 30, 2011.

52. Sugar interview; Dave Kitchell, "Fifth District Picks Buyer," *Logansport Pharos-Tribune*, November 4, 1992.

53. Kitchell, "Fifth District Picks Buyer"; Mark Skertic, "Jontz Returns to Kokomo Plant to Say Thanks," *Northwest Times*, November 5, 1992. Although the timber industry expressed

delight at Jontz's defeat in Indiana's Fifth District, it had much worse luck in the Pacific Northwest, as every major candidate it invested money in (approximately $750,000 in all) to promote its "environmental extremism" message lost at the polls in the State of Washington. "Shellshocked might be a pretty good world for how we feel," noted William Jacobs, executive director of the Washington Forest Protection Association, a lobbying group for the timber industry. See, Jim Simon, "Voters Do Slash-and-Burn on Candidates Supported by Timber-Industry Money," *Seattle Times*, November 10, 1992.

54. Rich James, "Jontz Falls after 18 Years on Edge," *Gary Post-Tribune*, November 5, 1992; "Buyer's Winning Strategy Began about a Year Ago," *Danville (IL) Commercial-News*, November 12, 1992; Britell e-mail; Mayes e-mail.

55. James, "Jontz Falls after 18 Years on Edge"; William Freyberg, "Jim Jontz: 5th District GOP Too Strong," *Rochester Sentinel*, November 4, 1992.

56. Sugar interview.

57. Mayes e-mail; author interview with Kathy Altman, May 12, 2010; George Stuteville, "Movin' On: Defeated Jontz Knew He was Living on Borrowed Time," *Indianapolis Star*, December 16, 1992.

Chapter 7

1. "Senate Challenger Jontz Pokes Fun at Dick Lugar's Geography," *Evansville Courier*, October 3, 1994. See also "Jontz Pokes Fun at Lugar Record," *Gary Post-Tribune*, October 3, 1994; "Jontz Tries to Turn Lugar Strength into a Negative," *Rochester Sentinel*, September 20, 1994. Lugar was not amused by his opponent's advertisements, telling a reporter: "I don't see much that's funny about it." He defended the foreign aid by noting it had domestic benefits, as the $5 billion in credits to Moscow were in the form of agriculture credits that had to be spent in the United States, and the funds to Mexico and Peru were to fight drugs. "Jontz Tries to Turn Lugar Strength into a Negative," *Madison Courier*, September 20, 1994.

2. See Richard G. Lugar, "Indiana in the Upper House," *Traces of Indiana and Midwestern History* 8 (Fall 1996): 12; Don McIntosh, "Former Congressman Builds Labor-Environmentalist Bridges," *Northwest Labor Press*, March 21, 2003.

3. Judith Barra Austin, "Jontz Hopes to Get Job with Clinton," *Marion Chronicle-Tribune*, December 20, 1992; Judith Barra Austin, "Will He Stay in the Arena?" *Lafayette Journal-Courier*, December 21, 1992; author interview with Tom Sugar, April 30, 2010.

4. John R. MacArthur, *The Selling of 'Free Trade': NAFTA, Washington, and the Subversion of American Democracy* (Berkeley: University of California Press, 2000), 187–88; Jennifer Lin, Kristin Huckshorn, and Chris Marquis, "NAFTA's Prospects Are Falling: House Members Heard an Outcry from Back Home," *Philadelphia Inquirer*, September 12, 1993.

5. Dave Phillips, "Jontz Hears Comments on Proposed NAFTA," *Kokomo Tribune*, September 16, 1992; "Free Trade Pact Will Cost American Jobs," *Local 1010 Steelworker*, April 1991, in Jim Jontz Papers, Calumet Regional Archives, Indiana University Northwest, Gary, IN.

6. Author interview with Scott Paul, August 6, 2010; Paul e-mail to author, August 24, 2011; "Jontz Finds New Life as a Lobbyist," *Northwest Times*, April 14, 1993. A list of organizations serving on the CTC's executive committee included the Sierra Club, Friends of the Earth, Public Citizen, the International Ladies Garment Workers Union, the National Farmers Union, the Institute for Agriculture and Trade Policy, the International Union of Electronic, Technical, Salaried Machine and Furniture Workers Union, and the Amalgamated Clothing and Textile Workers Union. See Frederick W. Mayer, *Interpreting NAFTA: The Science and Art of Political*

Analysis (New York: Columbia University Press, 1998), 226.

7. Carl M. Cannon, "Democratic Schism over NAFTA Could Leave Lasting Rift in Party," *Baltimore Sun*, September 18, 1993.

8. Keith Bradsher, "Last Call to Arms on the Trade Pact," *New York Times*, August 23, 1993; Dave Skidmore, "Buchanan Criticizes Fellow Republicans' Support of NAFTA," *Bangor (ME) Daily News*, August 27, 1993.

9. Mayer, *Interpreting NAFTA*, 203–4.

10. "Sides Prepare to Spend on NAFTA Ads," *Spokane Spokesman–Review*, September 21, 1993; Paul e-mail; Ian Austen, "Clinton Faces Uphill Battle for NAFTA," *Kitchenor–Waterloo (Ontario) Record*, November 13, 1993; Peter T. Kilborn, "The Free Trade Accord: Little Voices Roar in the Chorus of Free-Trade Foes," *New York Times*, November 13, 1993; "Both Sides Predict NAFTA Victory," *Ludington (MI) Daily News*, November 11, 1993.

11. Thomas B. Edsall, "Are Labor Tactics on NAFTA Real Threats or 'Tough Love'?" *Washington Post*, November 16, 1993; Nigel Hamilton, *Bill Clinton: Mastering the Presidency* (New York: PublicAffairs, 2007), 228–29; Mayer, *Interpreting NAFTA*, 314.

12. Austen, "Clinton Faces Uphill Battle"; "Clinton Comes Up Short in Votes for Trade Pact," *Charleston Post and Courier*, November 1, 1993; Patrick Howe and Carol Byrne, "The NAFTA Endgame," *Minneapolis Star-Tribune*, November 16, 1993; Paul e-mail; Taylor Branch, *The Clinton Tapes: Wrestling History with the President* (New York: Simon and Schuster, 2009), 83–84.

13. Paul e-mail; Jon Schwantes, "Jontz Bounces Back from Defeat, Will Take on Lugar," *Indianapolis Star*, December 13, 1993; David L. Haase, "Jontz May Seek Lugar Senate Seat," ibid., December 1, 1993.

14. "Opposing Lugar, Jontz is Taking on Formidable Odds," *Gary Post-Tribune*, May 1, 1994; Mary Beth Schneider, "Out of Touch or Out of Reach? Jim Jontz is Trying to Prevent Dick Lugar from Becoming Indiana's First Four-Term Senator," *Indianapolis Star*, October 30, 1994.

15. Mary Beth Schneider, "Lugar Undaunted by 4th-Term Specter: The Senator's Confident He'll be Re-elected but Hoosier Demorats Won't Concede the Race," *Indianapolis Star*, May 1, 1994, and "Jontz vs. Lugar for Senate," *Gary Post-Tribune*, May 4, 1994.

16. "It's a David vs. Goliath Senate Race," *Gary Post-Tribune*, October 23, 1994; John Krull, "Senate Campaign Snapshots Teem with Revelations," *Indianapolis News*, November 3, 1994; Mary Beth Schneider, "Jontz Hoping Lugar's Support of NAFTA Sends His Votes South," *Indianapolis Star*, January 16, 1994; and Schneider, "Senate Foes Jontz, Lugar Disagree on Economy's Outlook," *Indianapolis Star*, October 15, 1994.

17. David L. Haase, "U.S. Senate Race Goes to the Dogs: Jontz Says TV Ad Shows That Lugar Not a Hoosier Anymore," *Indianapolis Star*, October 11, 1994; "Jontz Ads Go for Funny Bone, Not Jugular," ibid., November 3, 1994; and Mary Beth Schneider, "Political Junkie Burned Out by Scorched-Earth Ad Campaigns,"ibid., November 6, 1994.

18. "Jontz Takes Small Steps in Uphill Campaign," *Gary Post–Tribune*, July 17, 1994; Krull, "Senate Campaign Snapshots Teem with Revelations;" "Jontz: Lugar out of Touch with Public," *Bloomington Herald-Times*, October 30, 1994.

19. John Krull, "Lugar-Jontz Debate Reveals Few Surprises: Neither Claims Win," *Indianapolis Star*, October 25, 1994; "Lugar, Jontz Hold Their Only Debate," *Warsaw Times-Union*, October 25, 1994.

20. Rex Buntain, "Weary Candidates Make Final Push Toward Election," *Bloomington*

Herald–Times, November 8, 1994.

21. John Krull, "Lugar's Plans are Now Topic of Speculation," *Indianapolis Star*, November 9, 1994; Hamilton, *Bill Clinton*, 359.

22. See Thomas R. Wellock, *Preserving the Nation: The Conservation and Environmental Movements, 1870–2000* (Wheeling, IL: Harlan Davidson, 2007), 238–41; David Helvarg, "Red Herrings of the Wise Use Movement–Endangered Species Act," *The Progressive* (November 1995), FindArticles.com, http://findarticles.com/p/articles/mi_m1295/is_n11_v59/ai_18008835/.

23. "Ex-Congressman Jim Jontz Thinking 'Green' in D.C.," *Kokomo Tribune*, October 22, 1995; David Helvarg, *The War against the Greens: The "Wise Use" Movement, the New Right, and the Browning of America* (Boulder, CO: Johnson Books, 2004), 296–97.

24. Author interview with Andy Kerr, July 18, 2011; Andy Kerr, "Message to Jim Jontz," April 3, 2007, in "Soul of a Hero: A People's Tribute to Jim Jontz," prepared by Brian Vincent, unpublished collection of tributes to Jontz, copy in author's collection; Roger Featherstone, "Remembering Jim," in "Soul of a Hero."

25. Mike Medberry, "Who Knows Best: Grassroots or Foundations?" *High Country News*, October 16, 1965; Douglas Bevington, *The Rebirth of Evironmentalism: Grassroots Activism from the Spotted Owl to the Polar Bear* (Washington, DC: Island Press, 2009), 188–89; Featherstone, "Remembering Jim." Pew critics claimed that by ousting Jontz and his staff the foundation had turned from a "grassroots initiative and became and extension of Washington electoral politics," and the coalition's position moderated from what it had been on the issue. See, Mark Dowie, *American Foundations: An Investigative History* (Cambridges: Massachusetts Institute of Technology Press, 2001), 100–101.

26. Featherstone, "Remembering Jim."

27. James Bornemeier, "Bipartisan Bid to Revamp Endangered Species Act Introduced in House," *Los Angeles Times*, September 8, 1995; Eric Pryne and Robert T. Nelson, "Endangered Species Act Upheld by Court," *Seattle Times*, June 29, 1995.

28. Featherstone, "Remembering Jim"; Scott Allen, "Battle Nears on Endangered Species Law," *Boston Globe*, September 10, 1995; "House GOP Targets Species Protections; Balance Would Shift to Property Rights," *Washington Post*, September 8, 1995; Robert T. Nelson, "Endangered Species Act to Survive as GOP Can't Agree," *Seattle Times*, October 5, 1995; "Weakening of Species Law is Losing Steam: New Opposition from Doctors, Church Leaders," *Salt Lake Tribune*, October 8, 1995.

29. Helvarg, *The War against the Greens*, 304; "Weakening of Species Law is Losing Steam;" "Endangered Species Act Pitting Politicians against Nature-Loving Churchmen," *Fredericksburg (VA) Free Lance-Star*, February 10, 1996; Heather Abel, "The Anecdotal War on Endangered Species is Running Out of Steam," *High Country News*, November 13, 1995; Richard Lacayo, "This Land is Whose Land?" *Time*, October 23, 1995; Larry Swisher, "GOP Wants Species Act to Go Away," *Eugene Register-Guard*, February 14, 2000.

30. "Northwest Forest Plan Marks 10 Years," Associated Press, April 13, 2004, http://www.citizenreviewonline.org/april2004/forestplan.htm; Scott Sonner, "Salvage Rider Threatens Forest Plan, Officials Say," *Eugene Register-Guard*, March 10, 1996; Brock Evans, "Remembering Jim Jontz" in "Soul of a Hero."

31. Glen Hodges, "Dead Wood," *Washington Monthly*, October 1, 1996, http://www.thefreelibrary.com/Dead+wood-a018750208; Paul Larmer, "Cut to the Past: Logging Wars Resume," *High Country News*, October 16, 1995, http://www.hcn.org/issues/45/1378; Tom

Kenworthy, "A Clear-Cut Solution for Loggers; 'Timber Rider' Expedites Sales from U.S. Land, Eliminates Recourse," *Washington Post*, February 20, 1996; "Audit Finds Timber Sale Targets Met," *Sonora (CA) Union Democrat*, March 11, 1997.

32. Kathie Durbin, *Tree Huggers: Victory, Defeat, and Renewal in the Northwest Ancient Forest Campaign* (Seattle, WA: The Mountaineers, 1996), 265–66; Tony Davis, "Last Line of Defense: Civil Disobedience and Protest Slow Down 'Lawless Logging,'" *High Country News*, September 2, 1996; George Stuteville, "Ex-Lawmaker Out on a Limb in His Crusade for Ecology," *Indianapolis Star*, February 3, 1996. There were some Hoosier conservationists who doubted the wisdom of Jontz's decision to take such forceful action. Gordon Durnil, a former chairman of the Indiana Republican Party and author of a book on his conversion to environmentalism, said by doing "outrageous things, you lose support of the public. The seriousness of the issue is lost and the chasm of misunderstanding becomes greater. You can't get to the work of real problem-solving." Stuteville, "Ex-Lawmaker Out on a Limb in His Crusade for Ecology."

33. Author interview with Brian Vincent, August 30, 2011; Evans, "Remembering Jim Jontz."

34. See Evans, "Remembering Jim Jontz"; Vincent interview; "Ex-Congressman Arrested in Protest," *Sacramento Bee*, October 31, 1995; Stuteville, "Ex-Lawmaker Out on a Limb in His Crusade for Ecology."

35. Jim Jontz is Arrested for Protest," *Fort Wayne Journal-Gazette*, January 26, 1996; "Repel the Rider, Repair the Damage!" Umpqua Watersheds, Inc., http://www.umpqua-water sheds.org/archive/unf/cdannounce.html.

36. "Lawmakers Launch Fight against Salvage Rider," *Eugene Register-Guard*, December 8, 1995; "Oregon's Furse, Republicans Clash over Salvage Logging Bill," *Moscow-Pullman (WA) Daily News*, December 20, 1995; Durbin, *Tree Huggers*, 286.

37. "Green-Drive Leaders See Comeback for the Trees," *Seattle Times*, February 5, 1996; Anne Semmes, "The 'Salvage Rider' Isn't Saving Forests, it's Decimating Them," *E–The Environmental Magazine*, August 31, 1996, http://www.emagazine.com/archive/946/; Steve Holmer, "Jim Jontz: Leader of the Forest Conservation Movement," in "Soul of a Hero"; "Salvage-Logging Rules Tightened," *Seattle Times*, July 3, 1996.

38. John H. Cushman Jr., "Administration Proposes Moratorium on New Logging Roads," *New York Times*, January 23, 1998; "GOP Defections Kill Bid for More U.S. Forest Logging," *Los Angeles Times*, March 28, 1998.

39. Holmer, "Jim Jontz"; "Fire-Risk Logging Bill Goes Down in Flames," *Eugene Register-Guard*, March 28, 1998; Swisher, "House Won't Go for More Logging in West," *Eugene Register-Guard*, March 31, 1998.

40. Don McIntosh, "Former Congressman Builds Labor-Environmentalist Bridges," *Northwest Labor Press*, March 21, 2003, http://www.nwlaborpress.org/2003/3-21-03Jontz.html; Americans for Democratic Action conference, June 13, 1998, C-Span Video Library, http://www.c-spanvideo.org/program/Americansfor.

Chapter 8

1. See Janet Thomas, *The Battle in Seattle: The Story Behind and Beyond the WTO Demonstrations* (Golden, CO: Fulcrum Publishing, 2000), 25–28; Alexander Cockburn, Jeffrey St. Clair, and Allan Sekula, *5 Days That Shook the World: Seattle and Beyond* (London: Verso, 2000), 16–17; "WTO Chronicles: Nancy Pennington Talks about Turtles," HistoryLink.org: The Free Online Encyclopedia of Washington State History, http://www.historylink.org/index .cfm?DisplayPage=output.cfm&file_id2871/.

2. "WTO Meeting and Protests in Seattle (1999), Part 2," HistoryLink.org: The Free Online Encyclopedia of Washington State History, http://www.historylink.org/index .cfm?DisplayPage=output.cfm&file_id=9213; "Rage Against the Machine," *Time*, December 13, 1999, http://www.time.com/time/magazine/article/0,9171,992808,00.html.

3. Patrick Harrington, "Nature Groups See WTO Pact as Threat," *Seattle Times*, June 29, 1999; Linda V. Mapes, "Fewer Timber Tariffs, Fewer Forests, Activists Warn," *Seattle Times*, November 30 1999.

4. Don McIntosh, "Former Congressman Builds Labor-Environmental Bridges," *Northwest Labor Press*, March 21, 2003, http://www.nwlaborpress.org/2003/3-21-03Jontz.html.

5. Steven Higgs, "Jontz: 'We Need to Build Our Power,'" *Bloomington Alternative*, December 7, 2002, http://www.bloomingtonalternative.com/node/7167/; Steven Greenhouse, "Longtime Foes to Promote Jobs and Earth," *New York Times*, October 4, 1999; "Houston Principles of the Alliance for Sustainable Jobs and the Environment," Alliance for Sustainable Jobs and the Environment, http://asje.info/principles.html/; author interview with David Foster, September 13, 2011; David R. Brower, "Economics on a Human Scale," *Earth Island Journal*, (Winter 2000–2001), https://www.earthislandprojects.org/eijournal/new_articles .cfm?articleID=51&journalID=43/.

6. News release from the United Steelworkers of America, February 21, 2003, The Free Library, http://www.thefreelibrary.com/NEWS+from+the+United+Steelworkers+of+America %3A+GrouGr+call+for+Public...-a098148006/; Don McIntosh, "Union-Led Campaign May Block Oregon Steel from Light-Rail Project," *Northwest Labor Press*, November 3, 2000, http://www.nwlaborpress.org/2000/11-3-00USWA.html; Higgs, "Jontz"; Jack Colwell, "Jontz Sees Dangers in Trade Agreements," *South Bend Tribune*, January 23, 2001.

7. Foster interview; author interview with Dan Leahy, September 9, 2011.

8. Clifton Brock, *Americans for Democratic Action: Its Role in National Politics* (Washington, DC: Public Affairs Press, 1962), 51, and Arthur M. Schlesinger Jr., *A Life in the 20th Century: Innocent Beginnings, 1917–1950* (Boston: Houghton Mifflin Company, 2000), 413.

9. Higgs, "Jontz"; Sylvia A. Smith, "Jim Jontz Elected to Head Liberal Lobby Group," *Fort Wayne Journal-Gazette*, June 16, 1998.

10. Author interview with Amy Isaacs, October 4, 2011.

11. "Workers' Rights are Human Rights," ADA National President Jim Jontz' Remarks to Organizing Conference, May 18, 2000, Americans for Democratic Action, http://www.adaction .org/pages/issues/all-policy-resolutions/economic-energy-amp-env/policy-brief-workers-rights-are.

12. Jim Jontz, "Political Accountability (and regime change), 2004," *Bloomington Alternative*, May 25, 2003, http://www.bloomingtonalternative.com/articles/2003/05/25/7303.

13. Speech by Jim Jontz, no date, Jim Jontz Papers, Calumet Regional Archives, Indiana University Northwest, Gary, IN (hereafter cited as Jontz Papers). John Kerry was not Jontz's candidate of choice during the 2004 Democratic primaries. In the Oregon Democratic presidential primary, Jontz said he voted for someone whose "last name begins with 'K' but his first name was Dennis," meaning Ohio congressman Dennis Kucinich.

14. Roger Featherstone, "Remembering Jim," in "Soul of a Hero: A People's Tribute to Jim Jontz," prepared by Brian Vincent, unpublished collection of tributes to Jontz, copy in author's collection.

15. Jim Jontz, "Bleeding Ohio: Can the Politics of Trade Change Red States to Blue?" January 13, 2005, in "Soul of a Hero."

16. Undated memo to Labor Friends from Jim Jontz on Working Families Win, Jontz

Papers. According to Amy Isaacs, the organizers who had worked with Jontz on the Regime Change 2004 project had come up with the Working Families Win program name, rejecting suggested titles offered by herself and Jontz. Isaacs interview.

17. Christine A. Cegelis, "Before There Were Progressives," April 15, 2007, http://mydd .com/users/christine-a-cegelis/posts/before-there-were-progressives/; author interview with Christine Cegelis, April 15, 2011.

18. Cegelis interview; Kusler interview.

19. Cegelis interview; author interview with Burton McInturff, September 21, 2011.

20. Cegelis, "Before There Were Progressives"; Working Families Win: A Project of Americans for Democratic Action presentation, Jontz Papers. The successful candidates touted by the WFW program in 2006 were Paul Hodges in New Hampshire's Second Congressional District, Bruce Braley in Iowa's First Congressional Distirct, Steve Kagen in Wisconsin's Eighth Congressinoal District, Jason Altmire in Pennsylvania's Fourth Congressional District, Chris Carney in Pennsylvania's Tenth Congressional District, Heath Schuler in North Carolina's Eleventh Congressional District, and Zack Space in Ohio's Eighteenth Congressional District.

21. Mary Lee Turk e-mail to author, August 21, 2011; Cegelis interview.

22. Turk e-mail.

23. Scott Paul, "With Appreciation—Former Congressman Jim Jontz," *Rensselaer Republican*, June 20, 2007; author interview with Scott Paul, August 6, 2010; Paul e-mail to author, September 12, 2011.

24. Lynn-Marie Crider, "Reflections about My Friend Jim," in "Soul of a Hero"; Turk e-mail; Cegelis interview.

25. Turk e-mail; McInturff interview; "Ex Rep Jim Jontz in Hospice Care for Cancer," *Chesterton Tribune*, April 12, 2007.

26. Isaacs interview.

27. "To Our Beloved Friend, Jim," Environmental Movement Colleagues, April 10, 2007, in "Soul of a Hero." Among the many signing the letter were Vincent of Big Wildlife, Brock Evans of the Endangered Species Coalition, Andy Kerr of the Larch Company, Roger Featherstone of Earthworks, Randi Spivak of the American Lands Alliance, Stevel Holmer of the American Bird Conservancy, Julie Norman of the Siskiyou Project, Roger Schlickeisen of Defenders of Wildlife, Pat Rasmussen of the World Temperate Rainforest Network, Ken Rait of the Campaign for America's Wilderness, Jeff Stant of the Hoosier Environmental Council, and Andy Stahl of the Forest Service Employees for Environmental Ethics.

28. Author interview with Brian Vincent, August 30, 2011.

29. "Ex-Indiana Rep. Jim Jontz, 55, Dies," *South Bend Tribune*, April 17, 2007; "Jim Jontz Worked to Serve us Well," *Marion Chronicle-Tribune*, April 23, 2007; "Political Notebook," *Fort Wayne Journal-Gazette*, June 10, 2007.

30. Author interview with Tom Sugar, April 30, 2010.

Select Bibliography

Archives

Committee on Crisis Biology material, Indiana University Archives, IU, Bloomington.

"Jim Jontz, 1951–2007: Eagle Scout, State Legislator, Congressman, Conservationist, Advocate for Working Families," author's collection.

"Soul of a Hero: A People's Tribute to Jim Jontz," prepared by Brian Vincent, author's collection.

Jim Jontz Papers, Calumet Regional Archives, Indiana University Northwest, Gary, Indiana.

Interviews

Altman, Kathy, May 12, 2010.

Arnold, Laura Ann, May 10, 2010.

Bauer, B. Patrick, August 15, 2011.

Bozell, David, March 16, 2011.

Buis, Tom, August 26, 2010.

Busch, Mike, January 31, 2011.

Campbell, Scott, May 6, 2010.

Cegelis, Christine, April 14, 2011.

Chilton, Bart, July 29, 2011.

Corbin, David, June 16, 2011.

Crafts, Rod, June 2, 2011.

Davis, Karen, January 10, 2011.

Dreyer, David, November 1, 2010.

Emmi, Elaine Caldwell, May 13, 2010.

Foster, David, September 13, 2011.

Goss, John, July 22, 2011.

Harmon, Tim, June 3, 2011.

Isaacs, Amy, October 4, 2011.

Jones, Stan, May 4, 2010.

Kaptur, Marcy, June 29, 2011.

Kerr, Andy, July 18, 2011.

Klose, Christopher, May 6, 2010.

Kusler, Don, September 28, 2011.

Leahy, Dan, September 9, 2011.

Lennon, Polly Jontz, April 22, 2010.

Mahern, Louie, January 25, 2011.

Martin, Fred, June 30, 2011.

Maxwell, Allen, July 11, 2011.

Mayes, Brian, May 12, 2010.

Meyers, Donlyn, September 7, 2011.

Monteith, James, October 7, 2011.

Mumford, Terry, September 6, 2011.

Paramenter, Bill, April 26, 2010.

Paul, Scott, August 6, 2010.
Peck, Larry, June 14, 2011.
Perdue, Phillip, January 12, 2010.
Riley, Michael, July 13, 2011.
Rodenkirk, Bob, April 29, 2010.
Schultz, Marilyn, August 10, 2011.
Shields, Kent, June 21, 2011.
Stotter, Dan, August 9, 2011.
Sugar, Tom, April 30, 2010.
Thompson, Jill Long, August 9, 2011.
Turk, Mary Lee, April 27, 2010.
Williams, Jack, July 19, 2011.

Books

Barone, Michael, and Grant Ujifusa. *The Almanac of American Politics 1986*. Washington, DC: National Journal, 1985.

_____. *The Almanac of American Politics 1988*. Washington, DC: National Journal, 1987.

_____. *The Almanac of American Politics 1990*. Washington, DC: National Journal, 1989.

Bevington, Douglas. *The Rebirth of Environmentalism: Grassroots Activism from the Spotted Owl to the Polar Bear*. Washington, DC: Island Press, 2009.

Biggs, Jeffrey R., and Thomas S. Foley. *Honor in the House: Speaker Tom Foley*. Pullman: Washington State University Press, 1999.

Bodenhamer, David J., and Robert G. Barrows, eds. *The Encyclopedia of Indianapolis*. Bloomington and Indianapolis: Indiana University Press, 1994.

Branch, Taylor. *The Clinton Tapes: Wrestling with History*. New York: Simon and Schuster, 2009.

Christofferson, Bill. *The Man from Clear Lake: Earth Day Founder Senator Gaylord Nelson*. Madison: University of Wisconsin Press, 2004.

Cockburn, Alexander, Jeffrey St. Clair, and Allan Sekula. *5 Days That Shook the World: Seattle and Beyond*. London: Verso, 2000.

Durbin, Kathie. *Tree Huggers: Victory, Defeat, and Renewal in the Northwest Ancient Forest Campaign*. Seattle: The Mountaineers, 1998.

Greene, John Robert. *The Presidency of George Bush*. Lawrence: University Press of Kansas, 2000.

Gulde, William F. *Hopes, Dreams, and Books: The Story of North Central High School, 1956–2004*. Indianapolis: Par Digital Imaging, 2004.

Hamilton, Nigel. *Bill Clinton: Mastering the Presidency*. New York: PublicAffairs, 2007.

Helvarg, David. *The War against the Greens: The "Wise-Use" Movement, the New Right, and the Browning of America*. 1994. Reprint, Boulder, CO: Johnson Books, 2004.

Johnson, Haynes. *Sleepwalking through History: America in the Reagan Years*. New York: W. W. Norton and Company, 1991.

Johnson, Leland R. *The Falls City Engineers: A History of the Louisville District, Corps of Engineers, United States Army, 1970–1983*. Louisville, KY: United States Army Engineer District, 1984.

Jontz, Jim, and David Dreyer. *Big Pine Creek: A Report on Big Pine Creek, Warren County, Indiana, and its Future*. Attica, IN: The Committee on Big Pine Creek, 1974.

Kline, Benjamin. *First Along the River: A Brief History of the Environmental Movement*. San Francisco: Acada Books, 1997.

Levy, Peter B. *Encyclopedia of the Reagan-Bush Years*. Westport, CT: Greenwood Press, 1996.

Libby, Ronald T. *Eco-Wars: Political Campaigns and Social Movements*. New York: Columbia University Press, 1998.

Lytle, Mark Hamilton. *The Gentle Subversive: Rachel Carson,* Silent Spring, *and the Rise of the Environmental Movement*. New York: Oxford University Press, 2007.

MacArthur, John R. *The Selling of 'Free Trade': NAFTA, Washington, and the Subversion of American Democracy*. Berkeley: University of California Press, 2000.

Madison, James H. *The Indiana Way: A State History*. Bloomington: Indiana University Press; Indianapolis: Indiana Historical Society, 1986.

Mayer, Frederick W. *Interpreting NAFTA: The Science and Art of Political Analysis*. New York: Columbia University Press, 1998.

Morgan, Judith, and Neil Morgan. *Dr. Seuss and Mr. Geisel: A Biography*. New York: Random House, 1995.

Ritchie. Donald A. *The U.S. Congress: A Very Short Introduction*. New York: Oxford University Press, 2010.

Sale, Kirkpatrick. *The Green Revolution: The American Environmental Movement, 1962–1992*. New York: Hill and Wang, 1993.

Sandbrook, Dominic. *Mad as Hell: The Crisis of the 1970s and the Rise of the Populist Right*. New York: Alfred A. Knopf, 2011.

Shabecoff, Philip. *A Fierce Green Fire: The American Environmental Movement*. New York: Hill and Wang, 1993.

Thomas, Janet. *The Battle in Seattle: The Story Behind and Beyond the WTO Demonstrations*. Golden, CO: Fulcrum Publishing, 2000.

Turner, Tom. *Roadless Rules: The Struggle for the Last Wild Forests*. Washington, DC: Island Press, 2009.

Walsh, Justin E. *The Centennial History of the Indiana General Assembly, 1816–1978*. Indianapolis: The Select Committee on the Centennial History of the Indiana General Assembly in cooperation with the Indiana Historical Bureau, 1987.

Watt, William J. *Bowen: The Years as Governor*. Indianapolis: Bierce Associates, 1981.

Wellock, Thomas R. *Preserving the Nation: The Conservation and Environmental Movements, 1870–2000*. Wheeling, IL: Harlan Davidson, 2007.

Articles and Pamphlets

Austin, Judith Barra, and Carol Bradley, "U.S. Rep. Jim Jontz: Preserving the Forest Primeval." *Lafayette Jouran and Courier*, June 16, 1991.

Blumm, Michael C. "Ancient Forests, Spotted Owls, and Modern Public Land Law." *Boston College Environmental Affairs Law Review*, August 1, 1991.

Brown, Sherry. "Jontz 'Lobbies' for Legislative Goals." *Lafayette Journal and Courier*, February 3, 1980.

Carpenter, Dan. "Rep. Jontz is Rare Official to See Forest for the Trees." *Indianapolis Star*, August 2, 1990.

Cavinder, Fred D. "The Nature Savers: Two Organizations in Indiana are Working to Preserve Wilderness." *Indianapolis Star Magazine*, January 9, 1972.

Caufield, Catherine. "The Ancient Forest." *The New Yorker*, May 14, 1990.

Craig, Bill. "The Campaign: See How Jontz Mingles with His Constituents." *Nuvo*, August 29–September 5, 1990.

Dinnen, S. P. "Jontz and the Fight over U.S. Forests." *Indianapolis Star*, January 6, 1993.

Duncan, Phil. "A Standout in the Heartland." *Congressional Quarterly*, October 29, 1988.

Groppe, Maureen. "You Have to Love a Parade if You Run for U.S. Congress." *Kokomo Tribune*, July 15, 1990.

Gup, Ted. "Owl vs. Man: Who Gives a Hoot?" *Time*, June 25, 1990.

Hays, Tom. "Calls from Home Make a Difference." *Gary Post-Tribune*, May 27, 1987.

Steven Higgs, "Jontz Urges Move beyond Endangered Species Act," *Bloomington Herald-Times*, January 30, 1993.

Jontz, Jim. "Interior's Argument Defies its Rhetoric." *Indiana Daily Student*, March 31, 1972.

_____. "'Sinkhole' Gets Down to Basics." *Indiana Daily Student*, April 7, 1972.

_____. "State Legislature Passes Weak Ecology Bill." *Indiana Daily Student*, April 14, 1972.

_____. "Corps Unsuccessful in Image Change." *Indiana Daily Student*, April 21, 1972.

Kitchell, Dave. "Jontz—Best Congressman on Two Wheels." *Logansport Pharos Tribune*, April 19, 2007.

McDaniel, Doug. "Forest Bill Puts Jontz in Middle of Controversy." *Indianapolis Star*, June 24, 1990.

Maxwell, John. "Fall Creek Gorge Nature Preserve: Hit the Potholes of Warren County." *Outdoor Indiana* (May/June 2010).

Moore, Martha T. "Party Lines Vague in House Race in Indiana." *USA Today*, September 15, 1988.

Noell, Debra. "Jontz: A Day in the Life of White County's First Congressman." *Monticello Herald Journal*, December 9, 1987.

Prendergast, Jane. "Jontz Wears Out Shoes, and His Associates," *Marion Chronicle-Tribune*, October 17, 1988.

Richardson, Doug. "Young Legislative Veteran Marches to Different Drummer." *Warsaw Times-Union*, April 9, 1985.

Rohn, David. "Indiana's Political Roadrunner." *Indianapolis Star*, January 18, 1994.

Sautter, Chris. "Jim Jontz, the Hoosier 'Roads Scholar,' Will Be Missed." *Roll Call*, May 3, 2007.

Siddons, Patrick. "'Unbelieveable': Jim Jontz, Possibly Youngest Member of House, Recalls His Close Victory." *Louisville Courier-Journal*, January 12, 1975.

Stuteville, George. "Ex-Lawmaker Out on a Limb in His Crusade for Ecology." *Indianapolis Star*, February 3, 1996

Thoele, Mike. "Hoosier Fights for Northwest Forests." *Eugene Register-Guard*, June 3, 1990

Witwer, Grace. "This Boy-Next-Door Legislator Gives a 'Damn about Dams.'" *Indiana Daily Student*, March 15, 1975.

Wynkoop, Mary Ann. "Dissent in the Heartland: The Student Protest Movement at Indiana University, Bloomington, Indiana, 1965–1970." PhD diss., Indiana University, Bloomington, 1992.

Index